State of the Art in Computer Graphics

Plate 1. Function-mapped surface to represent surface pressure, and particle traces to simulate oil flow traces on the surface of the space shuttle orbiter.

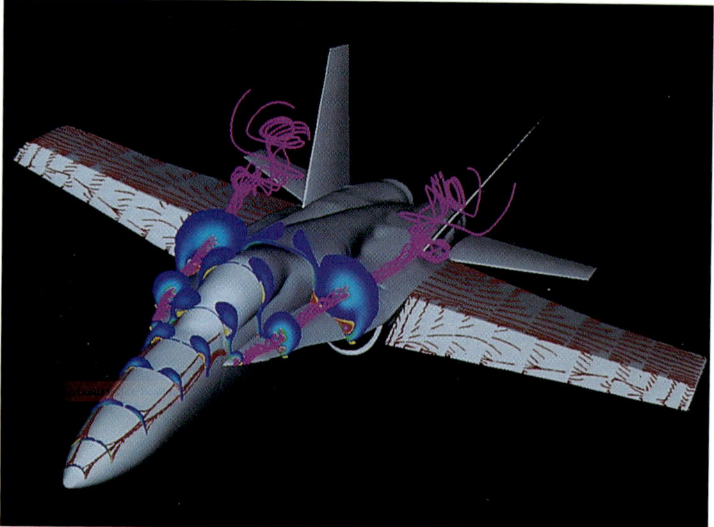

Plate 2. Function-mapped cutting planes used to depict helicity density in the flow field, and particle traces used to illustrate the vortex flow and to simulate oil flow traces on an F-18 aircraft.

David F. Rogers   Rae A. Earnshaw

Editors

State of the Art in Computer Graphics

Aspects of Visualization

With 101 Figures in 139 Parts, 36 in Color

Springer-Verlag

New York Berlin Heidelberg London Paris
Tokyo Hong Kong Barcelona Budapest

David F. Rogers
Aerospace Engineering Department
U.S. Naval Academy
Annapolis, MD 21402
USA

Rae A. Earnshaw
University of Leeds
Leeds LS2 9JT
United Kingdom

Front cover art: Scientific visualization of the CFD flow field about the Space Shuttle. Courtesy of Val Watson, NASA Ames.
Back cover art: Scientific visualization of the CFD flow field about an AV8 Harrier aircraft in slow flight. Courtesy of Merritt H. Smith, NASA Ames.

Library of Congress Cataloging-in-Publication Data
State of the art in computer graphics : aspects of visualization/
    David F. Rogers, Rae A. Earnshaw, editors.
        p. cm.
    Papers from an International Summer Institute on the State of the
Art in Computer Graphics held at Reading University, in July 1992;
sponsored by the British Computer Sociey, Computer Graphics and
Displays Group and Computer Graphics Society.
    Includes bibliographical references and index.
    ISBN 0-387-94164-9 (New York : acid-free paper). --
    ISBN 3-540-94164-9 (Berlin : acid-free paper)
    1. Computer graphics--Congresses.   2. Visualization--Congresses.
I. Rogers, David F., 1937- .   II. Earnshaw, Rae A., 1944 -
III. International Summer Institute on the State of the Art in
Computer Graphics (1992 : Reading University)   IV. British Computer
Graphics Society.
T385.S72   1993
003.366--dc20   93-33016

Printed on acid-free paper.

Production managed by Karen Phillips, manufacturing supervised by Jacqui Ashri.
Photocomposed pages prepared from $\TeX$ files prepared by Nancy A. Rogers.
Printed and bound by Edwards Brothers Inc., Ann Arbor, MI.
Color separations by Veriscan Color, Inc., New York, NY; color printing by New England Book Components, Hingham, MA.
Printed in the United States of America.

9 8 7 6 5 4 3 2 1

ISBN 0-387-94164-9 Springer-Verlag New York Berlin Heidelberg
ISBN 3-540-94164-9 Springer-Verlag Berlin Heidelberg New York

Contents

Introduction

State of the Art in Computer Graphics –
Aspects of Visualization

This is the fourth volume derived from a State of the Art in Computer Graphics Summer Institute. It represents a snapshot of a number of topics in computer graphics, topics which include visualization of scientific data; modeling; some aspects of visualization in virtual reality; and hardware architectures for visualization. Many papers first present a background introduction to the topic, followed by discussion of current work in the topic. The volume is thus equally suitable for nonspecialists in a particular area, and for the more experienced researcher in the field. It also enables general readers to obtain an acquaintance with a particular topic area sufficient to apply that knowledge in the context of solving current problems.

The volume is organized into four chapters — Visualization of Data, Modeling, Virtual Reality Techniques, and Hardware Architectures for Visualization. In the first chapter, Val Watson and Pamela Walatka address the visual aspects of fluid dynamic computations. They discuss algorithms for function-mapped surfaces and cutting planes, isosurfaces, particle traces, and topology extractions. They point out that current visualization systems are limited by low information transfer bandwidth, poor response to viewing and model accuracy modification requests, mismatches between model rendering and human cognitive capabilities, and ineffective interactive tools. However, Watson and Walatka indicate that proposed systems will correct most of these problems.

In the second paper in this chapter Ingrid Carlbom explores techniques in registration, segmentation, 3D reconstruction, and rendering that are common to applications that depend on visualizing experimental data. Her emphasis is on volumetric data sampled on regular grids. Next, Greg Nielson and John Tvedt describe and compare results for visualizing data on irregular grids, i.e., for scattered data. They describe an interesting interactive data visualization program used to conduct both objective and subjective experimental analysis of the effectiveness of several well-known scattered data visualization techniques. Together, these two papers represent a virtual tour de force of visualization techniques for experimental data.

In the second chapter, first Roy Hall and Mimi Bussan explore strategies for managing abstraction, context, and constraint that mimimize interaction and presentation ambiguities. They find that the key elements are to reduce screen complexity and to provide the designer with a variety of presentation options, thus allowing the designer to focus on important detail. However, an unfortunate side effect is that key features and interrelationships are then often hidden.

In the second paper in this chapter Professor Tosiyasu Kunii poses the question 'What is a visual computer?' and develops some fundamental requirements that allow linking computer vision with computer graphics. He uses both homotopy and singularity modeling to describe the garment wrinkle formation process. Then he uses a bifurcation model to illustrate forest growth and develops the concept of a Reeb graph to find the critical points during the growth.

The final paper in this chapter is by Dietmar Saupe and Wayne Tvedt. They consider approximation and rendering techniques for strange attractors that arise when mathematically modeling chaotic dynamical systems. The authors show that volume rendering of a strange attractor's invariant probability measure is an efficient technique for these interesting phenomena. They discuss efficient data structures and convergence criteria in the context of this model.

Stereo computer graphics is now an important part of scientific visualization and virtual reality applications. David McAllister opens the chapter on virtual reality techniques with an enlightening discussion of stereo in computer graphics. He explores some of the fundamental perception and implementation issues in the context of recent research in algorithms and graphical user interface design for stereo. A number of stereo color plates are included.

In the second paper in this chapter Warren Robinett, who is well known within the virtual reality community, proposes a classification taxonomy for virtual reality systems. The model is based on the concept of mediated interaction. The mediated interaction model assumes a sensor-display link from the world to the human user, and an action-actuator link from the human to the world. Using this model, he explores the dimensions of the synthetic experience.

In the final chapter, Turner Whitted explores computer architectures for 3D graphics display hardware. Based on wide experience with computer graphics, he concludes that the classical graphics pipeline has been stretched to nearly the breaking point in order to satisfy the high demands of current visualization systems. The author argues that it is due for replacement. He provides an overview of the continued growth in the capability of graphics hardware, with special emphasis on the rapid display of complex scenes and the addition of features that improve image quality while maintaining the flexibility required to serve a wide range of graphics applications.

Today computer graphics, in fact excellent computer graphics is just *accepted.* Many people not intimately concerned with the technology underlying computer graphics expect too much, too quickly. Basically they just do not understand the limitations of the current technology. The complexity required to generate accurate models of complex systems (aircraft and buildings, to cite just two examples), and the necessity to include nongeometric information in those models, far outstrips our technological understanding of 'how to do it', as well as the capabilities of either the software or hardware to support such understanding.

The second problem is interpretation. With the ever increasing computational power available, our ability to generate data far exceeds our ability to interpret, understand, and utilize that data. For example, a typical computational fluid dynamics program yields literally millions of pieces of information in a few hours of computation. How does the scientist or engineer interpret and understand that data? Although scientists and engineers have always used graphical techniques for interpretation and understanding, computer graphics techniques for scientific visualization are now crucial for interpreting and understanding these vast amounts of data. Fundamentally, if you do not have the tools to interpret and understand the data, there is little sense in generating it!

Virtual reality, in the guise of visually supported aircraft simulators, has been around for at least three decades. Flying a visually supported aircraft simulator is a synthetic experience. However, it is a controlled synthetic experience, subject to the known and predictable laws of physics. Today computer graphics is developing the technology to create synthetic experiences that are no longer subject to the known laws of physics. The development of this technology will yield new insights in as yet unknown directions.

Even given all the advances in computer graphics in the last three and a half decades, it is perhaps appropriate for those of us who work in computer graphics to clearly keep in mind that computer graphics is a support discipline, as is computation itself. To paraphase a well-known axiom from computer science, 'The purpose of computer graphics is insight, not pictures'.

Acknowledgments. The papers in this volume formed the basis of an International Summer Institute on The State of the Art in Computer Graphics held at Reading University, England, in July 1992. We are very grateful to our cosponsors: the British Computer Society (BCS) Computer Graphics and Displays Group, the Computer Graphics Society (CGS), and Springer-Verlag. We also thank the Association for Computing Machinery (ACM) for their cooperation and support.

We extend thanks and appreciation to Mrs. Frances Johnson of Concilia for all her help with the practical arrangements for the Institute, and to all those delegates who attended and contributed by their discussion, interaction, and inspiration. Especial thanks and appreciation go to Gerhard Rossbach of Springer-Verlag for his continued support of this series of Summer Institutes. Thanks are certainly due Nancy Rogers of NAR Associates, who computer typeset the book using TEX.

A volume such as this is the result of many months of planning and preparation, and we thank all those who have assisted us. Colleagues, students, contributors, and publisher — we thank you all for enduring our persistence in seeking to bring this project to a successful conclusion.

David F. Rogers
Annapolis, Maryland, USA

Rae A. Earnshaw
Leeds, United Kingdom

1 Visualization of Data

Visual Analysis of Fluid Dynamics

Val Watson and Pamela P. Walatka

Abstract

Many visual analysis systems have been created to enhance understanding of computer simulations of complex phenomena. Several visualization techniques have emerged as favorites for analysis of fluid dynamics: function-mapped surfaces, function-mapped cutting planes, and isosurfaces are widely used for viewing scalar values. The favorites for analysis of vector fields are particle traces and topology extractions. Algorithms used for these techniques are given. The major limitations of current visualization systems are the relatively low bandwidth of information from the workstation to the human, the inability to view or modify the accuracy of the rendering, the inability to match the human cognitive capabilities, and the ineffectiveness of the interactive controls for 3D viewing or manipulating 3D objects. Current research outlined in this paper indicates that these limitations are being overcome. Present trends are for an order of magnitude improvement in visualization capabilities each four years. Those wishing to create visualization software in the future are encouraged to design for the high-performance visualization hardware expected to be the norm in a few years, to make their systems fully 3D and interactive, to use pseudostandards such as Motif and Open GL, and to design scenes to match the human cognitive capabilities. Within a few years, the new visualization systems will make our current visualization systems as obsolete as computer punched cards.

Introduction

The increasing power of computers has permitted simulations of very complex physical events, such as the dynamics of air flow about high-performance aircraft. Extracting the important features of computer simulations is no longer a simple task, and presenting results as columns of numbers is no longer satisfactory. Because visual analysis techniques are particularly well suited to the human cognition capabilities, more emphasis has been placed on visual analysis tools for understanding computer simulations of complex phenomena. McKim [McKi80] and Friedhoff [Frie89] describe why the human is so well suited to visual analysis, and they provide the rationale for the current trend toward visual analysis. McCormick [McCo87] provides detailed documentation of the need for visual analysis in computational physics. The purpose of this paper is to describe current visualization tools, list current limitations in visualization systems, and provide recommendations for future visual analysis systems. The rate of change of visualization systems is extremely high — an order of magnitude increase in capability occurs every four years. Therefore, the description of current systems presented herein must be considered as merely a snapshot in time — in a few years, systems will be much more powerful and the techniques much more sophisticated.

Current Visualization of Fluid Dynamics

During the last five years, many software packages have been developed for visualizing computer simulations of physics. Table 1 lists some packages that are appropriate for visualizing results of 3D simulations.

VISUALIZATION TECHNIQUES

The most popular visual techniques used in these programs are:

for scalar fields:

viewing scalar values as color on a body surface;

An example is given in Plate 1, where the pressure on the surface of the space shuttle is represented by colors.

viewing scalar values as color on a cutting plane (2D cross section) that sweeps through the volume of interest;

An example is given in Plate 2, where the magnitude of helicity density (dot product of vorticity and velocity) is represented by colors on cross sections in the flow field near the body of the F-18. (The cross section planes are clipped when the helicity density is below a specified value.)

viewing the surface on which some scalar property has a constant value, for example constant Mach number.

for vector fields:

viewing vector fields as 3D vectors at grid points;

viewing particle traces, stream lines and surfaces, or streak lines;

Particle traces are simulations of the path of a weightless particle that moves with the fluid. Streamlines and stream surfaces are lines and surfaces at an instant in time that no mass is crossing. Streak lines are lines at an instant in time simulating smoke or weightless bubbles that have been released over time at a single point. For steady flow the particle traces, stream lines, and streak lines coincide.

Examples for steady flow (where all three coincide) are given in Plates 1 and 2. In Plate 2, particle paths are shown near the core of vortices to provide understanding of the vortex flow and vortex bursting. In Plates 1 and 2 the particle traces near the surface of the wing simulate oil flow traces, providing an understanding of the flow in the boundary layer of the wing or body.

viewing the topological features of a vector field, such as stagnation points, surfaces of flow separation, and vortex cores.

Table 1. Visualization software packages.

	Software	Source
Government	FAST	NASA Ames (Sterling Software)
	Rambo	Air Force (Aerospace Corp)
Universities	apE	Ohio Supercomputer Center
	Visual3	MIT
Vendors	AVS	Stardent
	Data Explorer	IBM
	Data Visualizer	Wavefront
	Explorer	Silicon Graphics
	Field View	Intelligent Light
	Flow Eyes	SOLIDRAY Co., LTD.
	FOCUS	Visual Kinetics
	IDL	Research Systems Inc.
	IVM	Dynamic Graphics, Inc.
	MPGS	Cray
	OMNI3D	Analytical Methods, Inc.
	PV Wave	Precision Visuals
	Spyglass	Spyglass, Inc.
	SSV	Sterling Software
	SUN View	SUN Microsystems
	TECPLOT	Amtec Engineering Inc.
	VCI PLOT3D	Visual Computing Inc.
	Voxel View	Vital Images

ALGORITHMS FOR VISUALIZATION TECHNIQUES

The algorithms usually used for the visualization techniques are:

for creating function-mapped surfaces (scalars represented as colors on surfaces):

The first step is to create a color map for mapping scalar values into colors. Usually, a number of specific colors are assigned to specific scalar values, and color ramps are created between these specific colors using the color ramp routines in the graphics language available on the workstation. The surface is normally represented by joined polygons, and the scalar values on the surface are normally specified on each polygon vertex. For rendering the surface, the color map entry for each vertex is obtained from the scalar value by linear interpolation. The polygons are then rendered by passing the geometric position and color map entry of each vertex to a Gouraud shading routine.

Most current visualization software permits interactive manipulation of the color map. This interaction makes the function-mapped surface tool much more effective, because specific regions can easily be emphasized or de-emphasized. One can also create special effects by manipulation of the color map, e.g., contour bands can be created by making the color map a 'staircase'.

For the Silicon Graphics Workstations, RGB mode rather than color map mode must be used in order to obtain some hardware features, such as transparency. Todd Plessel of Sterling Software [Ples92] has developed software for managing a color table, external to the graphics system, to determine colors at each vertex. In RGB mode, the RGB values of the color at each vertex are passed to the Gouraud shading routine, and the colors inside the polygons are actually interpolations in RGB space rather than interpolations in color map space. This technique works well as long as there are no large differences in scalar values between adjacent vertices.

for creating isosurfaces (surfaces of some constant scalar quantity):

The method of marching cubes described by Lorenson [Lore87] is used.

for creating arbitrary cutting planes:

The cutting plane (or any mathematical surface defined by $F\{x, y, z\} =$ constant) is created from the isosurface algorithm, where the scalar value that is held constant represents the constant in the plane equation (or in the equation for the mathematically defined surface).

for creating particle traces, streamlines, or streak lines:

Traditionally, Runge-Kutta algorithms are used because they are robust and require less storage than multistep methods. (Fourth-order Runge-Kutta methods are a good compromise between computing time and accuracy). However, storage for the typical number of particle traces, streamlines, or streak lines is usually not a problem, and multistep methods provide better accuracy for the same calculation effort. Therefore, multistep methods such as Hamming's Method [Carn69] probably should be used more often.

Capabilities Required to Achieve Effective Visualization

Based on our experience in visualization of fluid dynamics, the most important capabilities are real-time interaction, using a combination of visualization techniques, and viewing the dynamics of the fluids at a rate fast enough to understand the dynamics.

real-time interaction:

The capability to change the viewing position (rotate to a better line of sight or zoom in to get a closer view) must occur quickly enough for the scientists to maintain their train of thought. To speed up the response time, one can frequently represent the objects in the scene with less resolution, or even as bounding boxes, during the manipulation without loss of functionality, but the final scene must appear soon after the manipulation is complete.

combining visual techniques:

Plate 2 illustrates function-mapped clipping planes (in this case showing the helicity density) combined with particle traces that show the vortex flow. Combining various visualization techniques often illustrates 'cause and effect' useful for understanding the physical phenomenon.

dynamics:

In order to represent the time evolution of a scene rapidly enough to understand the dynamics, the scenes should be shown at a rate of 10 frames or more per second.

REQUIREMENTS TO MEET THE CAPABILITIES

The typical scenes currently viewed can be represented by approximately 10,000 polygons. These are normally four-sided, nonplanar polygons that average on the order of 100 pixels each. With a rate of 10 frames per second, this yields a requirement to render 100,000 polygons per second with shading and with hidden surfaces removed. First let us consider the hardware requirements.

The standard graphics benchmark most appropriate for visualization of scenes like Plate 2 is the NCGA GPC benchmark for the 'head' [NCGA92]. One GPC-mark for this benchmark represents a rendering rate of approximately 3,000 triangles per second. In order to render 100,000 four-sided polygons (or 200,000 triangles) per second, one needs more than 60 GPCmarks. We recommend 30 GPCmarks as a minimum for any workstation to be used for 3D interactive viewing of modestly complex scenes. At present, not many workstations have this capability, but the cost for obtaining this rendering rate is rapidly decreasing. We believe that shortly the cost for this interactive viewing capability will drop below the 'threshold of pain', and we believe that shortly most scientists will insist on this capability when purchasing workstations.

At NASA Ames Research Center, the fluid dynamics simulations are performed on supercomputers and the visualizations are typically done on high-performance graphical workstations. The Numerical Aerodynamic Simulation Division selected the Silicon Graphics 4D/320 VGX workstation for their standard visualization tool. The performance of this workstation is listed in Table 2.

The computing for visualization can be done on the supercomputer, but performing visualization computations on high-performance graphics workstations is much more cost-effective. Figure 1 illustrates that our current workstations perform graphics computations with their specialized graphics hardware at a rate of approximately one-tenth the rate of the supercomputers, but the cost of the supercomputers is approximately 100 times greater. Therefore, graphics computing on workstations has approximately 10 times the performance/price ratio of graphics computing on the supercomputers.

It is not enough to have good visualization hardware unless adequate software is available. Currently, the only software packages that provide high performance

Table 2. Workstation features (Silicon Graphics 4D/320VGX).

Basic Features	Arithmetic processor	12 MFLOPS
	Primary memory	48 MBytes
	Secondary memory	780 MBytes
Graphic Features	131 GPCmarks on the NCGA GPC benchmark for the 'head'	

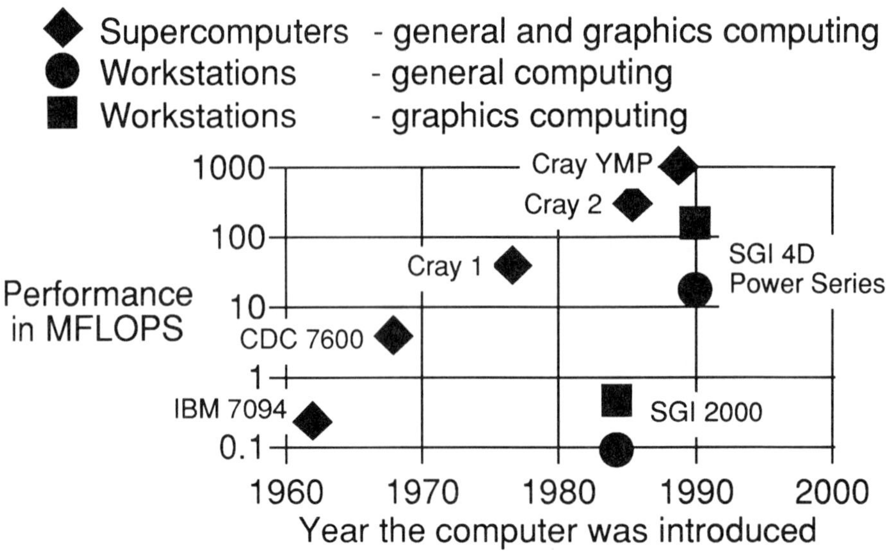

Figure 1. Performance trends of supercomputers and workstations.

for interactive visual analysis of complex simulations are those tailored to take advantage of the hardware in high-performance graphics workstations. Packages that are designed for 'lowest common denominator' workstations usually do not make optimum use of the hardware in high-performance graphics workstations and are not as effective for visual analysis of complex fluid dynamic simulations.

Although data flow programs, like Explorer and AVS, are excellent for prototyping or for production visualization of simpler simulations, the programs tailored specifically for fluid dynamic visualization are likely to be more effective.

Current Limitation to Visual Analysis

The factors limiting the effectiveness of visualization systems are:

the low bandwidth of information from the workstation to the human;

the inability to view or modify the accuracy of the rendering;

the inability to create scenes that match the human cognitive capability;

the ineffectiveness of the interactive controls for manipulating 3D objects or 3D viewing.

The bandwidth from the computer to the human is increased substantially by increasing the field of view of the display (only 1/25th the human field of view is used by the typical 19-inch monitors) by adding stereo vision, and by using sound. Except for the high-performance graphics workstations, rendering speed of the workstation is a major limitation. Picture and color resolution of current workstation displays is near the maximum the human can discern when viewing most dynamic scenes.

Most visualization programs provide no method for viewing the accuracy of the rendering approximation nor the ability to modify the accuracy. Therefore, the scientist cannot be sure that the rendering is not producing some artificial effects that mask or distort real effects.

A scientist just beginning to use the current visualization techniques is likely to create visual clutter. Creating scenes that extract the essence of the flow in an easily understood scene usually requires a long trial and error session with the data. The inability to easily extract the essence of a complex simulation is a major limitation.

Most visualization programs do not have interfaces for highly efficient manipulation of scenes. Examples of typical problems viewers have are:

> viewers frequently have the object of interest fly off the screen when attempting to rotate the view;
>
> the object frequently moves too rapidly or slowly during translation;
>
> the controls to move to the desired orientation are often not obvious;
>
> some popular rotation schemes have 'gimbal lock', where two of the rotation axes have coalesced so there is no single maneuver possible to get to some desired orientations.

There are no accepted standards for 3D manipulation, so as the scientists move from an interactive grid generator program to an interactive solution viewing program they have to change their method of 3D interaction. The speed of gaining understanding from visualization can be greatly improved by use of a good standard interface for 3D manipulation.

Efforts to Remove the Limitations on Visual Analysis

Some of the efforts aimed at eliminating the limitations listed above are:

> to improve the bandwidth between the computer and the human;
>
>> The primary efforts by workstation vendors for increasing the bandwidth between the computer and the human are aimed at increasing the rendering rates. These rates increase by approximately a factor of 10 every four years. Furthermore, the cost for a fixed performance workstation is decreasing by approximately the same factor. Therefore, it is likely that within five years most scientists will have access to a workstation where the rendering rates are not a limiting factor for visualization of most simulations as long as the usual approximate lighting methods are used.
>>
>> Other efforts to increase the bandwidth between the computer and the human are aimed at increasing the field of view, adding stereographics, and adding sound. Most of these efforts are tagged as virtual reality research. This research is being conducted at:
>>
>>> University of Washington: Tom Furness III;
>>>
>>> University of North Carolina: Henry Fuchs;

> Artificial Reality Corporation: Myron Kruger;
> NASA Ames: Ellis and McGreevy, Levit and Bryson.

Bryson [Brys91] describes a virtual reality environment applied to visualization of fluid dynamics, wherein the scientist walks around inside the flow field of a space shuttle orbiter and initiates particle traces from his or her finger.

to make the accuracy of rendering visible;

> Ning and Hesselink [Ning92] are conducting research at Stanford University on techniques to provide insight into the accuracy of rendering methods. Although their techniques are designed primarily to reduce the number of polygons to increase rendering speeds for a specified accuracy, a major benefit is that the viewer gains insight into the rendering accuracy.

> Butler [Butl89] proposed creation of data objects where the approximation techniques are bundled with the data base so that inappropriate approximations techniques are less likely to be used.

to permit extraction and display of key features;

> Helman and Hesselink at Stanford [Helm90], and Globus, Levit, and Lasinski at NASA Ames [Glob91] conducted research on extracting the topology of vector fields in order to create scenes with the essence of the flow field. A topology extraction module was created for FAST, an environment described in the next paragraph, which was found to be extremely useful. The user can quickly locate origins of vortices, separation bubbles, stagnation points, saddle points, and other topological features useful for determining which regions of a vector field to investigate.

to improve the interactive interface;

> As a start at improving the interface for 3D viewing, the interface for the NASA Ames software, FAST (Flow Analysis Software Toolkit), permits the user to select a variety of coordinate systems for manipulation. Therefore, if you want to rotate about the center of the screen so your object of interest will not fly off the screen, you can select that option. If you want to roll the object of interest about the roll axis of the object (a typical maneuver for manipulating aircraft), you can select that option.

> In order to keep the object translations at 'expected rates', the translation rates are normalized to screen coordinate units rather than to world coordinate units. When world coordinate units are used, the objects move very slowly across the screen when viewing far from the object and rapidly across the screen when viewing close to the object. Normalizing the translation rate to screen coordinate units causes the objects to move across the screen at the same rate regardless of the viewing distance from the object.

> In order to permit quick changes of the viewing region, research is being conducted on 3D zoom boxes within the FAST interface. For the 'zoom in' box the screen is filled with the area designated by the zoom box. For the 'zoom out' box, the contents of the current screen are placed within the bounds of the zoom box, and the surrounding scene is added to fill out the screen. The 'zoom in' box is a standard tool for working with 2D scenes, but the 'zoom out' box is a new concept that must be tested

to determine if it is easily understood and used. Although both are well defined for 2D scenes, both are ill defined for 3D scenes. In 3D one cannot just change the field of view to simulate the zooming, because that would make the display of stereo vision incorrect. One must actually move the objects by the proper amount in z space in the eye coordinate system. The proper amount depends on the z distance of the object of interest. If the z in the scene is varying, then one must determine or approximate the z of the point the user has in mind. Kevin McCabe, a coauthor of FAST, has developed a technique for approximating the z value to use for the 'zoom in' box, based on reading the z values in the zoom box from the Z-buffer and using some average of these z values to approximate the z desired by the user. For the 'zoom out' box the mode of the z values will probably be adequate.

Research is being conducted by van Dam et al. at Brown University [Conn92] on an effective interface for manipulating, sculpting, and viewing of 3D objects. Silicon Graphics performed research on an interface for 3D visualization and incorporated the results in a tool called Inventor, which was recently released. This tool has received good initial reviews. If third party developers adopt this tool it may become the much-needed pseudostandard for 3D visualization.

NASA Ames [Banc90] is conducting research on the creation of a single visual environment for all the tasks involved in fluid dynamic simulations so the user does not have to change environments between the preprocessing, simulation, and analysis tasks. The environment being developed is an expansion of FAST, described above. The FAST interface is highly visual and interactive, to promote efficiency in all phases of fluid dynamic simulations. Although the program is still in beta testing, a number of NASA, industry, and university sites are using FAST as an environment for developing simulation technology and are using FAST as a basis for sharing the technology developed.

Recommendations for Designing New Visualization Systems

For people who wish to design their own future visualization software we recommend:

Select software tools based on the complexity of the visualization task;

Use data flow software for simple analysis tasks and for prototyping complex analysis tasks, but use lower-level graphics software to create programs more tailored to tasks for routine analysis of complex phenomena.

Design for high-performance hardware to be the norm for visual analysis in the future;

Think 3D.

All future hardware for visual analysis is expected to be based on 3D. Use 3D as much as possible to take advantage of the human's ability to comprehend better in 3D.

Use real-time interaction fully.

Design for direct manipulation of scenes and rendering techniques to permit the 'what-if' mode of investigation.

Design for rapid response, reducing resolution during manipulations, if necessary, to maintain speed.

Assure utilization of hardware.

Use Open GL or other graphics languages that fully and efficiently utilize the graphics hardware of the workstations. Greenberg [Gree91] provides a good explanation of why PHIGS is not appropriate as a language for visual analysis software. Currently, PEX does not permit adequate access to the hardware, e.g., PEX does not permit reading values from the Z-buffer. Open GL is likely to become a pseudostandard for a graphics language for high-performance graphics workstations of the future.

Design for performing most of the visual analysis on workstations rather than on supercomputers.

Based on the comparison of performance/price ratios of graphics computing on workstations and supercomputers, it is unlikely that performing visualization tasks on the supercomputer will be as cost-effective as on the workstations in the foreseeable future.

Use standards for 'look and feel' and 3D manipulation tools when possible:

Use Motif for the standard 'look and feel' for the window system.

Use Inventor for 3D manipulations.

At present, Inventor appears the most likely to become a pseudostandard for 3D manipulation, but one should track this field in case some other tool becomes more prevalent.

Make approximation techniques appropriate to the data.

Develop visualization tools that expect the approximation techniques to be included with the data.

Provide a variety of approximation techniques so that the user can experiment with different approximation techniques and choose the most appropriate one.

Make accuracy of rendering evident.

Provide error bounds or some other illustration of the errors due to approximations in rendering the scenes.

Investigate and apply techniques for matching human cognitive capabilities.

Conclusions

Current visualization tools have greatly improved understanding of simulations of physics and especially of fluid dynamics. However, we have just begun to learn how to create and use visualization tools. Current tools are 'punched card' versions compared to tools expected in the future. Future visualization software will be designed to take advantage of the much greater bandwidth of information that future hardware will offer, and will be designed to match the human cognitive capabilities so that understanding is maximized.

REFERENCES

[Banc89]
Bancroft, G.V., Plessel, T., Merritt, F., Walatka, P.P., and Watson, V.R., Scientific visualization in computational aerodynamics at NASA Ames Research Center, *IEEE Comp. Jour.*, pp. 89–94, August, 1989. Anthologized in *Visualization in Scientific Computing*, Nielson, G.N., and Shriver, B., IEEE book number 1979, ISBN 0-8186-8979-X, pp. 237–244, 1990.

[Brys91]
Bryson, S., and Levit, C., The virtual windtunnel: An environment for the exploration of three-dimensional unsteady flows, *Proc. Visualization 91*, pp. 17–24, Los Alamitos, CA: IEEE Computer Society Press, 1991.

[Butl89]
Butler, D.M., and Pendley, M.H., The visualization management system approach to visualization in scientific computing, *Computers in Physics*, September/October 1989.

[Carn69]
Carnahan, B., Luther, H.A., and Wilkes, J.O., *Applied Numerical Methods*, New York: John Wiley & Sons Publishers, 1969.

[Conn92]
Conner, D.B., Snibe, S.S., Herndon, K.P., Robbins, D.C., Zeleznik, R., and van Dam, A., Three-dimensional widgets, *Proc. '92 SIGGRAPH Symposium on Interactive 3D Graphics*, Cambridge, MA, March 29–April 1, 1992, pp. 183–188.

[Frie89]
Friedhoff, R., and Benzon, W., *Visualization — The Second Computer Revolution*, New York: Harry N. Abrams Publishers, 1989.

[Glob91]
Globus, A., Levit, C., and Lasinski, T., A tool for visualizing the topology of three-dimensional vector fields, *Proc. Visualization 91*, pp. 33–40, Los Alamitos, CA: IEEE Computer Society Press, 1991.

[Gree91]
Greenberg, D., More accurate simulations at faster rates, *IEEE Comput. Graph. and Appl.*, Vol. 11, No. 1, pp. 23–29, January 1991.

[Helm90]
Helman, J.L., and Hesselink, L., Surface representations of two- and three- dimensional fluid flow topology, *Proc. Visualization 90*, pp. 6–13, Los Alamitos, CA: IEEE Computer Society Press, 1990.

[Lore87]
Lorenson, W.E., and Cline, H.E., Marching cubes: a high resolution 3D surface construction algorithm, *Comput. Graph.*, Vol. 21, No. 4, pp. 163-169, 1987 (SIGGRAPH 87).

[McCo87]
McCormick, B.H., DeFanti,T.A., and Brown, M.D., Eds., Visualization in scientific computing, *Comput. Graph.*, Vol. 21, No. 6, November 1987.

[McKi80]
McKim, R.H., *Experiences in Visual Thinking*, Boston, MA: PWS Publishers/ Wadsworth, 1980.

[NCGA92]
The PLB Overview, *The GPC Quarterly Report*, Vol. 2, No. 2, National Computer Graphics Assoc., 2nd Qtr. 1992.

[Ning92]
Ning, P., and Hesselink, L., Octree pruning for variable-resolution isosurfaces, in *Visual Computing: Integrating Computer Graphics with Computer Vision*, Kunii, T.L., Ed., Tokyo: Springer-Verlag, pp. 349–363, 1992.

[Ples92]
Plessel, T., Private communication, 1992.

Modeling and Visualization
of Empirical Data

Ingrid Carlbom

Abstract

Many engineering and scientific applications in such diverse disciplines as medicine, biomedical research, geophysics, and robotics depend on the modeling and visualization of empirical data. Although the sources of data for each of these applications differ and considerable domain knowledge may be necessary to interpret the data, there is a great deal of commonality in the required modeling and visualization techniques. In this paper, we explore techniques in registration, segmentation, 3D reconstruction, and rendering, which are common to applications that depend on empirical data. The emphasis is on volumetric data sampled on regular grids, with examples from radiology, neuroscience, embryology, geophysics, and computer vision.

Introduction

Engineering, medical, and scientific applications depend on the modeling and visualization of empirical data. Robot-controlled vehicles use empirical data from their surroundings for navigation. Physicians use empirical data for medical diagnosis, surgery planning, and treatment planning. Neuroscientists use such data to model the structure and function of the central nervous system, and embryologists use empirical data to study the mechanisms of human development. Exploration geophysicists collect data to describe subsurface formations to determine the location, amount, and producability of hydrocarbon and mineral deposits. In these applications, data is collected from different sources and combined into models which are used to measure, simulate, and understand the structure and any relationships that may exist.

Although the sources of data for each of these applications differ and considerable domain knowledge may be necessary to interpret the data, there is a great deal of commonality in the required modeling and visualization techniques. In this paper, we explore techniques in registration, segmentation, 3D reconstruction, and rendering, which are common to most of these applications. Topics in registration include manual techniques for registering serial sections, semiautomatic, feature-based registration for comparative and composite analysis of 3D objects, and automatic techniques based on optical flow. Segmentation topics include statistical classification, region- and boundary-based techniques, and user-assisted techniques based on interactive deformable contours. Topics in 3D reconstruction include reconstruction from 2D contours, 3D surface samples, 3D volume samples, and shape-based interpolation. Finally, topics in volume rendering include volume ray-casting and voxel projection, implicit surface rendering, and parallel algorithms for volume rendering. We restrict our treatment to data sampled on regular grids and emphasize practical approaches to real applications, with examples from radiology, neurology, embryology, geophysics, and computer vision.

Each section starts with an overview of the most commonly used techniques and then explores a current research area. Before we begin our treatment of the first major topic, registration, we discuss two topics that underlie the remainder of the paper: digital filter design, and affine transformations for image and volume data.

Digital Filter Design

Digital filtering is a crucial operation in volume reconstruction and visualization. Lowpass filters are needed for subsampling and minification. Interpolation filters are needed for registration and magnification, and to compensate for geometric distortions introduced by scanners. Interpolation filters are also needed in volume rendering for ray-casting and slicing.

The accuracy of the lowpass and interpolation filters affects significantly the quality of the output. Insufficient attention to good filter design can lead to undesirable visual artifacts. However, visual inspection of an image or a volume is not always the most reliable criterion for determining if a filter is suitable. In fact, while a filter may yield visually pleasing results, the same filter can give rise to problems in registration or in performing certain calculations on the resulting 3D model.

There is, of course, no universally suitable lowpass or interpolation filter for volume reconstruction and visualization. Consequently, many different filters have been proposed [Mitc88; Wolb90]. The appropriate filter is highly dependent on the characteristics of the data, the sampling rate, and the desired result. Filter design also requires tradeoffs between computational expense and accuracy. Undoubtedly, different filters must be used at different stages in volume reconstruction and visualization.

In this section, we describe a method for digital filter design which is based on visual inspection of the filter frequency response. We also show how a judicious choice of filter parameters can improve filter accuracy. Finally, we compare the resulting filter with the most commonly used filter in volume visualization: the linear interpolation filter. For readers unfamiliar with sampling theory, the appendix contains some commonly used terms. More details can be found in standard signal or image processing texts [Duda73; Oppe75; Rose76; Gonz77; Dudg84; Lim90; Wolb90].

FILTER DESIGN BY THE WINDOW METHOD

We start with the ideal frequency response of a filter and derive the ideal impulse response from this frequency response. Since the resulting impulse response is of infinite duration, we restrict the impulse response to a finite duration interval by multiplying the impulse response by a finite-duration window. Finally, we adjust the filter and window parameters to get the best possible correspondence between the frequency response of the ideal filter and the windowed ideal filter in the finite duration interval (see also [Oppe75; Dudg84; Lim90]).

Lowpass Filter

A subsampling operation must be preceded by a lowpass filtering operation to remove high frequency components that can cause aliasing in the subsampled signal. The frequency response of the ideal lowpass filter is

$$H(u) = \begin{cases} 1 & \text{if } -u_0 \leq u \leq u_0 \\ 0 & \text{otherwise} \end{cases} \tag{1}$$

It is called the ideal lowpass filter because the low frequencies in the passband $-u_0 \leq u \leq u_0$ are retained (passed) with no attenuation, and the higher frequencies in the stopband are completely attenuated. The variable u_0 is called the cutoff frequency.

The impulse response $h(m)$ of the ideal lowpass filter is the inverse Fourier transform of the frequency response

$$h(m) = \frac{\sin(2\pi u_0 m)}{\pi m} \tag{2}$$

where m ranges over the sampling points and u_0 is the cutoff frequency. The impulse response is of infinite duration; hence, we must restrict the length of the filter to a finite interval to arrive at a practical implementation. One way to do this is by multiplying the impulse response by a rectangular window

$$g_r(m) = \begin{cases} 1 & \text{if } |m| \leq \dfrac{(L-1)}{2} \\ 0 & \text{otherwise} \end{cases} \tag{3}$$

where L is the width of the window. In Figure 1 we show the impulse response and the frequency response of the ideal filter windowed with a rectangular window.[†] We note three problems with the windowed ideal filter: the impulse response exhibits significant ringing, which results in undesirable 'rippling' effects around sharp transitions in the sampled signal; the frequency response has significant side lobes outside the cutoff frequency, which results in aliasing in the

---

[†]The actual filter impulse response is discrete. What is plotted here is the corresponding bandlimited, continuous-parameter counterpart.

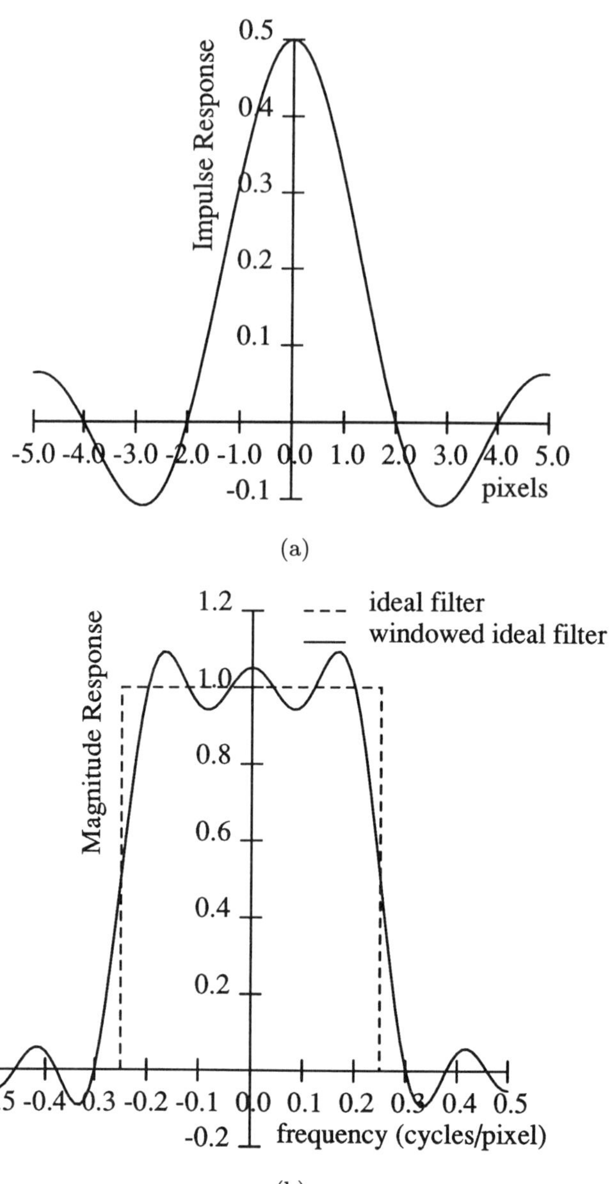

Figure 1. Impulse and frequency magnitude response for an ideal lowpass filter, with a rectangular window, for subsampling by a factor of two (i.e., $u_0 = 0.25$). (a) Impulse response; (b) frequency response.

sampled signal; and the frequency response exceeds unity, which causes some distortion in the sampled signal.

To improve upon this filter, we multiply it with a window that tapers smoothly to zero at each end of the filter. We choose a raised cosine

$$g_c(m) = \begin{cases} (1-k) + k\cos \dfrac{2\pi m}{L+1} & \text{if } |m| \le \dfrac{(L-1)}{2} \\ \\ 0 & \text{otherwise} \end{cases} \tag{4}$$

where L is the width of the window. (For $k = 0.5$, the resulting window is called a Hanning window [Oppe75] or a Hann window [Wolb90].)

Two variables determine the shape of the lowpass filter $(g_c(m)h(m), |m| \le (L-1)/2)$, the filter length L and the frequency cutoff u_0. To select a suitable value for L, for several values of L we plot the frequency response magnitude for the filter (Figure 2a). Similarly, to select a suitable value for u_0, for several values of u_0 we plot the frequency response magnitude for the filter (Figure 2b). We choose values for L and u_0 which give good agreement between the desired frequency response and the actual frequency response.

The raised cosine reduces the side lobes in the frequency response significantly, as well as some of the ringing in the impulse response, but at the expense of a more gradual transition between the passband and the stopband.

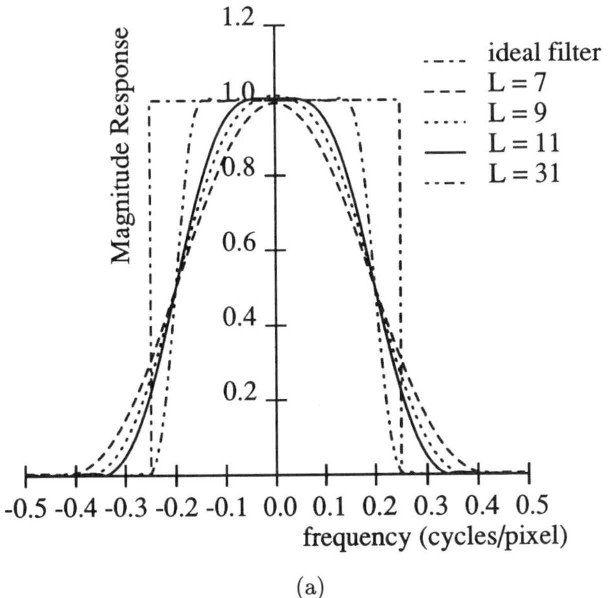

(a)

Figure 2. Frequency magnitude response for windowed ideal lowpass filter. (a) Different filter lengths; (b) different cutoff frequencies.

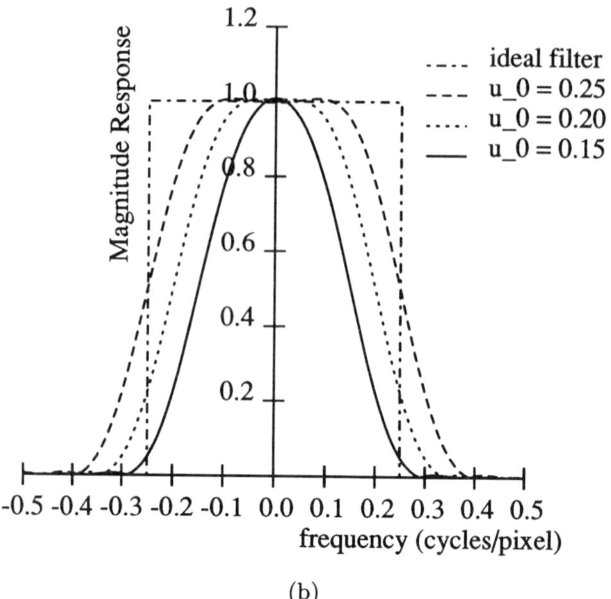

(b)

Figure 2. (*Continued.*)

Interpolation Filter

The simplest and most often used method of interpolation is linear interpolation; that is, an interpolated sample is computed as the weighted average of the
surrounding samples. Linear interpolation can be implemented by a convolution
with a filter whose impulse response is

$$h_l(m, \tau) = \begin{cases} 1 - \tau & \text{if } m = 0 \\ \tau & \text{if } m = 1 \\ 0 & \text{otherwise} \end{cases} \tag{5}$$

where τ, $(0 \le \tau \le 1)$, is the fractional distance to the nearest sample. As we
shall see later, the linear interpolator performs well only for low frequencies.
We proceed by designing an interpolation filter that performs better for higher
frequencies, again using the window design method.

An interpolation filter is equivalent to a filter that shifts or delays a signal
by a noninteger number of sampling periods; that is, shifting in the frequency
domain is equivalent to interpolation in the spatial domain.

If a signal $e^{i2\pi ut}$ is delayed by τ, then the delayed signal is of the form

$$e^{i2\pi u(t-\tau)} = e^{i2\pi ut} e^{-i2\pi u\tau} \tag{6}$$

Thus, the frequency response of the ideal shift filter is $H_\tau(u) = e^{-i2\pi u\tau}$. The impulse response of the ideal filter is the inverse Fourier transform of the frequency response[†]

$$h_i(m, \tau) = \frac{\sin\left(\pi(m - \tau)\right)}{\pi(m - \tau)} \tag{7}$$

where m ranges over the sampling points, and τ is the fractional delay.

The impulse response is of infinite duration; again we apply a Hanning window. In this case there is one variable, the filter length L, which determines the shape of the frequency response. For several values of L we plot the frequency response and choose a value which gives good agreement between the desired frequency response and the actual frequency response. A shift filter, in contrast to the lowpass filter above, is not a zero-phase filter, and we must get good agreement in both magnitude and phase.

In Figure 3 we see that the linear interpolator performs well only for low frequencies ($-0.1 \leq u \leq 0.1$), which means that linear interpolation gives good results only if the sampling rate is at least five times the Nyquist rate. In contrast, we see that the windowed ideal shift filter with eleven filter coefficients performs well for frequencies in the interval $-0.35 \leq u \leq 0.35$, and gives good results for a correspondingly lower sampling rate.

Two- and Three-dimensional Filters

The filters just discussed are separable filters, that is, they are two-dimensional filters which can be implemented as a cascade of two one-dimensional filters, one operating in the x direction, the other in the y direction [Dudg84]. Similarly, a three-dimensional filter can be implemented as a cascade of three one-dimensional filters.

However, sometimes it is computationally advantageous to apply a 2D or 3D filter directly, instead of a sequence of two or three 1D filters. Given a one-dimensional filter $h(m)$, $0 \leq m \leq L$, the corresponding two-dimensional filter is $g(m, n) = h(m) h(n)$, $0 \leq m, n \leq L$, and the corresponding three-dimensional filter is $f(m, n, k) = h(m) h(n) h(k)$, $0 \leq m, n, k \leq L$.

Affine Transformations of Images and Volumes

Affine transformations are used in registration and sometimes also in rendering of volume data. Registration of, for example, two CT (computer tomography) data sets of the same subject requires 3D rotation and translation of one of the data sets to align it with the other. Similarly, registration of 3D volumes from different modalities, such as CT and MR (magnetic resonance) data, requires

---

[†]Since this filter is not shift-invariant (it varies with τ), we make τ a parameter, contrary to other definitions of shift filters.

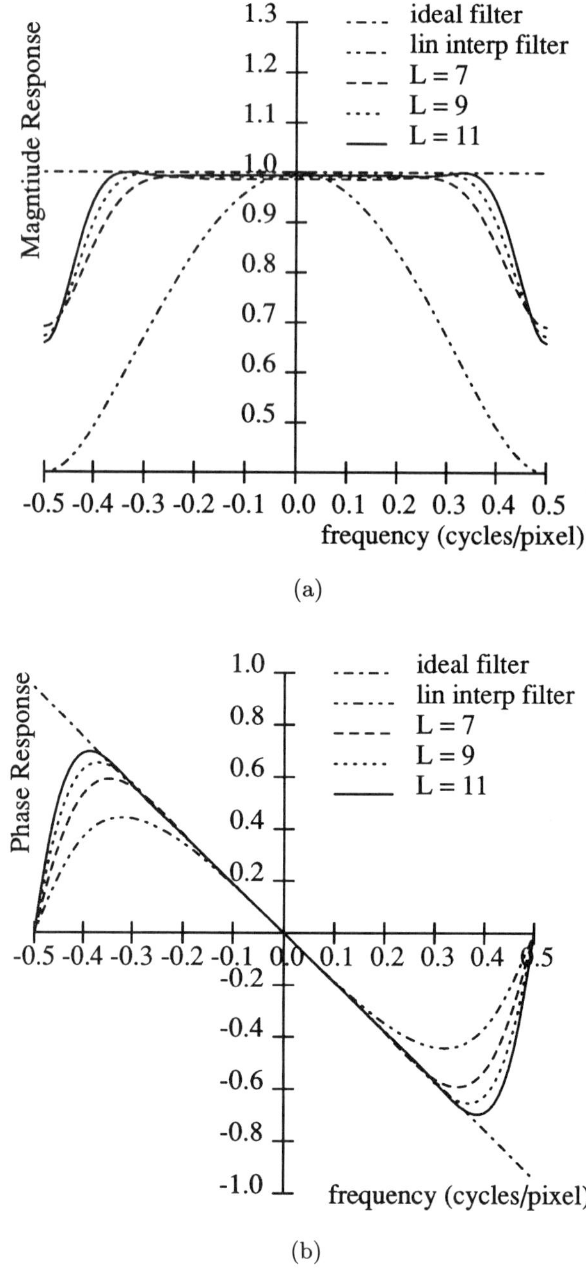

Figure 3. Frequency response for a windowed ideal shift filter; $\tau = 0.3$. (a) Magnitude response; (b) phase response.

3D rotation, scaling, and translation. Finally, as we shall see in a later section, volume rendering sometimes also depends on 3D rotation and scaling to align the 3D volume with the projection plane.

All affine transformations, except translations by integer values or rotations of multiples of 90 degrees, require resampling of the image or volume using a fractional interpolation filter. Also, if we are reducing the size of the image or volume the application of a lowpass filter is necessary. In the remainder of this section we describe algorithms for 2D image transformations; 3D extensions are straightforward.

Assume that an image is transformed by an affine transformation $[T]$, which can be expressed as a homogeneous matrix

$$\begin{bmatrix} x' \\ y' \\ 1 \end{bmatrix} = \begin{bmatrix} a & b & c \\ d & e & f \\ 0 & 0 & 1 \end{bmatrix} \begin{bmatrix} x \\ y \\ 1 \end{bmatrix} \tag{8}$$

Traverse the transformed image in row order, and for each pixel find the corresponding position in the original image, using the inverse of $[T]$ as illustrated in Figure 4. This position, in general, lies between pixels and not exactly on a pixel. Thus, we use an interpolation filter to find the value for the pixel in the transformed image.

An affine transformation can be implemented as a two-pass algorithm in the 2D case [Smit87] and a three-pass algorithm in the 3D case [Hanr90]. This approach is based on the observation that a 2D affine transformation can be decomposed into six transformations: a scaling, shearing, and translating in one axis, followed by a scaling, shearing, and translation in the other axis. That is,

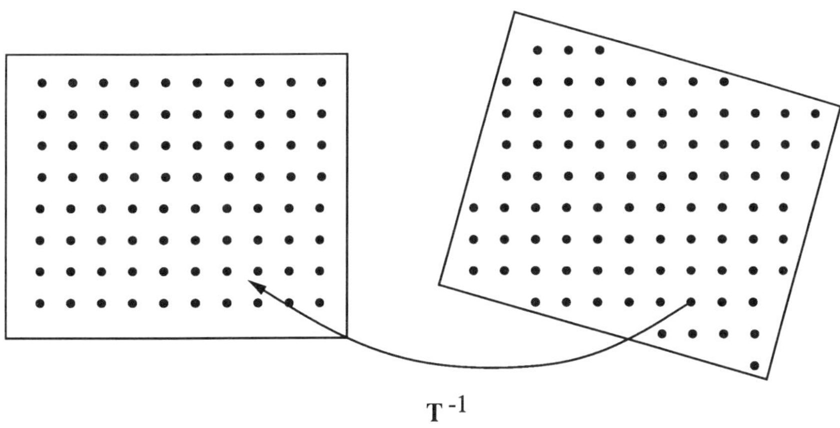

Figure 4. Image transformation.

$[T]$ can be written as

$$\begin{bmatrix} a & b & c \\ d & e & f \\ 0 & 0 & 1 \end{bmatrix} = \begin{bmatrix} 1 & 0 & 0 \\ d' & e' & f' \\ 0 & 0 & 1 \end{bmatrix} \begin{bmatrix} a & b & c \\ 0 & 1 & 0 \\ 0 & 0 & 1 \end{bmatrix} \tag{9}$$

or
$$[T] = [T_y][T_x] \tag{10}$$

The matrix $[T_x]$ is a product of a translate, a shear, and a scale matrix in x, and the matrix $[T_y]$ is a product of a translate, a shear, and a scale matrix in y. The transformation $[T_x]^{-1}$ requires fractional interpolation in the x direction only, as illustrated in Figure 5; similarly, $[T_y]^{-1}$ requires fractional interpolation in the y direction only.

This two-pass algorithm has two potential advantages: a one-dimensional interpolation filter can be used for each transformation, and the convolutions require fewer operations than in the first algorithm. In addition, the formulation of a 2D transformation into two separate transformations of this form results in a matrix access pattern that may lend itself to efficient parallel implementation.

Registration

Registration refers to the alignment of data from the same or different modalities, or sensors. Alignment is required to compensate for: misregistration, such as that occurring in temporal image sequences from the same scene; physical changes over time or space, such as in images of a beating heart; or a combination of the two, such as the alignment of sections from serial microscopy. The first example requires only a rigid body transformation, while the second requires a nonlinear

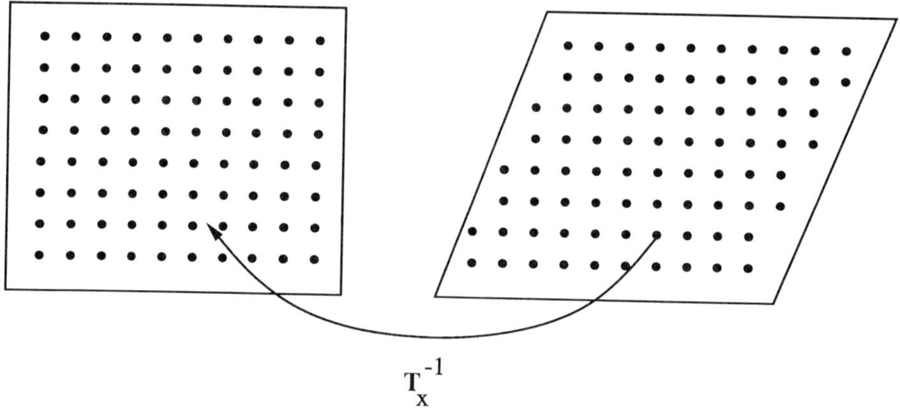

Figure 5. Image shearing.

transformation (image or volume warping). The last example requires a combination of a linear transformation to bring the sections into approximate alignment, followed by a nonlinear transformation to account for distortions in the tissue preparation process and the physical changes in the tissue between slices.

The registration techniques discussed in the literature are classified into three broad categories: manual techniques using color and motion, semiautomatic techniques based on feature or landmark extraction, and automatic techniques based on intensity or color constancy. No technique performs effectively on a broad variety of data. The most reliable results are obtained when registration is accomplished with a linear transformation based on reliable landmarks. Nonlinear registration, although also important, has received much less attention in the literature to date.

We first discuss two manual techniques for registration of 2D data. Next we discuss semiautomatic techniques based on landmarks and on feature extraction. Finally, we describe registration based on optical flow, a method used in computer vision for the registration of temporal image sequences.

MANUAL REGISTRATION

One manual technique is an interactive digital blink comparator, which uses perceived visual motion to align pairs of images [Carl91]. One image of the image pair is held stationary, and the user translates and rotates the other image while the two images are alternately shown on a graphics screen. There is an illusion of movement when the images are misaligned, and the movement is reduced by translating and rotating the image. The images are aligned when the sum of the motion between the two images is minimized. We obtain comparisons at a frequency of about 2 Hz for a 640×496 pixel image on a DECstation 5000/240HX. This frequency is adequate to obtain good alignment, although a higher speed would be desirable.

Another manual technique for aligning two images is similar to the blink comparator, in that the user translates and rotates one of the images while the other is held stationary. This method uses color instead of motion to guide the registration. The two images are encoded using two distinct colors, and the images are added to form a third distinct color. Perfect alignment maximizes the area of the third color. The advantage of this method over the blink comparator is that it is easier to evaluate the accuracy of the alignment. The disadvantages are: it is harder to determine the direction to move the image; color image addition and display often consume more compute time than display of monochrome images; and this method does not work well for images with a large amount of detail, especially when the discrepancy between the images is large. Plate 3 shows two sections from an embryo heart, (a) before registration and (b) after registration with the color merging method. Plate 4 shows two sections of a nerve cell that have also been aligned using color merging. In both Plates 3 and 4, one image is blue, the other yellow; regions that overlap are some shade of grey. As is illustrated, color merging does not work well for the nerve cell due to the discrepancy between adjoining sections, but it works much better for the embryo heart.

FEATURE-BASED REGISTRATION

Many semiautomatic methods are discussed in the literature for registration of both 2D and 3D data. These techniques require feature or landmark extraction through manual or semiautomatic means, as well as determination of feature or landmark correspondence. In some applications, fiducial marks (extrinsic landmarks) are used to aid the registration, and in some biomedical applications registration marks are inserted in the tissue itself before the tissue is sectioned and imaged. However, in many cases, such as for internal living organs, landmarks must be selected after the imaging.

Cross correlation is used to register retinal images in [Byrn90], where edges of common features in adjoining images are employed in the correlation process. Giertsen et al. [Gier90] propose a method to align electron micrographs which uses both control points and moments. They manually trace the membrane and internal substructures of a pancreatic cell in serial sections and specify connectivity relations among successive contours. Using contour shape features (centroids and mean radii), they determine linear transformations between successive contours and refine the alignment using residuals between the original and smoothed data.

Methods for 3D object matching include matching of characteristic curves [Guez91]. These curves are B-spline representations of, for example, surface borders, borders of holes, or ridge points. After the curves are selected they are matched using rigid body transformations. Another example is matching 3D anatomical surfaces to 2D X-rays [Lava91]. The authors assume that the anatomical surface is already extracted and develop a method for matching the projection of the surface with the corresponding contour in the X-ray, by minimizing the distances along the projectors from the surface to the contour.

Comparative analysis is used to measure change over time in, for example, pre- and postoperative CT scans. Registration is necessary to compensate for variations in subject positioning during the scans. One example of comparative analysis is motivated by the desire to quantitatively evaluate the result of bone-graft surgery [Toen89,90]. Pre- and postoperative scans are defined in a scanner coordinate system. Since the same subject and the same modality are used, registration requires a composite translation and rotation to align the pre- and postoperative subject data. First, a set of landmarks is identified interactively from each scan,[†] and then these landmarks are used to find the composite transformation. If the locations of the landmarks were completely accurate, then three landmarks should suffice for registration. However, operator and quantization errors make it desirable to base the transformation on a larger number of landmarks. To accomplish this, the composite transformation is derived using principal component analysis. A covariance matrix is found for each set of landmarks, whose origin is the centroid of the landmarks, and whose eigenvalues form

---

[†]Herman and Abbott [Herm89] describe a methodology for selecting a set of 24 landmarks on CT scans of the head, including the left condylion (the head of the mandible) and the nasale (the tip of the nose ridge bone).

an orthogonal coordinate system. The composite translation and rotation transformation that aligns the subject data is the same transformation that aligns the two coordinate systems formed by the eigenvectors of the covariance matrices. The accuracy of the landmarks is determined using cross validation, whereby a subset of the landmarks is used to predict whether the remaining landmarks increase or decrease the accuracy of the transformation. The authors report errors in the registration on the order of one voxel. (Other minimization techniques can be used, for example, based on least-squares fitting of the two landmark sets [Arun87; Horn90].)

Composite analysis is used to combine data from multiple modalities, such as CT, MR, and PET (positron emission tomography). Here registration is also necessary to compensate for variations in subject positioning during the scans. In addition, differences in resolution must be considered. As a result, registration requires a composite translation, rotation, and scaling transformation. One way to proceed is by basing the registration on matching anatomical surfaces, such as the outer (skin) surface in the data sets [Levi88; Peli89]. The surfaces are extracted slice-by-slice by a semiautomatic contouring program. The longest scan is represented as a set of contours, referred to as the 'head', and the second scan as a subset of the points on the contours, the 'hat'. The hat is fitted onto the head by minimizing the distance between hat and head points in a least-squares sense. Finally, one of the data sets is resampled along the slices of the second set, and the two data sets are overlaid. The authors report errors of similar magnitude as in the previous example, namely on the order of one voxel in the lower resolution scan.

OPTICAL FLOW

Optical flow is an automatic registration technique where the local pixel motion is estimated by assuming that points move between images but keep the same intensity. The optical flow between two images is a set of vectors between corresponding pixels in the two images [Horn81]. To register two images, we find the flow that best aligns the pixels in the two images. Using the approach in [Berg92], we minimize

$$E(\{\vec{u}\}) = \sum_{\hat{x}} \left[I_1(\hat{x}) - I_2(\hat{x} - \vec{u}(\hat{x})) \right]^2 \tag{11}$$

where E denotes the error, $I(\hat{x})$ the image intensity at position $\hat{x} = [\, x \quad y \,]^T$, $[\vec{u}(\hat{x})] = [\, u(\hat{x}) \quad v(\hat{x}) \,]^T$ the flow at position $\hat{x}$, and $\{\vec{u}\}$ the entire flow field. Optical flow has been used for registration of motion sequences in computer vision and for data compression of image sequences [Berg92], but could apply also to registration of other types of image or volume data.

A brute-force search for optimum alignment is very time consuming; hence, a search strategy involving a pyramid of images and an iterative minimization method is employed. The pyramid contains a collection of images, where each level is a blurred and subsampled version of the previous image. The low-resolution images enable large displacements between images to be computed quickly; higher resolution images are then used to improve the accuracy. Registration proceeds as follows: two pyramids are constructed, one for each image; an optical flow model is selected and applied to the images starting at the apex of the pyramids and moving toward the base; at each iteration, one image is resampled during flow computation.

Given the current flow estimate $\{\vec{u}\}$, we estimate the incremental error $\{\delta\vec{u}\}$ using a first-order expansion [Berg92]

$$E(\{\vec{u} + \delta\vec{u}\}) = \sum_{\hat{x}} \left[\Delta I(\hat{x}) - \nabla I_2^T(\hat{x} - \vec{u}(\hat{x})) \delta\vec{u}(\hat{x}) \right]^2 \tag{12}$$

where
$$\Delta I(\hat{x}) = I_1(\hat{x}) - I_2(\hat{x} - \vec{u}(\hat{x})) \tag{13}$$

is the difference between the images using the current flow estimate, and $\nabla = [\partial/\partial x \quad \partial/\partial y]^T$ denotes the gradient.

We describe two flow models, a global model for affine flow and a local model for general flow. Other flow models are described in [Berg92]. The affine model could be used for composite analysis of data from multiple modalities; for comparative analysis of data from one modality, a rigid body transformation results in better registration. The general flow model could be used for nonlinear registration of, for example, serial tissue sections.

An affine flow model is expressed as

$$\begin{bmatrix} u(\hat{x}) \\ v(\hat{x}) \end{bmatrix} = \begin{bmatrix} a & b & c \\ d & e & f \end{bmatrix} \begin{bmatrix} x \\ y \\ 1 \end{bmatrix} \tag{14}$$

This equation is rewritten as

$$[\vec{u}(\hat{x})] = [X(\hat{x})][\hat{a}] \tag{15}$$

where $[\hat{a}] = [a\ b\ c\ d\ e\ f]^T$ and

$$[X(\hat{x})] = \begin{bmatrix} x & y & 1 & 0 & 0 & 0 \\ 0 & 0 & 0 & x & y & 1 \end{bmatrix} \tag{16}$$

If $[\hat{a}]$ is the current flow estimate, an incremental estimate for $[\hat{a} + \delta\hat{a}]$ is found by substituting into Eq. (11)

$$E(\hat{a} + \delta\hat{a}) = \sum_{\hat{x}} \left\{ \Delta I(\hat{x}) - \nabla I_2^T(\hat{x} - [X(\hat{x})][\hat{a}]) [X(\hat{x})]\delta\hat{a} \right\}^2 \tag{17}$$

which is minimized with respect to $[\delta\hat{a}]$ to get a new flow estimate.

The affine flow model is a global model where the flow is identical over the entire image; a general flow model is a local model where the flow varies over the image. Bergen et al. [Berg92] suggest a model that is constant over a small window (5 × 5 pixels), which leads to the error estimate

$$E(\vec{u} + \delta\vec{u}) = \sum_{\hat{x}} \left\{ \Delta I(\hat{x}) - \nabla I_2^T(\hat{x} - \vec{u})\delta\vec{u} \right\}^2 \qquad (18)$$

where the sum is taken over the small window.

Optical flow is used for stereo matching of images [Okut90], for depth estimation in image sequences [Matt89], for matching of temporal image sequences [Anan84], and for reconstructing 3D models of an object rotating in front of a camera [Szel90]. In this last application, an object, like the tea can in Figure 6a, is placed on a turntable, and an image sequence of the rotating object is recorded. The author computes a flow field using a local flow model (Plate 5a). Since the flow calculation depends on local variation in the images, certain areas, like the background, result in a noisy flow. A certainty map (Plate 5b) is used to filter out the noise. The resulting points on the images are mapped into 3D, using knowledge of the object rotation angle and the camera position. The position of the points are subsequently refined as the object turns and new measurements of the points are added (Figure 6b).

Segmentation

Segmentation refers to the process of extracting meaningful regions from images or volumes. Such regions typically correspond to objects of interest or their parts. Many techniques have been developed for 2D and 3D image segmentation.

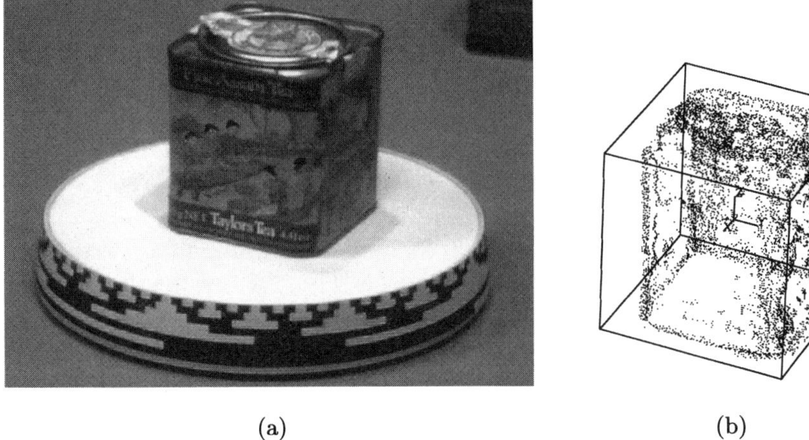

(a)   (b)

Figure 6. Object reconstruction from optical flow. (a) One of the original images; (b) model point cloud. (Courtesy Richard Szeliski, Digital Equipment Corporation).

They can be categorized into statistical classification methods, region growing methods, and boundary methods [Rose76; Gonz77; Ball82]. None of these general techniques performs well on a broad variety of data, even within the same domain. This deficiency prompted the development of ad hoc techniques tailored to individual types of data and problems.

We now describe a statistical classification technique based on Bayesian estimation. Next we describe techniques based on region and boundary detection. All of these methods require well-defined boundaries without holes. We end this section with a user-assisted technique which uses interactive deformable contours to localize meaningful regions that need not have well-defined boundaries.

STATISTICAL CLASSIFICATION

The simplest classification method, intensity thresholding, was used in [Vann83; Farr85; Frie85] to segment CT data and in [Wolp88] to segment seismic data. Thresholding tends to introduce aliasing; each voxel is classified as being of one material or another, even though it may contain a mixture of the two. Aliasing is reduced by employing a linear ramp instead of a step function to map the sample values to opacities or color [West91].

Another way to reduce aliasing is to assign to the voxel the percentages of different materials present in the voxel. A probabilistic classifier is employed to derive the probability that a certain material is present in the voxel, and this probability is used to estimate the percentage of the material.

A Bayesian model is a statistical classifier which relates a sensor model $P(I|m_i)$ (the sensor's response I to material m_i) and a prior model $P(m_i)$ (which gives the probability of the presence of material m_i) to the posterior model $P(m_i|I)$ (the probability that a sensor response I was the result of material m_i) [Fell57; Szel89]. Bayes' rule is expressed as

$$P(m_i|I) = \frac{P(I|m_i)P(m_i)}{P(I)} \tag{19}$$

where
$$P(I) = \sum_i P(I|m_i)P(m_i) \tag{20}$$

$P(I|m_i)$ and $P(m_i|I)$ are shown for two different materials in Figure 7. The dashed vertical line indicates the cutoff point for thresholding.

If we want to classify voxels from CT data, the materials m_i are air, fat, soft tissue, and bone; and the sensor model $P(I|m_i)$ represents the probability distributions of the CT attenuation for the different materials. If we assume that the presence of any material is equally likely, that is, $P(m_i)$ are identical for all i, then we get a maximum likelihood classifier. This type of classification was used in [Dreb88; Ney90]. Plate 6 shows the result of maximum likelihood classification of one CT slice. The top image is the original slice, and the left image is a color representation of the classified slice. Blue represents fat, red soft tissue, and green bone. Yellow represents a mixture of soft tissue (red) and bone

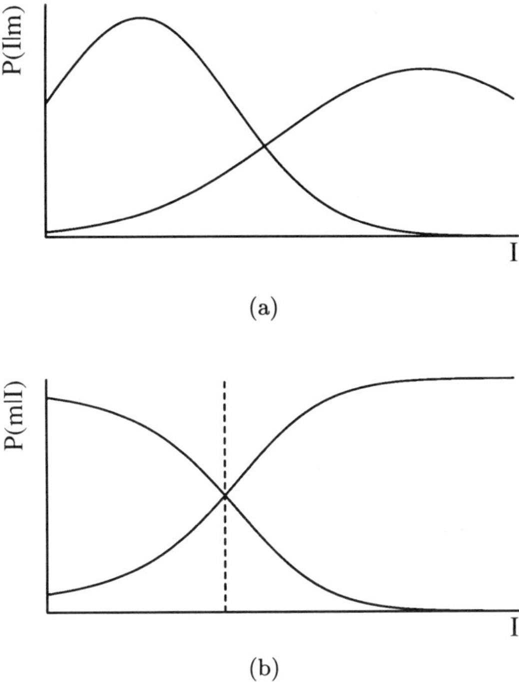

Figure 7. Simple example of Bayesian modeling. (a) Sensor models; (b) classification. (Reproduced from [Szel89].)

(green). The right image shows the opacity resulting from the classification. Plate 7 shows the result of maximum likelihood classification of several 3D CT data sets. Reading Plate 7 left to right, the top row shows the lateral view of a skull; a thigh melanoma; a shoulder, in which the upper part shows a humeral fracture and the lower part soft tissue. The middle row shows a frontal view of the pelvis, the upper part showing bone and the lower part soft tissue; a lung specimen; a pelvis and sacrum. The bottom row illustrates the base of a skull; a humeral fracture; a knee, the upper part showing bone and the lower part soft tissue.

REGION-BASED SEGMENTATION

Region-based segmentation algorithms can be divided into region-growing algorithms that use a bottom-up approach, and split-and-merge algorithms that use a top-down approach. Region-growing algorithms start from a seed point and find neighboring points belonging to the same region. These algorithms use some search strategy, generally neighboring horizontal spans, and can employ different inclusion criteria, such as intensity, color, gradient, and texture. Region-growing algorithms are similar to region-fill algorithms in computer graphics [Fole90].

A region-growing algorithm starts with a seed point and finds the one region containing that seed point, while connected component labeling algorithms find all connected regions in an image without requiring seed points. A connected component algorithm can be implemented in three phases [Same81]:

> The image is traversed in row order, and all adjacencies are explored. The pixels are assigned pixel classes, each class containing adjacent pixels of the same or similar intensity. Should pixel classes be found equivalent, the class labels are added to a list of equivalences; this is illustrated in Figure 8. In this figure there are only two regions. However, when traversing row i we note three pixel classes. Not until row k do we note that the three classes found in row i represent only two different connected components;

> The pairs of equivalences are processed to give the minimum number of connected regions;

> The image is traversed, and the pixels are labeled according to their class.

An example of a connected component labeling algorithm for medical data is found in [Rhod79].

A split-and-merge algorithm starts with a high-level partition of the image into initial regions. Each region is examined, and if it contains elements with different properties (e.g., intensity, color, texture) the region is further divided. If neighboring regions contain elements with the same property the neighboring regions are merged. The algorithm halts when no more regions can be split or merged [Ball82].

Region-based algorithms yield a low-level segmentation, using only local information. To group some of the smaller regions into larger, more meaningful regions, multiresolution techniques are employed, where images are described by tree structures which link features in successively blurred versions of the original images [Cull90; Lifs90; Pize90; Vinc90]. The segmented images generally need

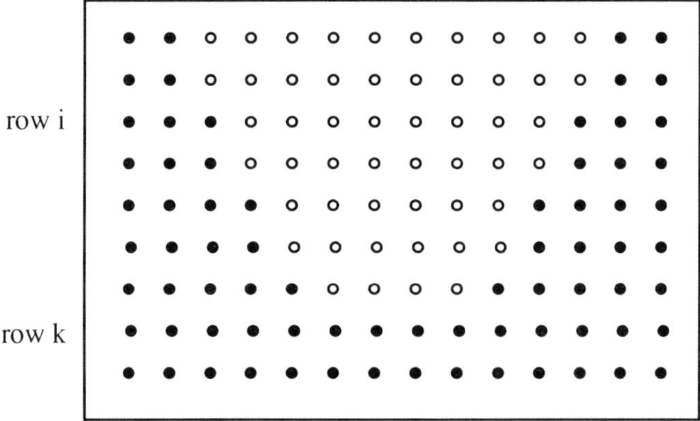

Figure 8. Connected component labeling of an image; samples have two intensities indicated by filled and unfilled circles.

postprocessing to correct for minor errors, and to group segmented regions into, for example, anatomically meaningful regions [Fred90].

BOUNDARY-BASED SEGMENTATION

Boundary-based segmentation techniques are based on various 3D edge detectors, which are often generalizations of 2D edge detectors. They fall into three categories. The first category fits surface patches to a neighborhood of a voxel in a volume. These patches may be planar [Morg81; Zuck81] or quadratic [Morg81; Sand90; Mong91], and are generally best-fitting in a least-squares sense. The iso-surface approximation discussed in the section on three-dimensional reconstruction is a special case of this category, and could equally well be described here.

A second category is surface-tracking algorithms. These algorithms start by picking an initial boundary element (generally interactively) and then find the next boundary element according to some criteria, such as proximity, gradient, or local curvature. These algorithms need some method for backtracking or eliminating boundaries that do not close. Examples of this type are found in [Liu77; Capp89]. A special class of surface tracking algorithms is developed for binary images [Gord89; Udup90]. These algorithms assume that the segmentation is completed, and are used to find a surface representation of the segmented object. Dynamic programming is also used to track boundaries of regions according to some criteria [Ball82].

The third category applies a 3D operator to the volume. A simple example is the gradient operator, which is used to render surfaces in a volume; this technique is discussed in a later section on shading models for volume data. Although that section is about volume rendering, gradient shading is in fact an implicit segmentation technique, in that it highlights one or more surfaces bounding some area of interest. Another operator, which works on a larger neighborhood of a voxel than the gradient, is the 3D extension to the Marr-Hildreth operator [Hohn88,89,90; Boma90]. The Marr-Hildreth operator is the Laplacian of a Gaussian

$$I'(x, y, z) = \nabla^2 \big(G_\sigma(x, y, z) * I(x, y, z)\big) \tag{21}$$

where I represents the original volume. $G_\sigma(x, y, z)*$ represents convolution with the Gaussian operator

$$G_\sigma(x, y, z) = \frac{1}{\sqrt{(2\pi)^3 \sigma^3}} \, e^{\frac{-(x^2 + y^2 + z^2)}{2\sigma^2}} \tag{22}$$

and
$$\nabla^2 G(x, y, z) = \frac{\partial^2 G}{\partial x^2} + \frac{\partial^2 G}{\partial y^2} + \frac{\partial^2 G}{\partial z^2} \tag{23}$$

the Laplacian.

The Marr-Hildreth operator first smooths the volume data, thereby removing high frequency components. The gradient has high values at surface boundaries, while the Laplacian has zero crossing. The zero crossings of I' are considered to be the object boundary. The resulting surfaces do not always correspond to correct anatomical structures. The errors are removed in a postprocessing step by filling holes and eliminating thin passages between objects.

INTERACTIVE DEFORMABLE CONTOURS

Snakes, or interactive deformable contours, are a model-based image feature localization and tracking technique [Kass88; Carl91]. The user quickly traces a contour which approximates the desired boundary, then starts a dynamic simulation that enables the contour to locate and conform to the true boundary. Where necessary, the user guides the contour using a mouse to apply simulated forces. With some guidance from the user, snakes exploit the coherence between adjoining images to quickly extract a sequence of regions. Snakes are dynamic models that differ substantially from manual contouring approaches. Snakes are attracted to image boundaries through forces, which not only reduces the contouring time but also increases the accuracy of the tracing.

The ability of snakes to conform to complex biological shapes such as cells, and to track their nonrigid deformations across image sequences, makes them attractive tools for biomedical image analysis. In [Leym90] snakes are used to track living cells moving on a planar surface. Ayache et al. [Ayac89] use snakes to find edges in cross sections of MR data. A 3D version of snakes is also used to segment MR data [Cohe91]. Variations on snakes based on B-splines are applied to the segmentation of CT and MR data [Leit90]. Other model-based CT and MR data segmentation methods closely related to snakes include the Fourier curve models proposed by Duncan et al. [Dunc90] and the deformable templates of Lipson et al. [Lips90].

Deformable Contour Models[†]

A snake can be thought of as a dynamic deformable contour in the xy image plane. We define a discrete deformable contour as a set of n nodes indexed by $i = 1, \ldots, n$, with time varying positions $[\hat{x}_i(t)] = [x_i(t) \quad y_i(t)]^T$. The behavior of an interactive deformable contour is governed by the first-order dynamic system of equations

$$\gamma \frac{d[\hat{x}_i]}{dt} + \vec{\alpha}_i + \vec{\beta}_i = \vec{f}_i \qquad i = 1, \ldots, n \qquad (24)$$

where γ is a velocity-dependent damping constant, the $\vec{\alpha}_i(t)$ are 'tension' forces which make the snake act like a series of springs that resist deformation, the $\vec{\beta}_i(t)$ are 'rigidity' forces which make the snake act like a thin wire that resists bending, and the $\vec{f}_i(t)$ are forces in the image plane applied to the contour.

Let l_i be the given reference length of the spring connecting node i to node $i + 1$, and let $\vec{r}_i(t) = [\hat{x}_{i+1}] - [\hat{x}_i]$ be the separation of the nodes. Given the

---

[†]This section is adapted from [Carl91].

deformation $e_i(t) = \|\vec{r}_i\| - l_i$, we define

$$\vec{\alpha}_i = \frac{a_i e_i}{\|\vec{r}_i\|}\,\vec{r}_i - \frac{a_{i-1}e_{i-1}}{\|\vec{r}_{i-1}\|}\,\vec{r}_{i-1} \tag{25}$$

It is convenient to create contours that gradually stretch or shrink in a viscoelastic manner under a sustained applied force. A viscoelastic contour results from setting

$$\frac{dl_i}{dt} = \nu_i e_i \tag{26}$$

where ν_i is a coefficient of viscoelasticity. To give the contours some rigidity, we introduce the variable b_i and define rigidity forces

$$\vec{\beta}_i = b_{i+1}\big([\hat{x}_{i+2}] - [2\hat{x}_{i+1}] + [\hat{x}_i]\big) - 2b_i\big([\hat{x}_{i+1}] - [2\hat{x}_i] + [\hat{x}_{i-1}]\big)$$

$$+\, b_{i-1}\big([\hat{x}_i] - [2\hat{x}_{i-1}] + [\hat{x}_{i-2}]\big) \tag{27}$$

Note that in the absence of external forces, if the nodes are separated more than l_i, are equally spaced, and lie on a straight line, $\vec{\alpha}_i$ and $\vec{\beta}_i$ vanish and the contour is at equilibrium. Tension and rigidity are locally adjustable through the a_i and b_i variables.

To compute the dynamic deformable contour, we integrate the system of ordinary differential equations (Eqs. 24 and 26) forward through time using a semi-implicit Euler procedure [Pres86; Terz87].

Image Segmentation Using Deformable Contours

The deformable contour is responsive to an image force field which influences the contour's shape and motion. It is convenient to express the force field as the gradient of a potential function $P_I(x, y)$ computed from an image $I(x, y)$ by

$$\vec{f}_i = \nabla P_I(\hat{x}_i) \tag{28}$$

where $\nabla = [\partial/\partial x \ \ \partial/\partial y]^T$. By substituting Eq. (24) into Eq. (28) and integrating the resulting equation numerically, the ravines (extended local minima) of $P_I(x, y)$ act as attractors to deformable contours. The contours 'slide downhill' and stabilize at the bottoms of the nearest ravines.

In one application [Carl91], we are interested in localizing nerve cell membranes, which appear dark in positive micrographs (see Plate 8). We therefore convert the micrograph image $I(x, y)$ into a 2D potential function whose ravines coincide with dark cell membranes

$$P_I(x, y) = G * I(x, y) \tag{29}$$

where $G*$ denotes convolution with a 2D Gaussian smoothing filter. The filter broadens the ravines of $P_I(x, y)$ so that they attract the contours from some distance away.

The user initializes a closed deformable contour by quickly sketching with a mouse an approximate trace around the dark membrane of a dendrite of interest. Plate 8a shows an initial deformable contour sketched near a cell membrane. The user then initiates the snake simulation. In a few simulation time steps, the deformable contour equilibrates at the bottom of the nearest ravine in $P_I(x,y)$ (Plate 8b). By interacting with the contour using interactive simulated forces, or springs (green lines in Plate 8c), the user helps it to quickly localize the membrane ravine and produce an accurate profile of the dendrite (Plate 8d).

In another application, we want to segment an embryo heart from the surrounding tissue (see Figure 9a). In this case, since there is no dark membrane to act as an attractor, we apply some standard image processing techniques to enhance the boundary

$$P_I(x,y) = VLSG * I(x,y) \tag{30}$$

where V denotes image inversion (of black to white), L a logarithmic ramp, and S the Sobel operator. In Figure 9b we see the section shown in Figure 9a processed according to Eq. (30).

Three-dimensional Reconstruction

After segmentation we proceed to reconstruct a three-dimensional model of the segmented object. With a set of serial sections, this means stacking the extracted regions and interpolating between the regions if the sampling rate in the stacking direction is less than the sampling rate of each section (which is generally the case). With data sampled on a 3D grid, such as CT or MR scans, reconstruction means interpolation between slices, since the interslice resolution is usually less than the intraslice resolution.

There are two basic approaches to reconstructing a 3D model. One results in a surface model, and the other in a volumetric model. Surface reconstruction algorithms can be classified based on their input data: planar domain samples, cross sections, 3D surface samples, and 3D volume samples [Tonn92]. The first method reconstructs single-valued surfaces from planar domain samples, and does not apply to the types of data discussed here; we give examples of the three remaining methods. The second approach, which reconstructs a 3D volumetric model, refers to resampling of the volume data to obtain isotropic resolution. This interpolation generally gives better results if performed prior to segmentation. We end this section with a review of an approach to volume interpolation for segmented data, called shape-based interpolation [Raya90].

RECONSTRUCTION FROM CROSS SECTIONS

The reconstruction of 3D surfaces from a set of planar contours can be broken into four subproblems: the correspondence problem, the tiling problem, the branching problem, and the surface fitting problem [Meye91]. The correspondence problem arises whenever there is more than one contour in a cross section,

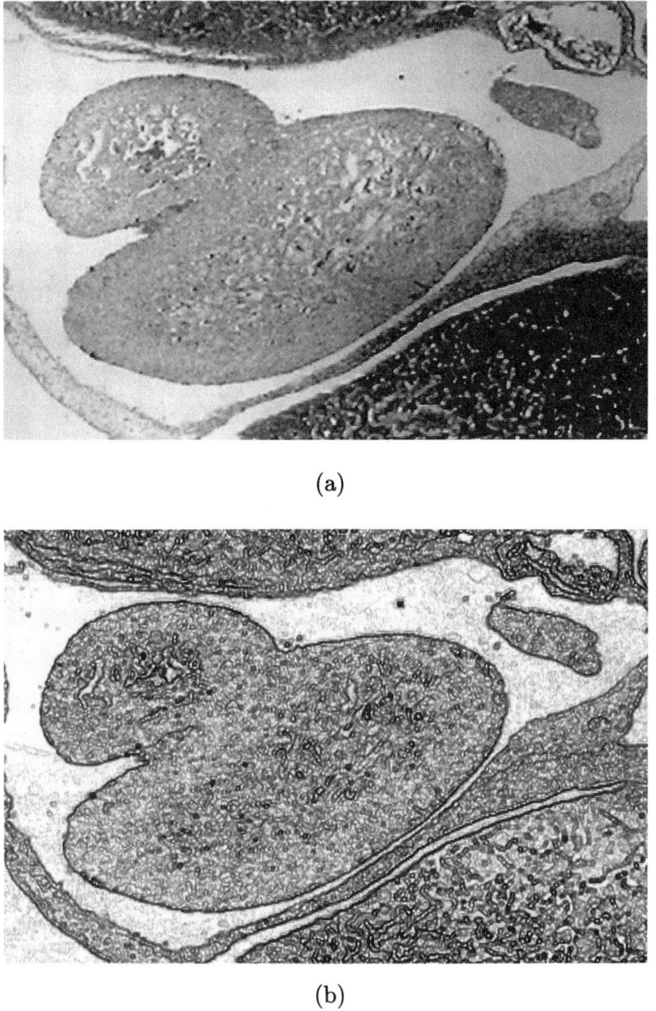

(a)

(b)

Figure 9. Section of an embryo heart. (a) Original section; (b) section processed to enhance heart boundary. (Data courtesy Michael Doyle, University of Illinois at Chicago.)

and it is necessary to determine which contours in adjoining sections are connected. If there is little disparity between adjoining sections, determining which contours overlap in the stacking, or slicing, direction may be sufficient. In the general case the correspondence problem is unsolved, but Meyers et al. [Meye91] suggest a method which solves the correspondence problems as long as there are no interior holes in the resulting objects by using a minimum spanning tree to group adjacent contours.

The tiling problem consists of finding a polygonal surface between adjoining contours, generally using triangles. Tiling is reduced to the problem of finding an optimum path in a directed graph [Kepp75]. Many solutions to this problem have been proposed using different measures of optimum fit, for example minimum surface area [Fuch77] and shortest edges connecting the two contours [Chri82].

The branching problem arises when there are a different number of contours in adjoining slices that should be connected, as illustrated in Figure 10. One way to solve this problem is to tile all pairs of contours in the sections; the solution is then the union of the tiled surfaces [Lin89]. Another way is to insert a new node between two contours in a section, assigning a coordinate in the stacking direction that is halfway between the sections, as illustrated in Figure 10 [Chri82]. This approach requires user intervention, in particular when there is a great deal of disparity between the sections.

The resulting polygonal surface may be an adequate surface representation for rendering. However, sometimes a smooth surface is desirable. The fitting of smooth surfaces to a polygonal mesh is the subject of much research; one general reference on the subject is [Fari88].

RECONSTRUCTION FROM 3D SURFACE SAMPLES

Reconstruction from 3D surface samples is, in general, beyond the scope of this paper; we assume that the data is collected on regular grids, which makes the surface reconstruction problem simpler, since the node proximity is always known. However, we review one method based on Voronoi diagrams, which have been used in generation of surface models from planar contours.

Given a set of points in the plane, a Voronoi diagram partitions the plane into a set of regions [Prep85], each of which is the locus of the points (x, y) closer to one point in the set than to any other points in the set (see Figure 11a). By connecting those vertices whose Voronoi polygons share an edge, we obtain the dual of the Voronoi diagram, also called a Delaunay triangulation (Figure 11b). It can be shown that such a triangulation can always be found [Prep85].

Delaunay triangulation has a 3D equivalent, where tetrahedra tessellate 3D space from a set of points on an object surface. The union of the tetrahedra fills the interior of the convex hull of the object points. To find a polygonal representation of the object surface, the tetrahedra are removed until all points of the object surface lie on the boundary of the polyhedral representation [Bois84]. Three-dimensional Delaunay triangulation is used to solve the contour reconstruction problem [Bois88]. This algorithm forms a tessellated volume between pairs of contours and prunes these subvolumes to find a polyhedral boundary. The algorithm becomes more efficient than general 3D Delaunay triangulation by taking advantage of the explicit neighbor relationship that exists between points in adjacent contours. It also handles branches and interior holes in the object correctly, without user intervention.

RECONSTRUCTION FROM VOLUME SAMPLES

Direct surface reconstruction from volume samples is a form of segmentation, in that it selects a set of volume samples that constitute a surface that bounds an interesting portion of the volume. We discuss one such method, marching cubes,

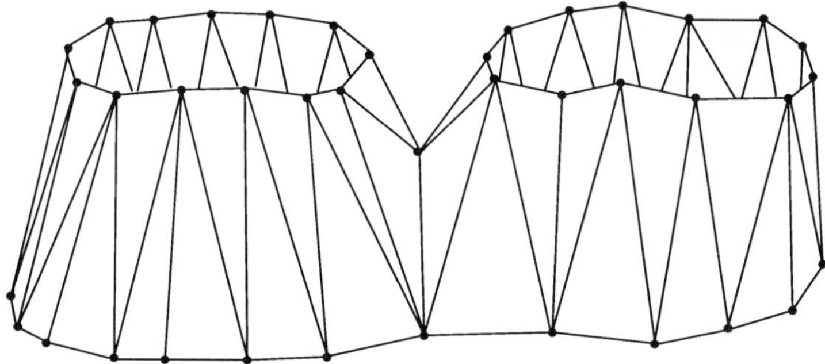

Figure 10. A solution to the two-way branching problem (adapted from [Tonn92]).

which constructs 3D polygonal representations of constant density surfaces from volumetric data [Lore87].

The marching cube algorithm proceeds as follows:

select a surface density value;

build cubes from eight adjoining samples (see Figure 12);

for each cube, test if the surface intersects the cube, that is, if at least one corner of the cube has a density value larger than the selected density value, and at least one corner has a value that is less. Two possible types of intersection are illustrated in Figure 12;

use the table of the 256 possible types of intersections that can occur between the isosurface and cubes in the grid to determine the intersection points of the surface and the cube edges. Interpolate along the cube edge to locate the cube/surface intersection points, and triangulate if there are more than three intersection points;

find the surface normal.

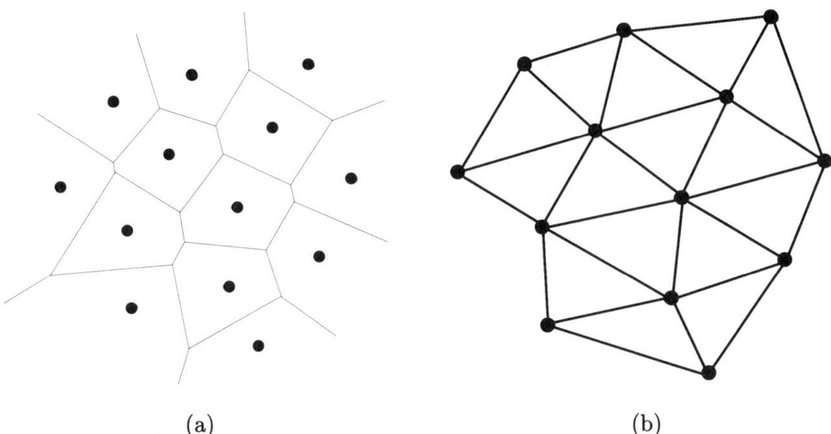

(a)   (b)

Figure 11. Voronai diagrams. (a) Two-dimensional Voronoi diagram; (b) dual Delaunay triangulation (from [Tonn92]).

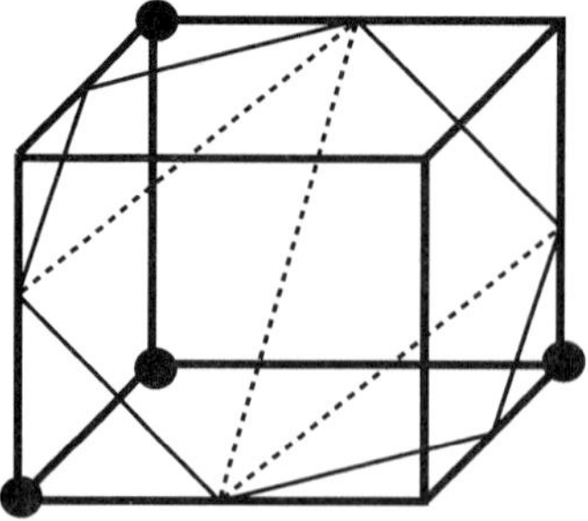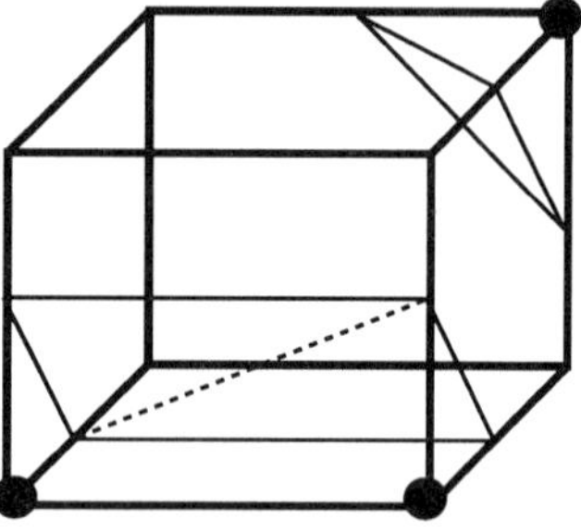

Figure 12. Two examples of a surface dividing eight adjoining samples in a volume; the dotted lines represent the triangulation of the surface patches.

Figure 13 shows hard and soft facial tissue surfaces extracted from CT data with the marching cube algorithm. The original data was represented by 256 × 256 × 113 voxels. Each resulting surface representation has about 500,000 polygons! This observation led to the dividing cube algorithm [Clin88], where each surface cube is subdivided to the desired screen resolution of the final image, and then a point and an associated normal is generated for each subcube.

SHAPE-BASED INTERPOLATION

Volume reconstruction, or resampling, is generally performed prior to segmentation, since reconstruction of already segmented data leads to inaccuracies at the boundaries. This is particularly noticeable when there is a large disparity between adjoining sections. As a result, the segmentation must be performed on a much larger volume than the original data, which is particularly cumbersome on data where automatic segmentation methods fail, and manual or user-assisted techniques must be used. Shape-based interpolation is a scheme for interpolating volume data after the segmentation phase [Raya90].

Shape-based interpolation proceeds in three steps:

segment the slices of the volume into binary images;

convert the binary images into a distance map, where each sample contains distance to the boundary of the object, positive for pixels inside the object and negative for the pixels outside the boundary (see Figure 14);

interpolate in the stacking or slicing direction.

The positive voxels in the resulting volume represent the reconstructed volume. Raya and Udupa [Raya90] show that the accuracy of the volume computation of an object reconstructed with shape-based interpolation is much better than for an object reconstructed with linear interpolation. This interpolation method can be extended to work in conjunction with the Bayesian classification discussed earlier. We can define probabilistic distances to the boundary, where each distance is weighted by the probability associated with the boundary sample value.

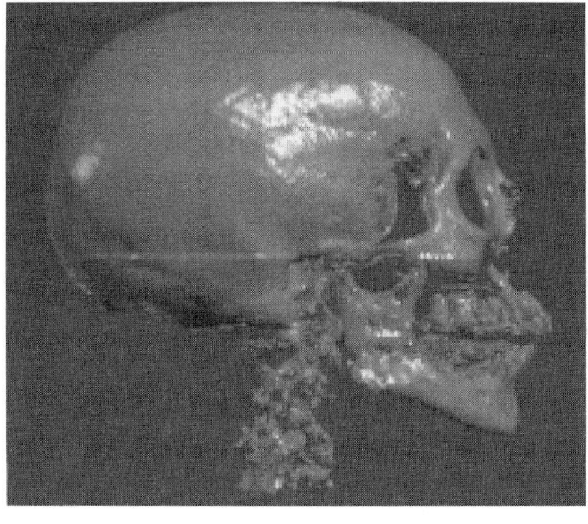

(a)

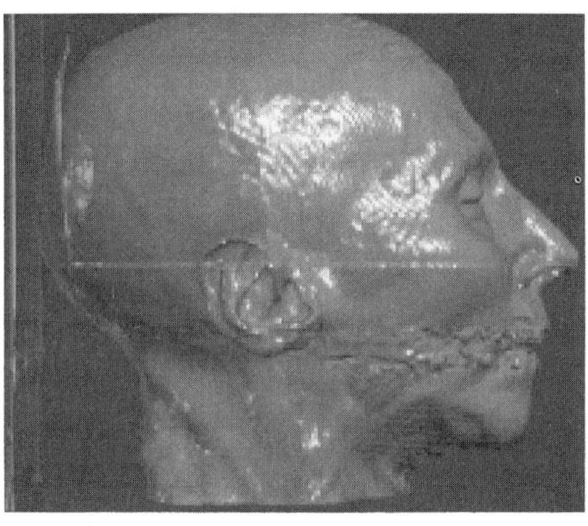

(b)

Figure 13. Surfaces generated from CT data using the marching cube algorithm. (a) Bone surface; (b) skin surface. (Images courtesy Keith Waters, Digital Equipment Corporation; data courtesy North Carolina Memorial Hospital.)

Volume Rendering

Volume rendering refers to the direct rendering of scalar or vector data sampled in three dimensions. These techniques differ from traditional computer graphics techniques in that explicit surfaces need not be extracted from the data before display. Rather, the entire 3D volume of data is used for display. Yet, by displaying only the portions of the volume that have a given density or a

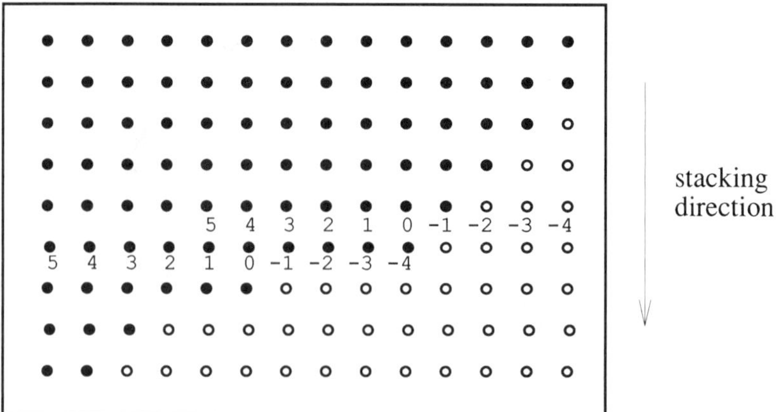

Figure 14. Cross section of a set of slices, where the solid dots indicate samples inside the object and the empty dots indicate samples outside the object. The numbers indicate the distance to the boundary of the object.

high gradient, features and surfaces are elicited without explicit representation [Fole90; Kauf91].

RENDERING METHODS

Volume rendering (or projection) can be classified into two methods, forward mapping (voxel projection) and backward mapping (ray-casting). In the voxel projection method [Dreb88; Upso88; West90,91], the 3D point samples, or voxels, are traversed, and their contributions are added to one or more pixels in the projection plane. In the ray-casting method [Sabe88; Upso88; Levo90d], rays are cast from a viewpoint through each pixel in the projection plane, and the values for each pixel are calculated by integrating, or summing, sample values along the ray.

We now make two assumptions, that voxels are point samples on a regular grid; and that projectors are parallel, which is the projection most commonly used in volume visualization. Extension to perspective projections is fairly straightforward.

We begin the description of the two rendering methods using some simplifying assumptions: one major axis of the volume is parallel to the projection plane normal; the resolution of the projection plane is identical to the volume sampling resolution (see Figure 15); and the voxels are completely opaque. Later we relax these assumptions. Figure 15 shows a 2D slice of the 3D volume. Here voxels are indicated as dots, and sample positions in the projection plane are indicated as triangles. Figure 15a shows the volume projection with projectors indicated as arrows; Figure 15b shows ray-casting, with rays indicated as arrows.

In the voxel projection method, we traverse the volume voxel by voxel, either in a back-to-front [Frie85] or front-to-back [Vann83; Farr85] order, writing the

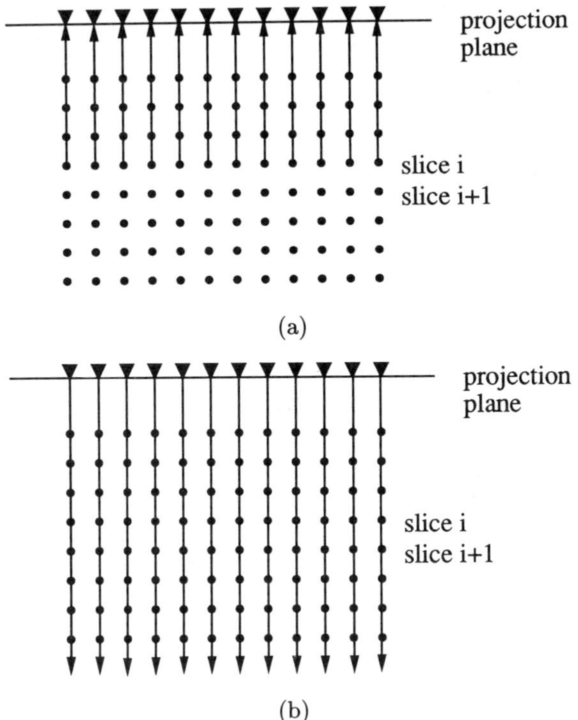

Figure 15. Volume rendering with projection plane parallel to one major axis. (a) Voxel projection; (b) ray-casting.

voxels to the pixels in the projection plane as we proceed. In the back-to-front method, we select a traversal order starting with the voxel at the largest distance to the projection plane and ending with the closest voxel (when the normal of the projection plane is parallel to one of the volume axes, we start with any voxel in the most distant slice). In the front-to-back method we proceed in the opposite order, halting the processing along a ray after the first filled voxel is encountered. By using the segmentation methods described previously, we can select for display portions of the volume of particular interest. The advantage of the back-to-front method is that the observer sees the image being accumulated and thus sees features in the volume that may become obscured later. The advantage with the front-to-back method is that the computation time may be reduced by terminating the ray processing before all voxels are traversed.

In volumetric ray-casting, we cast rays through each pixel in the projection plane and fill the pixel with the first voxel that is found along the ray. Ray-casting is identical to front-to-back mapping in the simple case when the projection plane is parallel to one major plane in the volume and has the same resolution, and when the voxels are completely opaque.

Let us relax the assumption that all voxels are completely opaque, and assume that the user wants to see some of the features embedded in the volume. Assume also that each voxel has an associated opacity α (in the range 0 to 1) and an associated color or intensity I. The current accumulated value is denoted by i, and the current sample, or voxel, by s. We interpolate between background color and a transparent foreground color using rules for compositing digital images [Port84]. Back-to-front accumulation is expressed as

$$I_{i+1} = I_i(1 - \alpha_s) + I_s\alpha_s \tag{31}$$

where the first term models absorption of the background color by the new voxel and the second term models emitted light. Front-to-back accumulation is expressed as

$$I_{i+1} = I_i + I_s\alpha_s(1 - \alpha_i) \tag{32}$$

$$\alpha_{i+1} = \alpha_i + \alpha_s(1 - \alpha_i) \tag{33}$$

In this case, part of the emitted light of the new voxel is absorbed by the accumulated opacity, which increases as the accumulation moves farther from the projection plane. In the front-to-back case, accumulation terminates when the opacity value indicates complete opacity.

By relaxing the remaining two assumptions, we have the completely general case. With an arbitrary orientation of the projection plane, the rays in general do not intersect the voxels, but rather pass between them (Figure 16a). Similarly, the projectors do not intersect the projection plane at a pixel location (Figure 16b). There are two ways to proceed: transform the volume such that the rays or the projectors align with one major axis of the volume, and such that the resolution of the volume is identical to that of the projection plane [Farr85; Dreb88]; or resample the volume along the rays or the projectors [Levo90d; West90]. In the first case we proceed as described above. When ray-casting a volume with an arbitrary orientation, the rays are sampled at regular intervals. Both the intensity and opacity are calculated at the new sample points using a 3D interpolation filter. The resulting values are accumulated using Eqs. (32) and (33).

Voxel projection is somewhat more difficult to understand in the general case. We insert a buffer parallel to the projection plane between the volume and the projection plane, as illustrated in Figure 16b. The volume is processed a slice at a time,[†] accumulating each resampled slice in the buffer. When one slice has been processed, we use Eq. (31), or Eqs. (32) and (33), to accumulate the buffer values into the projection plane.

Assuming that the slices are parallel to the xy plane of the volume, recall from the section on digital filter design that the interpolated values are of the form

$$g(x - \tau_x, y - \tau_y, z) = \sum_{m_x=-\frac{(L-1)}{2}}^{\frac{(L-1)}{2}} \sum_{m_y=-\frac{(L-1)}{2}}^{\frac{(L-1)}{2}} f(x - m_x, y - m_y, z)h(m_x, \tau_x)h(m_y, \tau_y) \tag{34}$$

[†]It is always possible to find a slice processing order in which the voxels in one slice occlude or partially occlude the voxels in an adjoining slice.

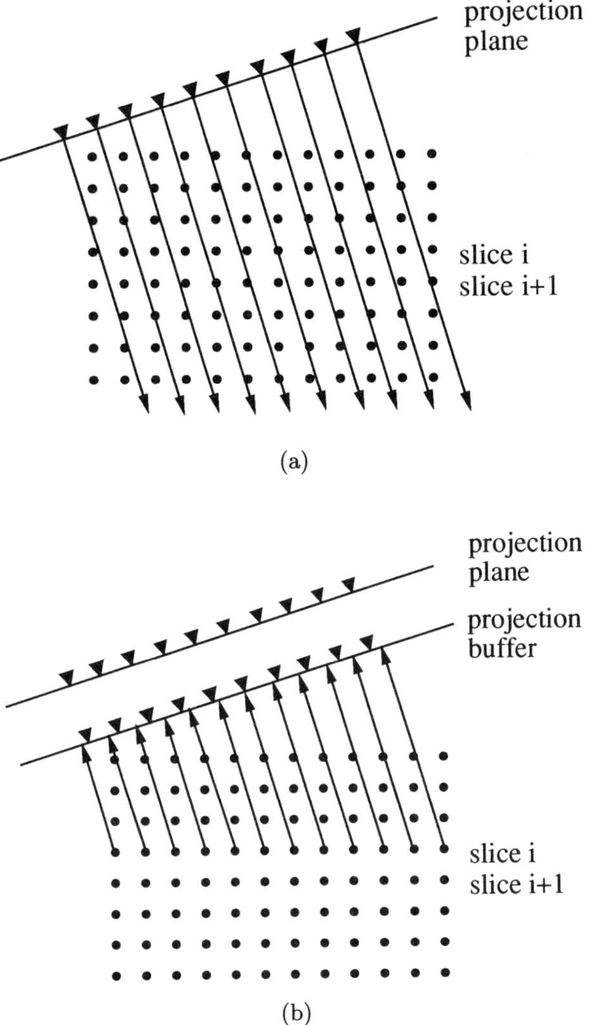

Figure 16. Volume rendering with projection plane in an arbitrary position. (a) Ray-casting; (b) voxel projection.

where g denotes the interpolated value, f the voxel color or intensity, h a fractional pixel interpolation filter for a fraction τ, and L the filter length. We observe that the contribution of a voxel at the position $(x - m_x, y - m_y, z)$ to position $(x - \tau_x, y - \tau_y, z)$ is

$$c(x-\tau_x, y-\tau_y, z)_{(x-m_x, y-m_y, z)} = f(x-m_x, y-m_y, z)h(m_x, \tau_x)h(m_y, \tau_y) \qquad (35)$$

The complete algorithm proceeds as follows: traverse the voxels in front-to-back or back-to-front order, one slice at a time, and distribute the contribution of each voxel to L elements of the buffer. After each slice, accumulate the buffer content into the projection plane using Eq. (31), or Eqs. (32) and (33). Volume projection by distributing contributions of each voxel to an image buffer is called splatting [West90].

Volume projection is significantly faster than ray-casting, since each voxel is visited only once, and only 2D interpolation is used [West91]. However, ray-casting is more accurate; the ray is sampled at the same rate for all viewing angles, yielding better results but at a higher computational cost.

Shading Models for Volume Data

Shading increases the user's perception of depth and helps accentuate the 3D shape of an object. Many different shading models are used for rendering surfaces in volumes, ranging from models using only ambient light and depth queuing [Vann83; Farr85; Wolp88], to models incorporating ambient and diffuse light [Gord85; Upso88; Ney90], and to those also incorporating specular reflection [Dreb88; Levo88; Tied90; West90]. Others have used more accurate light scattering methods [Sabe88; Mein91] and shadows [Yage91] to enhance the perception of volume data.

Here we describe a popular shading model developed by Phong [Phon75], which models ambient, diffuse, and specular light, as well as depth queuing. A detailed description of this model for polygonal data is found in [Fole90]; we focus only on the differences between polygonal and volume shading. The Phong shading model is expressed as

$$I_\lambda(\hat{x}) = I_{a\lambda}k_{a\lambda} + \frac{I_{p\lambda}}{c_1 + c_2 d(\hat{x})} \left[k_{d\lambda}\big(\vec{N}(\hat{x})\cdot\vec{L}\big) + k_{s\lambda}\big(\vec{N}(\hat{x})\cdot\vec{H}\big)^n \right] \tag{36}$$

where

$I_\lambda(\hat{x})$ is the color at voxel $\hat{x}$, $\lambda = (R, G, B)$;

$I_{a\lambda}$ is the ambient light color component;

$I_{p\lambda}$ is the point light source color component;

$k_{a\lambda}$ is the ambient reflection coefficient;

$k_{d\lambda}$ is the diffuse reflection coefficient;

$k_{s\lambda}$ is the specular intensity reflection coefficient;

c_1 and c_2 are constants used for depth queuing;

$d(\hat{x})$ is the distance from voxel $\hat{x}$ to projection plane;

$\vec{N}(\hat{x})$ is the projection plane normal at voxel $\hat{x}$;

$\vec{L}$ is a normalized vector in direction of light source;

$\vec{H}$ is a normalized vector in direction of maximum highlight, which is equal to the vector halfway between the viewer and the light source;

n is an exponent chosen for optimal highlight.

The only difference between polygonal and volumetric Phong shading lies in the normal calculation. While in polygonal meshes the local surface normal can be calculated exactly, in volume shading the normal $\vec{N}(\hat{x})$ is estimated with the normalized gradient vector at voxel $\hat{x}$. The gradient is estimated with the central finite difference formula

$$\nabla f(x_i, y_j, z_k) = \begin{bmatrix} \frac{1}{2}\big(f(x_{i+1}, y_j, z_k) - f(x_{i-1}, y_j, z_k)\big) \\ \frac{1}{2}\big(f(x_i, y_{j+1}, z_k) - f(x_i, y_{j-1}, z_k)\big) \\ \frac{1}{2}\big(f(x_i, y_j, z_{k+1}) - f(x_i, y_j, z_{k-1})\big) \end{bmatrix} \tag{37}$$

A large gradient magnitude indicates a large difference in density between neighboring voxels, which in turn indicates a surface boundary. To render the surfaces, one renders only those voxels where the gradient magnitude exceeds a certain value. This may give rise to aliasing effects similar to those experienced with density thresholding. Westover [West91] uses the magnitude of the gradient to determine the opacity values: a low magnitude gives low opacity, making the voxels more translucent; a high magnitude makes the voxels more opaque. By using a smooth function instead of a step function to map the gradient magnitudes to opacities, aliasing is reduced. Another way to reduce aliasing is to let the opacity values go to zero smoothly over a user-specified number of voxels, at a rate inversely proportional to the gradient magnitude [Levo88]. Examples of surface rendering of a data set that used a maximum likelihood classifier is seen in Figure 17. Figure 17a shows the data set supersampled in the vertical direction with four rays per slice to compensate for anisotropic sampling. Figure 17b shows an isotropic data set reconstructed using a cubic B-spline interpolator, and subsequently rendered with one ray per CT slice.

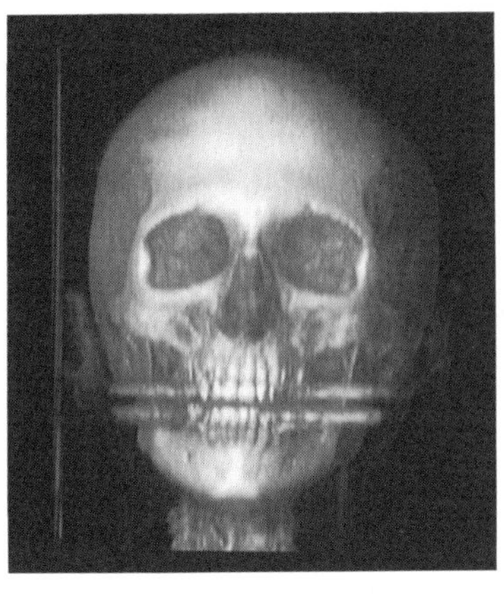
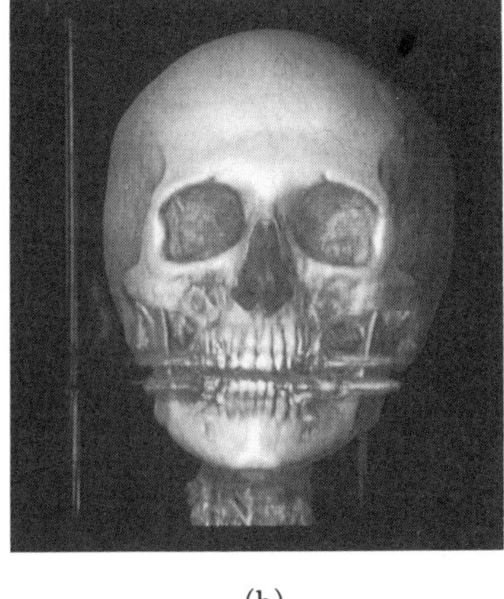

(a)   (b)

Figure 17. Surface shaded CT data. (a) The data set supersampled in the vertical direction with four rays per slice; (b) an isotropic data set rendered with one ray per CT slice. (Reproduced from [Levo88] ©1988 IEEE.)

Mixing Geometric and Volume Data

In some applications, it is desirable to render a combination of geometric and voxel data. For example, in a geophysical application one might want to render seismic data of some formation, combined with the location of boreholes defined by some path through the formation. In a medical application, one may want to see some instruments inserted into an anatomical model, or show a radiation treatment beam superimposed on an anatomical model.

One obvious approach to this problem is to convert all data to voxel data and render the result with the methods discussed earlier. This was done in the geophysical application shown in Plate 9 [Sabe89] and in biomedical applications [Yage91]. Plate 9 shows a reservoir with four heavily faulted sands, displayed in yellow, green, blue, and red. The fault surfaces are shown in light blue. The well data was collected from an off-shore platform, and six wells are shown with their gamma ray log values. (The gamma ray log represents a measurement of natural radiation from a formation.) In the green sand, where the wells intersect the sand, two perforation areas are indicated in blue. The horizontal surface is the oil-to-water contact surface, and the vertical surface is a seismic section.

Another more elegant approach is the hybrid ray-caster described in [Levo90b, 90c]. Here, rays are simultaneously cast through the polygon and the volume data. For the polygons, the intersections between the rays and the polygons are calculated and shaded, yielding a color and an opacity value at each intersection point. The volume data is ray-cast using the shading method described previously, also yielding color and opacity values at each resampled voxel. In the last stage of processing, the color and opacities are composited using Eqs. (32) and (33). Selective supersampling is used to reduce aliasing around polygonal edges and around volume-polygon intersections. Plate 10 shows the use of this algorithm for radiation treatment planning. In Plate 10 a polygonally defined target volume is rendered in purple and a polygonally defined radiation beam is displayed in red. A portion of the volume is cut away, and the raw MR data is mapped onto the cutting plane.

In Pursuit of Real-time Rendering of Volume Data

The time to render a volume of $256 \times 256 \times 256$ voxels is still measured in tens of seconds to minutes on a workstation [Levo90a]. As a result, it is often hard to select a good view of an object, and motion parallax to discern 3D shape is far from being achieved. Although high-quality shading produces very attractive images, shading also smooths voxel data and thus fine detail in the data is sometimes lost. Our goal must be to achieve real-time rendering with high data fidelity where motion parallax can be used to discern 3D shape.

Many methods have been proposed to speed up the ray-casting and voxel projection algorithms described previously:

> *Preprocessing.* Some of the computation for volume rendering can be done in a pre-processing pass. Examples include gradient calculation [Dreb88] and labeling of groups of empty voxels that require no further processing;

Table lookup. Much of the computation can be done by table lookup. Examples include filter coefficients and shading parameters [West91];

Successive refinement. Low quality images are displayed initially, and, if the user does not change the viewing parameters, the image begins to improve. Candidates for successive refinement are [West89,91]:

> image resolution — the image is initially computed at a lower resolution and the resulting image is interpolated;

> filter quality — the interpolation starts with nearest-neighbor interpolation and proceeds to better interpolation;

> shading model — starts with flat shading and successively adds diffuse and specular components to the model;

> ray termination — terminate ray-casting early, at first nonempty voxel.

Adaptive refinement. Two methods for adaptive refinement have been suggested by Levoy [Levo90a,90d]:

> adaptive ray termination — the ray accumulation stops when the accumulated opacity is $1 - \epsilon$, where ϵ is determined empirically;

> adaptive ray computation — rays are initially traced on a sparse grid, and additional rays are added in areas of high image complexity.

Specialized software and hardware have also been developed to facilitate real-time manipulation of medical data [Meag82,84], seismic data [Chak86], and arbitrary volume data [Vita90]. Other attempts at real-time manipulation of volume data are done through coarse-grain parallel algorithms for a set of Sun Workstations [West91], or fine-grain parallel algorithms on a Thinking Machine CM-200 [Schr91], on a MasPar MP-1 [Vezi92], and on a DECmpp 12000 [Hsu92].

There are two basic approaches to volume rendering on a massively parallel system: volume rotation (i.e., move data between processors) to align the volume with the projection plane followed by rendering, and direct rendering (i.e., keep data stationary) of the nonaligned volume. In the first case, the data is transformed using a sequence of eight shearing transformations [Schr91] or a four-pass algorithm which includes perspective projections [Vezi92]. (This is a generalization of the three-pass algorithm discussed in the section on affine transformations of images and volumes, to include perspective.) The resulting volume is rendered by summing, in parallel, along a processor axis. Schröder et al. [Schr91] report a total processing time of 324ms for a volume $128 \times 128 \times 128$ on a 64K processor CM-2. Vezina et al. [Vezi92] report a total processing time of 595ms for a volume $128 \times 128 \times 128$ on a 16K processor MP-1. It is impossible to compare these timings, since details of the rendering algorithms are not described.

Hsu [Hsu92] takes a different approach, holding the data stationary while accumulating the opacity and intensity along the rays in parallel. This algorithm has the advantage that errors are not introduced into the data by a sequence of transformations, but the ray accumulation is, of course, more complex. Although this algorithm is still under development, initial results indicate computation times comparable to the times of algorithms based on volume transformation.

Summary and Future Research

In this paper we surveyed techniques for modeling and visualization of empirical data sampled on regular 3D grids. We gave an overview of existing techniques and explored some research directions in registration, segmentation, 3D reconstruction, and volume rendering. Although all these steps are necessary in building models from and visualizing empirical data in many vastly different applications, no commercial system to date incorporates all these processing steps. As we have seen, registration, segmentation, 3D reconstruction, and rendering rely on techniques from computer graphics, image processing, and computer vision. And therein lies a large part of the problem: computer graphics and image processing hardware and software architectural paradigms are fundamentally different; we do not yet understand how to reconcile the different paradigms for a unified visualization environment [Carl92].

Also notice that most techniques described in this paper are highly specialized to narrow classes of data. For example, rarely are methods that are successful in medicine used in geophysics, and vise versa. One encouraging exception is that many computer vision techniques developed for model building are also being applied to medical data.

We conclude with a list of research topics:

widely applicable, (semi-)automatic registration techniques, including non-linear registration;

widely applicable (semi-)automatic segmentation techniques, including soft tissue segmentation;

better interpolation methods for volume data. One way to accomplish this might be to combine optical flow with high-quality interpolation. This is akin to motion-compensated interpolation, which is a key feature of the MPEG standard [Lega91];

rendering with high data fidelity combined with quantification of the loss of accuracy in the data due to rendering;

real-time volume rendering, where motion parallax is used to convey 3D shape;

better digital filters for volume resampling, combined with a better understanding of the relationships between quality of interpolation and the quality of registration, rendering, and model quantification.

Appendix: Sampling Theory Definitions

Signal. A signal is a one- or multi-dimensional function of space or time. For our purposes, a 2D signal is an image while a 3D signal is a volume. In the frequency domain, a signal is expressed as the sum of a sequence of sinusoids of different frequencies $e^{i2\pi un}$, where u is the frequency and n is the spatial variable. A signal is transformed from the spatial domain to the frequency domain by a

Fourier transform. In what follows, we define terms for the 1D case only. All concepts and terms have obvious 2D and 3D counterparts.

Bandlimited signal. A signal is said to have bandwidth u_m if it has no frequency components outside the interval $-u_m \leq u \leq u_m$. Most optical imaging systems produce an analog spatially bandlimited signal [Born84].

Nyquist rate. The Nyquist rate of a signal is twice its bandwidth.

The sampling theorem. If a signal is bandlimited, and if it is sampled on an infinite interval at a rate higher than the Nyquist rate, then the continuous signal can be exactly recovered from the samples through appropriate interpolation. In what follows, we consider signals to have a bandwidth of $1/2$, which gives rise to a Nyquist rate of one, or equivalently, we use a nondimensional frequency in units of cycles per pixel.

Discrete impulse. A discrete impulse, or the unit sample sequence $\delta(n)$ is defined by

$$\delta(n) = \begin{cases} 1 & \text{if } n = 0 \\ 0 & \text{otherwise} \end{cases} \qquad (A1)$$

Filter. A filter is a system that maps an input signal $f(n)$ to an output signal, or response, $g(n)$. When a filter is applied to $\delta(n)$, the result is called the filter impulse response.

Response. The response $g(n)$ of a filter to a discrete function $f(n)$ is

$$g(n) = f(n) * h(n) = \sum_{k=-\infty}^{\infty} f(k)h(n-k) \qquad (A2)$$

where $*$ denotes convolution and $h(n)$ the discrete filter impulse response. The filter $h(n)$ is also called the convolution kernel, and each $h(n_i)$ is called a filter coefficient.

Discrete-space Fourier transform. A discrete function $f(n)$ is mapped to a continuous function in the frequency domain by the discrete-space Fourier transform

$$F(u) = \sum_{n=-\infty}^{\infty} f(n)e^{-i2\pi un} \qquad -\frac{1}{2} \leq u \leq \frac{1}{2} \qquad (A3)$$

Similarly, a continuous function $F(u)$ in the frequency domain is mapped to a discrete function in the spatial domain by the inverse discrete-space Fourier transform

$$f(n) = \int_{u=-1/2}^{1/2} F(u)e^{i2\pi un}du \qquad -\infty \leq n \leq \infty \qquad (A4)$$

Magnitude. $F(u)$ is a complex function of the form $R(u) + iI(u)$, and the amplitude, or magnitude, of $F(u)$ is expressed as

$$\|F(u)\| = \sqrt{R^2(u) + I^2(u)} \tag{A5}$$

Phase.   The phase, or phase angle, of $F(u)$ is expressed as

$$\phi(u) = \arctan \frac{I(u)}{R(u)} \tag{A6}$$

Frequency response.   The Fourier transform of a filter impulse response is called its frequency response. If the input to a filter is the complex sinusoid $e^{i2\pi un}$, then the output of the filter is the same sinusoid, multiplied by the complex filter frequency response. We use the filter frequency magnitude response and phase response as criteria for filter design.

Aliasing.   Aliasing manifests itself as artifacts in the sampled or subsampled signal, e.g., jagged edges. Aliasing occurs if a signal is not bandlimited or is not sampled above the Nyquist rate. It can also occur when a sampled signal is subsampled, since the sampling periods may overlap in the frequency domain, and high frequencies may appear as lower frequencies in the subsampled signal.

Acknowledgments.   The author thanks the Director of Digital Equipment Corporation's Cambridge Research Lab, Victor Vyssotsky, for his support of this work. Special thanks go to Richard Szeliski for explaining optical flow. The author also thanks those who read and commented on the manuscript: Dick Beane, William Hsu, Sing Bing Kang, Gudrun Klinker, Richard Szeliski, Demetri Terzopoulos, and Keith Waters.

REFERENCES

[Anan84]
   Anandan, P., Computing dense displacement fields with confidence measures in scenes containing occlusion, *Image Understanding Workshop*, New Orleans, LA, December 1984, pp. 236–246; McLean, Va: Science Applications Int. Corp.

[Arun87]
   Arun, K.S., Huang, T.S., and Blostein, S.D., Least-squares fitting of two 3-D point sets, *IEEE Trans. Patt. Anal. Mach. Intell.*, Vol. 9, No. 5, pp. 698–700, September 1987.

[Ayac89]
   Ayache, N., Boissonnat, J.D., Brunet, E., Cohen, L., Chieze, J.P., Geiger, B., Monga, O., Rocchisani, J.M., and Sander, P., Building highly structured volume representations in 3D medical images, *Proc. 3rd Internat. Symposium on Computer Assisted Radiology, CAR'89*, pp. 765–772, June 1989, New York: Springer-Verlag.

[Ball82]
Ballard, D.H., and Brown, C.M., *Computer Vision*, Englewood Cliffs, NJ: Prentice-Hall, 1982.

[Berg92]
Bergen, J.R., Anandan, P., Hanna, K.J., and Hingorani, R., Hierarchical Model-based Motion Estimation, in *Second European Conference on Computer Vision (ECCV'92)*, Sandini, G., Ed., Santa Margherita Liguere, Italy, May 1992, pp. 237–252, Berlin: Springer-Verlag.

[Bois84]
Boissonnat, J.D., Geometric structures for three-dimensional shape representation, *ACM TOG*, Vol. 3, pp. 266–286, 1984.

[Bois88]
Boissonnat, J.D., Shape reconstruction from planar cross-sections, *Comput. Vis., Graph. and Image Process.*, Vol. 44, pp. 1–29, 1988.

[Boma90]
Bomans, M., Höhne, K.H., Tiede, U., and Riemer, M., 3-D segmentation of MR images of the head for 3-D display, *IEEE Trans. on Medical Imaging*, Vol. 9, No. 2, pp. 177–183, June 1990.

[Born84]
Born, M., and Wolf, E., *Principles of Optics*. Oxford: Pergamon Press, 1984.

[Byrn90]
Byrne, J.P., Undrill, P.E., and Phillips, R.P., Feature based image registration using parallel computation methods, *First Conf. on Visualization in Biomedical Computing*, Atlanta, GA, May 1990, Los Alamitos, CA: IEEE Computer Society Press, pp. 304–310.

[Capp89]
Cappelletti, J.D., and Rosenfeld, A., Three-dimensional boundary following, *Comput. Vis., Graph. and Image Process.*, Vol. 48, pp. 80–92, 1989.

[Carl91]
Carlbom, I., Terzopoulos, D., and Harris, K.M., Reconstructing and Visualizing Models of Neuronal Dendrites, in *Scientific Visualization of Physical Phenomena*, Patrikalakis, N.M., Ed., Tokyo: Springer-Verlag, 1991, pp. 623–638. Presented at CGI '91: Visualization of Physical Phenomena, Cambridge, MA, June 26–28, 1991.

[Carl92]
Carlbom, I., Chakravarty, I., and Hsu, W.M, SIGGRAPH'91 workshop report: Integrating computer graphics, computer vision, and image processing in scientific applications, *Comput. Graph.*, Vol. 26, No. 1, pp. 8–17, 1992.

[Chak86]
Chakravarty, I., Nichol, B., and Ono, T., The integration of computer graphics and image processing techniques for the display and manipulation of geophysical data, *Proc. Comp. Graph. Tokyo '86*, Tokyo, Japan, 1986. Reprinted in *Advanced Computer Graphics*, Kunii, T., Ed., Tokyo: Springer-Verlag, 1986.

[Chri82]
Christiansen, H.N., and Sederberg, T.W., Conversion of complex contour line definitions into polygonal element mosaics, *Comput. Graph.*, Vol. 12, pp. 187–192, 1982 (SIGGRAPH 82).

[Clin88]
Cline, H.E., Lorensen, W.E., Ludke, S., Crawford, C.R., and Teeter, B.C., Two algorithms for the three-dimensional reconstruction of tomograms. *Medical Physics*, Vol. 15, No. 3, pp. 320–327, May/June 1988.

[Cohe91]
Cohen, L.D., and Cohen, I., Finite element methods for active contour models and balloons from 2D to 3D, Technical Report 9124, CEREMADE, Université Paris IX, Paris, France, December 1991.

[Cull90]
Cullip, T.J., Frederiksen, R.E., Gauch, J.M., and Pizer, S.M., Algorithms for 2D and 3D image description based on the IAS, *First Conf. on Visualization in Biomedical Computing*, Atlanta, GA, May 1990, Los Alamitos, CA: IEEE Computer Society Press, pp. 102–107.

[Dreb88]
Drebin, R.A., Carpenter, L., and Hanrahan, P., Volume rendering, *Comput. Graph.*, Vol. 22, pp. 65–74, 1988 (SIGGRAPH 88).

[Duda73]
Duda, R.O., and Hart, P.E., *Pattern Classification and Scene Analysis*, New York: J. Wiley and Sons, 1973.

[Dudg84]
Dudgeon, D.E., and Mersereau, R.M., *Multidimensional Digital Signal Processing*, Englewood Cliffs, NJ: Prentice Hall, 1984.

[Dunc90]
Duncan, J.S., Staib, L.H., Birkholzer, T., Owen, R., Anandan, P., and Bozma, I., Medical image analysis using model-based optimization, *First Conf. on Visualization in Biomedical Computing*, Atlanta, GA, May 1990, Los Alamitos, CA: IEEE Computer Society Press, pp. 370–377.

[Fari88]
Farin, G., *Curves and Surfaces for Computer-Aided Geometric Design: A Practical Guide*, San Diego, CA: Academic Press, 1988.

[Farr85]
Farrell, E.J., Yang, W.C., and Zappulla, R.A., Animated 3D CT imaging, *IEEE Comput. Graph. and Appl.*, Vol. 5, No. 12, pp. 26–32, December 1985.

[Fell57]
Feller, W., *An Introduction to Probability Theory and Its Applications*, New York: John Wiley and Sons, 1957.

[Fole90]
Foley, J.D., van Dam, A., Feiner, S.K., and Hughes, J.F., *Computer Graphics: Principles and Practice*, Reading, MA: Addison-Wesley, 1990.

[Fred90]
Frederiksen, R.E., Coggins, J.M., Cullip, T.J., and Pizer, S.M., Interactive object definition in medical images using multiscale, geometric image descriptions, *First Conf. on Visualization in Biomedical Computing*, Atlanta, GA, May 1990, Los Alamitos, CA: IEEE Computer Society Press, pp. 108–114.

[Frie85]
Frieder, G., Gordon, D., and Reynolds, R.A., Back-to-front display of voxel-based objects, *IEEE Comput. Graph. and Appl.*, Vol. 5, No. 1, pp. 52–60, January 1985.

[Fuch77]
Fuchs, H., Kedem, Z.M., and Uselton, S.P., Optimal surface reconstruction from planar contours, *CACM*, Vol. 20, No. 10, pp. 693–702, 1977.

[Gier90]
Giertsen, C., Halvorsen, A., and Flood, P.R., Graph-directed modeling from serial sections, *The Visual Computer*, Vol. 6, pp. 284–290, 1990.

[Gonz77]
Gonzalez, R.C., and Wintz, P., *Digital Image Processing*, Reading, MA: Addison-Wesley, 1977.

[Gord85]
Gordon, D., and Reynolds, R.A., Image space shading of 3-dimensional objects, *Comput. Vis., Graph. and Image Process.*, Vol. 29, pp. 361–376, 1985.

[Gord89]
Gordon, D., and Udupa, J.K., Fast surface tracking in three-dimensional binary images, *Comput. Vis., Graph. and Image Process.*, Vol. 45, pp. 196–214, 1989.

[Guez91]
Guéziec, A., and Ayache, N., Smoothing and matching of 3-D space curves, Technical Report 1544, INRIA, France, October 1991.

[Hanr90]
Hanrahan, P., Three-pass affine transforms for volume rendering, *Comput. Graph.*, Vol. 24, No. 5, pp. 71–78, 1990.

[Herm89]
Herman, G.T., and Abbott, A.H., Reproducibility of landmark locations on CT-based three-dimensional images, *Proc. NCGA '89*, Fairfax, VA, April 1989, pp. 144–148, National Computer Graphics Association.

[Hohn88]
Höhne, K.H., Bomans, M., Pommert, A., Riemer, M., and Tiede, U., 3D segmentation and display of tomographic imagery, *Proc. Int. Conf. on Pattern Recognition*, Rome, Italy, pp. 1271–1276, Los Alamitos, CA: IEEE Computer Society Press, 1988.

[Hohn89]
Höhne, K.H., Bomans, M., Pommert, A., Riemer, M., Schiers, C., Tiede, U., and Wiebecke, G., 3D Visualization of Tomographic Volume Data Using the Generalized Voxel-model, in *Proc. Volume Visualization Workshop*, Upson, C., Ed., Dept. Computer Science, University of North Carolina, Chapel Hill, NC, pp. 51–57, 1989.

[Hohn90]
Höhne, K.H., Bomans, M., Pommert, A., Riemer, M., Schiers, C., Tiede, U., and Wiebecke, G., 3D visualization of tomographic volume data using the generalized voxel model, *The Visual Computer*, Vol. 6, pp. 28–36, 1990.

[Horn81]
Horn, B.K.P., and Schunck, B.G., Determining optical flow, *Artificial Intelligence*, Vol. 17, pp. 185–203, 1981.

[Horn90]
Horn, B.K.P., Relative orientation, *Int. Jour. Comp. Vision*, Vol. 4, pp. 59–78, January 1990.

[Hsu92]
Hsu, W.M, Personal communication, 1992.

[Kass87]
Kass, M., Witkin, A., and Terzopoulos, D., Snakes: Active contour models, *Int. Jour. Comp. Vision*, Vol. 1, No. 4, pp. 321–331, 1987.

[Kauf91]
Kaufman, A., *Volume Visualization*, Los Alamitos, CA: IEEE Computer Society Press, 1991.

[Kepp75]
Keppel, E., Approximating complex surfaces by triangulation of contour lines, *IBM Research and Development*, Vol. 19, pp. 2–11, 1975.

[Lava91]
Lavalleé, S., Szeliski, R., and Brunie, L., Matching 3-D smooth surfaces with their 2-D projections using 3-D distance maps, *SPIE Vol. 1570 Geometric Methods in Computer Vision*, San Diego, CA, The International Society for Optical Engineering, pp. 322–336, July 1991.

[Lega91]
Le Gall, D., MPEG: A video compression standard for multimedia applications, *CACM*, Vol. 34, No. 4, pp. 46–58, 1991.

[Leit90]
Leitner, F., Marque, I., LaVallee, S., and Cinquin, P., Dynamic segmentation: Finding the edge with differential equations and 'spline snakes', Technical Report TIMB - TIM 3 - IMAG, Faculté de Médecine, 38700 La Tronche, France, 1990.

[Levi88]
Levin, D.N., Pelizzari, C.A., Chen, G.T.Y., Chen, C.T., and Cooper, M.D., Retrospective geometric correlation of MR, CT, and PET images, *Radiology*, Vol. 169, No. 3, pp. 817–823, December 1988.

[Levo88]
Levoy, M., Display of surfaces from volume data, *IEEE Comput. Graph. and Appl.*, Vol. 8, No. 3, pp. 29–37, May 1988.

[Levo90a]
Levoy, M., Volume rendering by adaptive refinement, *The Visual Computer*, Vol. 6, pp. 2–7, 1990.

[Levo90b]
Levoy, M., A hybrid ray tracer for rendering polygon and volume data, *IEEE Comput. Graph. and Appl.*, Vol. 10, No. 2, pp. 33–40, March 1990.

[Levo90c]
Levoy, M., Fuchs, H., Pizer, S.M., Rosenman, J., Chaney, E.L., Sherouse, G.W., Interrante, V., and Kiel, J., Volume rendering in radiation treatment planning, *First Conf. on Visualization in Biomedical Computing*, Atlanta, GA, May 1990, Los Alamitos, CA: IEEE Computer Society Press, pp. 4–10.

[Levo90d]
Levoy, M., Efficient ray-tracing of volume data, *ACM TOG*, Vol. 9, pp. 245–261, 1990.

[Leym90]
Leymarie, F., "Tracking and Describing Deformable Objects Using Active Contour Models", Master's thesis, Computer Vision and Robotics Laboratory, McGill Research Centre for Intelligent Machines, McGill University, Montreal, Canada, February 1990.

[Lifs90]
Lifshitz, L.M., and Pizer, S.M., A multiresolution hierarchical approach to image segmentation based on intensity extrema, *IEEE Trans. Patt. Anal. Mach. Intell.*, Vol. 12, pp. 529–540, June 1990.

[Lim90]
Lim, J.S., *Two-Dimensional Signal and Image Processing*. Englewood Cliffs, NJ: Prentice Hall, 1990.

[Lin89]
Lin, W.C., Chen, S.Y., and Chen, C.T., A new surface interpolation technique for reconstructing 3D objects from serial cross sections, *Comput. Vis., Graph. and Image Process.*, Vol. 48, pp. 124–143, 1989.

[Lips90]
Lipson, P., Yuille, A.L., O'Keeffe, D.O., Cavanaugh, J., Taaffe, J., and Rosenthal, D., Automated bone density calculation using feature extraction by deformable templates, *First Conf. on Visualization in Biomedical Computing*, Atlanta, GA, May 1990, Los Alamitos, CA: IEEE Computer Society Press, pp. 477–484.

[Liu77]
Liu, H.K., Two and three dimensional boundary detection, *Comput. Graph. and Image Process.*, Vol. 6, pp. 123–134, 1977.

[Lore87]
Lorensen, W.E., and Cline, H.E., Marching cubes: A high resolution 3D surface construction algorithm, *Comput. Graph.*, Vol. 21, pp. 163–169, 1987 (SIGGRAPH 87).

[Matt89]
Matthies, L.H., Kanade, T., and Szeliski, R., Kalman filter-based algorithms for estimating depth from image sequences, *Int. Jour. Comp. Vision*, Vol. 3, pp. 209–236, 1989.

[Meag82]
Meagher, D., Geometric modeling using octree encoding, *Comput. Graph. and Image Process.*, Vol. 19, pp. 129–147, 1982.

[Meag84]
Meagher, D., Interactive solids processing for medical analysis and planning, *Proc. National Computer Graphics Association, NCGA'84*, May 1984.

[Mein91]
Meinzer, H.P., Meetz, K., Scheppelmann, D., Engelmann, U., and Baur, H.J., The Heidelberg ray tracing model, *IEEE Comput. Graph. and Appl.*, Vol. 11, No. 6, pp. 34–43, November 1991.

[Meye91]
Meyers, D., Skinner, S., and Sloan, K., Surfaces from contours: The correspondence and branching problems, *Graphics Interface '91*, Calgary, Alberta, Canada, Canadian Information Processing Society, June 1991.

[Mitc88]
Mitchell, D.P., and Netravali, A.N., Reconstruction filters in computer graphics, *Comput. Graph.*, Vol. 22, pp. 221–228, 1988 (SIGGRAPH 88).

[Mong91]
Monga, O., Ayache, N., and Sander, P., From voxel to curvature, *IEEE Comp.*

Soc. Conf. on Comp. Vision and Pattern Recognition (CVPR'91), Maui, HI, June 1991, pp. 644–649; Los Alamitos, CA: IEEE Computer Society Press.

[Morg81]
Morgenthaler, D.G., and Rosenfeld, A., Multidimensional edge detection by hypersurface fitting, *IEEE Trans. Patt. Anal. Mach. Intell.*, Vol. 3, No. 4, pp. 482–486, July 1981.

[Ney90]
Ney, D.R., Fishman, E.K., Magid, D., and Drebin, R.A., Volume rendering of computed tomography data: Principles and techniques, *IEEE Comput. Graph. and Appl.*, Vol. 10, No. 2, pp. 24–32, March 1990.

[Okut90]
Okutomi, M., and Kanade, T., A signal matching algorithm: An adaptive window based on a brownian motion model, *Third International Conference on Computer Vision (ICCV'90)*, Osaka, Japan, December 1990, pp. 190–199; Los Alamitos, CA: IEEE Computer Society Press.

[Oppe75]
Oppenheim, A.V., and Schafer, R.W., *Digital Signal Processing*, Englewood Cliffs, NJ: Prentice Hall, 1975.

[Peli89]
Pelizzari, C.A., Chen, G.T.Y., Spelbring, D.R., Weichselbaum, R.R., and Chen, C.T., Accurate three-dimensional registration of CT, PET, and/or MR images of the brain, *Jour. Comp. Assisted Tomography*, Vol. 13, No. 1, pp. 20–26, January/February 1989.

[Phon75]
Phong, B.T., Illumination for computer generated pictures, *CACM*, Vol. 18, pp. 311–317, June 1975.

[Pize90]
Pizer, S.M., Gauch, J.M., Cullip, T.J., and Frederiksen, R.E., Descriptions of image intensity structure via scale and symmetry, *First Conf. on Visualization in Biomedical Computing*, Atlanta, GA, May 1990, Los Alamitos, CA: IEEE Computer Society Press, pp. 94–101.

[Port84]
Porter, T., and Duff, T., Compositing digital images, *Comput. Graph.*, Vol. 18, pp. 253–259, 1984 (SIGGRAPH 84).

[Prep85]
Preparata, F.P., and Shamos, M.I., *Computational Geometry*, New York: Springer-Verlag, 1985.

[Pres86]
Press, W.H., Flannery, B.P., Teukolsky, S.A., and Vetterling, W.T., *Numerical Recipes: The Art of Scientific Computing*, Cambridge, UK: Cambridge University Press, 1986.

[Raya90]
Raya, S.P., and Udupa, J.K., Shape-based interpolation of multidimensional objects, *IEEE Trans. on Medical Imaging*, Vol. 9, No. 1, pp. 32–42, March 1990.

[Rhod79]
Rhodes, M.L., An algorithmic approach to controlling search in three-dimensional image data, *Comput. Graph.*, Vol. 13, pp. 134–142, 1979 (SIGGRAPH 79).

[Rose76]
Rosenfeld, A., and Kak, A.C., *Digital Picture Processing*, New York: Academic Press, 1976.

[Sabe88]
Sabella, P., A rendering algorithm for visualizing 3D scalar fields, *Comput. Graph.*, Vol. 22, pp. 51–58, 1988 (SIGGRAPH 88).

[Sabe89]
Sabella, P., and Carlbom, I., An object-oriented approach to solid modeling for empirical data, *IEEE Comput. Graph. and Appl.*, Vol. 9, No. 5, pp. 24–35, September 1989.

[Same81]
Samet, H., Connected component labeling using quadtrees, *JACM*, Vol. 28, No. 3, pp. 487–501, July 1981.

[Sand90]
Sander, P.T., and Zucker, S.W., Inferring surface trace and differential structure from 3-D images, *IEEE Trans. Patt. Anal. Mach. Intell.*, Vol. 12, No. 9, pp. 833–854, September 1990.

[Schr91]
Schröder, P., and Salem, J.B., Fast Rotation of Volume Data on Data Parallel Architectures, in *Proc. Visualization '91*, Nielson, G.M., and Rosenblum, L., Eds., San Diego, CA, October 1991, pp. 50–57, Los Alamitos, CA: IEEE Computer Society Press.

[Smit87]
Smith, A.R., Planar 2-pass texture mapping and warping, *Comput. Graph.*, Vol. 21, pp. 263–272, 1987 (SIGGRAPH 87).

[Szel89]
Szeliski, R., *Bayesian Modeling of Uncertainty in Low-Level Vision*, Dordrecht, The Netherlands: Kluwer Academic Publishers, 1989.

[Szel90]
Szeliski, R., Shape from rotation, Technical Report 90/13, Digital Equipment Corporation, Cambridge Research Lab, December 1990.

[Terz87]
Terzopoulos, D., On matching deformable models to images: Direct and iterative solutions, *Topical Meeting on Machine Vision*, Washington, D.C., Optical Society of America, pp. 160–167, March 1987.

[Tied90]
Tiede, U., Höhne, K.H., Bomans, M., Pommert, A., Riemer, M., and Wiebecke, G., Investigation of medical 3D-rendering algorithms, *IEEE Comput. Graph. and Appl.*, Vol. 10, No. 2, pp. 41–53, March 1990.

[Toen89]
Toennies, K.D., Udupa, J.K., and Herman, G.T., Segmentation of implanted bone grafts using anatomical landmarks, *Proc. NCGA'89*, pp. 207–214, Fairfax, VA, National Computer Graphics Association, April 1989.

[Toen90]
Toennies, K.D., Udupa, J.K., Herman, G.T., Wornom III, I.L., and Buchman, S.R., Registration of 3D objects and surfaces, *IEEE Comput. Graph. and Appl.*, Vol. 10, No. 3, pp. 52–62, May 1990.

[Tonn92]
Tonnesen, D., Extracting surface structure from 3D data, unpublished manuscript, April 1992.

[Udup90]
Udupa, J.K., and Ajjanagadde, V.G., Boundary and object labeling in three-dimensional images, *Comput. Vis., Graph. and Image Process.*, Vol. 51, pp. 355–369, 1990.

[Upso88]
Upson, C., and Keeler, M., V-buffer: Visible volume rendering, *Comput. Graph.*, Vol. 22, pp. 59–64, 1988 (SIGGRAPH 88).

[Vann83]
Vannier, M.W., Marsh, J.L., and Warren, J.O., Three dimensional computer graphics for craniofacial surgical planning and evaluation, *Comput. Graph.*, Vol. 17, pp. 263–273, 1983 (SIGGRAPH 83).

[Vezi92]
Vezina, G., Fletcher, P.A., and Robertson, P.K., Volume rendering on the Maspar MP-1, Technical Report TR-HJ-92-07, CSIRO Division of Information Technology, Australia, April 1992.

[Vinc90]
Vincken, K.L., de Graaf, C.N., Koster, A.S.E., Viergever, M.A., Appelman, F.J.R., and Timmens, G.R., Multiresolution segmentation of 3D images by the hyperstack, *First Conf. on Visualization in Biomedical Computing*, Atlanta, GA, May 1990, Los Alamitos, CA: IEEE Computer Society Press, pp. 115–122.

[Vita90]
VitalImages, Inc., VoxelView/PLUS 1.4, *The Interactive Volume Rendering System*, Fairfield, IA, 1990.

[West89]
Westover, L., Interactive Volume Rendering, in *Proc. Volume Visualization Workshop*, Upson, C., Ed., Dept. Computer Science, University of North Carolina, Chapel Hill, NC, pp. 9–16, 1989.

[West90]
Westover, L., Footprint evaluation for volume rendering, *Comput. Graph.*, Vol. 24, pp. 367–376, 1990 (SIGGRAPH 90).

[West91]
Westover, L.A., "Splatting: A Parallel, Feed-Forward Volume Rendering Algorithm", Ph.D. diss., Dept. of Computer Science, University of North Carolina at Chapel Hill, Chapel Hill, NC, 1991.

[Wolb90]
Wolberg, G., *Digital Image Warping*, Los Alamitos, CA: IEEE Computer Society Press, 1990.

[Wolp88]
Wolphe Jr., R.H., and Liu, C.N., Interactive visualization of 3D seismic data: A volumetric method, *IEEE Comput. Graph. and Appl.*, Vol. 8, No. 4, pp. 24–30, July 1988.

[Yage91]
Yagel, R., Kaufman, A., and Zhang, Q., Realistic Volume Imaging, in *Proc. Visualization '91*, Nielson, G.M., and Rosenblum, L., Eds., San Diego, CA, October 1991, pp. 226–231, Los Alamitos, CA: IEEE Computer Society Press.

[Zuck81]
Zucker, S.W., and Hummel, R.A., A three-dimensional edge operator, *IEEE Trans. Patt. Anal. Mach. Intell.*, Vol. 3, No. 3, pp. 324–331, May 1981.

Comparing Methods of Interpolation
for Scattered Volumetric Data

Gregory M. Nielson and John Tvedt

Abstract

This report describes the methodology and some of the results of an empirical study devoted to comparing methods of interpolating scattered volumetric data. The data is represented by $(x_i, y_i, z_i;\ F_i)$, $i = 1, \ldots, N$, where $P_i = (x_i, y_i, z_i)$ represents the independent data variables, and F_i is the dependent data variable. No assumptions about the distribution of independent data sites is made except that the points are distinct. Several methods for constructing a function F such that $F(P_i) = F_i$, $i = 1, \ldots, N$, are described and compared. The comparisons are based upon test functions, data sets, and an interactive program for visualizing and comparing the graphs of different models.

Introduction

This paper describes the methodology and some of the results of a study devoted to comparing methods of interpolating scattered volumetric data. Scattered data arises in many areas of science and engineering. It results from computer simulations and from physical measurements taken during experiment. Here, we are interested in data where one variable is dependent on several others. In particular, we are interested in the case where the independent data domain is three-dimensional. Samples of the data are represented by $(x_i, y_i, z_i; F_i)$, $i = 1, \ldots, N$, where $P_i = (x_i, y_i, z_i)$ represents the independent data variables and F_i is the dependent data variable. Examples include measurements of temperature at various locations in a furnace; mineral concentrations known at various depths of scattered bore hole locations; density measurements at various locations inside a human body; and economic performance levels known at various times, interest rates, and unemployment levels. A major problem for the scientist or engineer is to understand the relationship that is inferred by the data. We denote this relationship by $F(x, y, z)$ so that $(x_i, y_i, z_i; F_i)$ represents a sampling of the graph $(x, y, z, F(x, y, z))$. A visualization of the graph is a great help in understanding the relationship and can possibly aid in understanding the underlying process which produced the data. Here we are interested in ways of constructing F so as to provide a means of graphing or visualizing the data. In this regard, we are not so interested in the form of F as in the results of the model and how easily it can be used to provide information for visualizing the graph. As the dimension of the independent data increases, the need to interpolate the data for graph creation increases. While it may be of some visual aid, often in the case of univariate data, a graph of the 'raw' data does not significantly benefit from adding the graph of an interpolating or fitting function (e.g., see Figure 1).

In the case of bivariate scattered data, it is much more difficult to infer any relationship from a plot of the raw data. Here the graph of an interpolating function can aid considerably (see Figure 2). The situation for trivariate data is even more pronounced. It is very difficult to infer anything from a graph of scattered trivariate data, and so the need to develop a model for graph creation is much more important.

In the past several years, several methods for 'graphing' trivariate relationships have been developed. These methods run the gamut from simple slicing methods to computationally intensive ray-cast volume rendering methods. A survey of these methods is found in [Niel93a]. For the most part, these standard methods require that the relationship $F(x, y, z)$ be sampled on a uniform cuberille grid (see Figure 3). This is where scattered data interpolation comes in. The raw data is passed to the interpolation method, which is used to provide samples on a uniform grid for the visualization tool.

Unfortunately, there is no single, general purpose method for the interpolation of scattered data. Each of the various methods has varying levels of success in different situations. This is one of the main reasons for this study. Our goal is not to provide precise, directive information for the selection of a particular method for a particular situation, but rather to convey a rough assessment of the quality of the various methods in a variety of situations.

In some ways, this project is an abbreviated trivariate version of the very comprehensive work by R. Franke on critical comparison of methods of interpolating bivariate scattered data [Fran82]. The basic plan for the study, adopted from

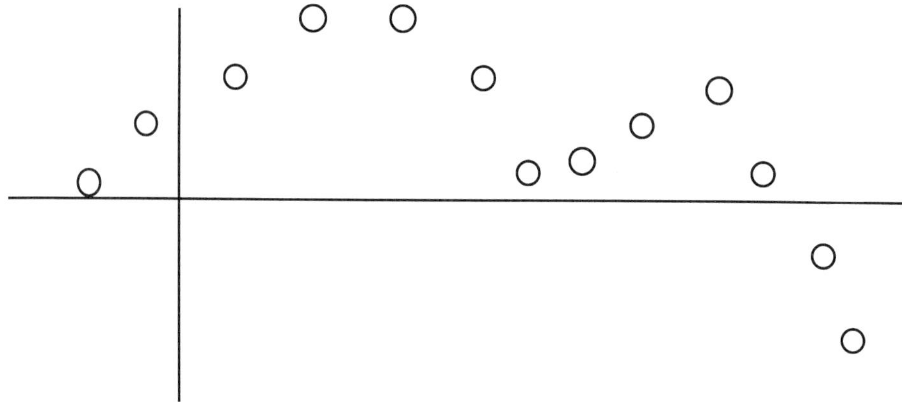

Figure 1. A scatter plot of the 'raw' univariate data without interpolation.

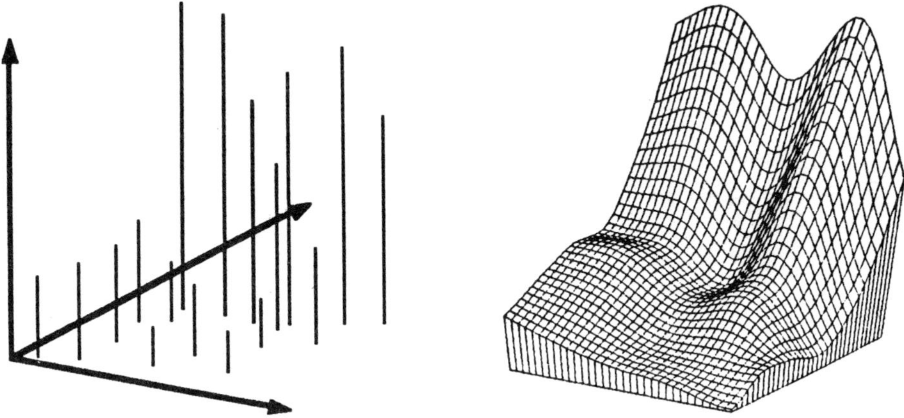

Figure 2. Scatter plot of bivariate data, and graph of interpolating function.

Franke's previous work, consists of applying a variety of methods in a variety of situations and comparing the results. Test functions and data sets are used. The test function $F(x, y, z)$ is used to generate the dependent data and to serve as a baseline for the evaluation of the performance of the method. Given a dependent data set (x_i, y_i, z_i), $i = 1, \ldots, N$, and a test function $F(x, y, z)$, a particular method for scattered data interpolation is used to produce an approximation $A(x, y, z)$, which is then compared to $F(x, y, z)$. Comparisons consist of numerical statistics and subjective assessments based upon the analysis of the 'graphs' of F and A. We now present the three components of the study: methods, data sets, and test functions.

Components of the Study

METHODS

The methods used in this study were selected in hopes they would be representative of all trivariate scattered data interpolation methods.

Modified Quadratic Shepard's Method

The basic Shepard's method, an inverse distance-weighted approximation which is very easy to describe and implement, is written in the form

$$S(P) = \frac{\displaystyle\sum_{i=1}^{N} \frac{F_i}{(x - x_i)^2 + (y - y_i)^2 + (z - z_i)^2}}{\displaystyle\sum_{i=1}^{N} \frac{1}{(x - x_i)^2 + (y - y_i)^2 + (z - z_i)^2}} = \frac{\displaystyle\sum_{i=1}^{N} \frac{F_i}{||P - P_i||^2}}{\displaystyle\sum_{i=1}^{N} \frac{1}{||P - P_i||^2}} \tag{1}$$

where $||P - P_i||$ represents the distance from P to P_i.

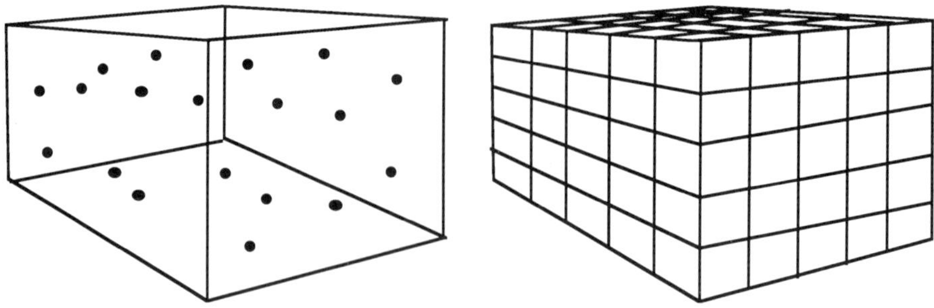

Figure 3. Scattered volumetric data, and a uniform cuberille grid.

In this form it is not easy to see that $F(P_i) = F_i$, $i = 1, \ldots, N$: but if both the numerator and denominator are multiplied by the appropriate factor, we have

$$S(P) = \frac{\displaystyle\sum_{i=1}^{N} \left(\prod_{i \neq j} ||P - P_i||^2 \right) F_i}{\displaystyle\sum_{i=1}^{N} \prod_{i \neq j} ||P - P_i||^2} = \sum_{i=1}^{N} F_i W_i(P) \tag{2}$$

where it is now easy to see that $W_i(P_j) = \delta_{ij}$; thus interpolation is guaranteed.

While this basic method is very simple, it has some shortcomings which eliminate it from practical application. Its main value is as a starting point for the development of other methods. Its main deficiency is that it does not reproduce any of the local shape properties inferred by the data, since

$$\frac{\partial S}{\partial x}(P_i) = \frac{\partial S}{\partial y}(P_i) = \frac{\partial S}{\partial z}(P_i) = 0 \qquad i = 1, \ldots, N$$

An example in the bivariate case is shown in Figure 4.

In the case of bivariate data, Franke and Nielson [Fran80] developed a modification which eliminates the deficiencies of the basic Shepard's method. They call this method the Modified Quadratic Shepard's method (MQS). The primary changes involve modifying the weight function $||P - P_i||$ to localize the overall approximation, and replacing F_i with a suitable 'local approximation', $Q_i(x, y)$. Their method has the general form

$$Q(P) = \frac{\displaystyle\sum_{i=1}^{N} \frac{Q_i(P)}{\rho_i^2(P)}}{\displaystyle\sum_{i=1}^{N} \frac{1}{\rho_i^2(P)}}$$

where

$$\frac{1}{\rho_i(P)} = \frac{(r_w - ||P - P_i||)_+}{r_w ||P - P_i||}$$

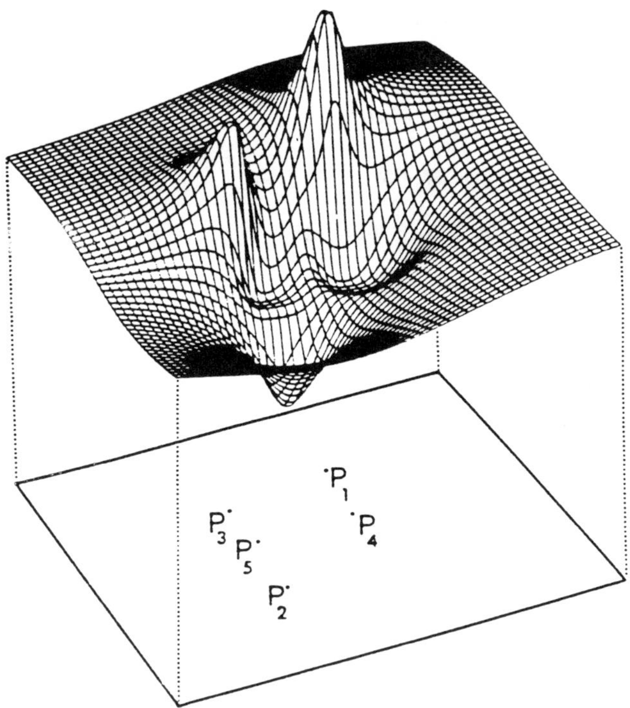

Figure 4. Shepard's method (Wixom and Gordon [Wixo78]).

for some constant r_w. Here the subscript $+$ denotes the truncated power function, hence the weight is zero at distances greater than r_w from the data point. The $Q_i(P)$ are assumed to be quadratic polynomials obtained by a weighted least-squares fit, constrained to take on the value F_i at P_i. The weights in the least-squares process are of the same form as the weight functions of the interpolant, but with r_w replaced by another value, r_q. The ideas of the bivariate MQS method of Nielson and Franke extend in a straightforward manner to the trivariate case. The algorithm used for this study consists of first selecting N_q and N_w in order to define

$$\frac{1}{\rho_i(P)} = \frac{\left(r_w - ||P - P_i||\right)_+}{r_w||P - P_i||} \qquad r_w = \frac{D}{2}\sqrt{\frac{N_w}{N}}$$

$$\frac{1}{\mu_i(P)} = \frac{\left(r_q - ||P - P_i||\right)_+}{r_q||P - P_i||} \qquad r_q = \frac{D}{2}\sqrt{\frac{N_q}{N}}$$

where $\qquad D = \max_{i,j} ||P_i - P_j||$

and the default values of N_q and N_w are 54 and 27, respectively. The following

72   Gregory M. Nielson and John Tvedt

least-squares problem is then solved

$$\min_{a_{kj},\,j=2,\ldots,10} \sum_{\substack{i=1 \\ i\neq k}}^{N} \frac{1}{\mu_i^2(x_k,y_k,z_k)} \big[f_k + a_{k2}(x_i - x_k) + a_{k3}(y_i - y_k)$$

$$+ a_{k4}(z_i - z_k) + a_{k5}(x_i - x_k)^2 + a_{k6}(y_i - y_k)^2$$

$$+ a_{k7}(z_i - z_k)^2 + a_{k8}(x_i - x_k)(y_i - y_k)$$

$$+ a_{k9}(x_i - x_k)(z_i - z_k) + a_{k10}(y_i - y_k)(z_i - z_k) - f_i \big]^2$$

in order to define

$$Q_k(x,y,z) = f_k + a_{k2}(x - x_k) + a_{k3}(y - y_k) + a_{k4}(z - z_k) + a_{k5}(x - x_k)^2$$

$$+ a_{k6}(y - y_k)^2 + a_{k7}(z - z_k)^2 + a_{k8}(x - x_k)(y - y_k)$$

$$+ a_{k9}(x - x_k)(z - z_k) + a_{k10}(y - y_k)(z - z_k)$$

which completes the definition of the final interpolant Q.

Note that the function is locally determined. The influence of any point does not extend further than a distance $r_w + r_q$ from each data point. Assuming a somewhat uniform density of data, constant values for r_w and r_q are appropriate. If the data are not of reasonably uniform density, then it may be desirable to let the radii r_w and r_q depend on i.

Volume Splines

This method is a straightforward generalization to volumetric data of the distance function approach to natural cubic splines (see [Niel93a]). The form of the modeling function is

$$F(P) = \sum_{i=1}^{N} c_i \|P - P_i\|^3 + a + bx + cy + dz$$

The unknown coefficients are obtained from the following system of equations, which represent the interpolation requirements with constraints analogous to end conditions

$$\begin{bmatrix} & & & 1 & P_1 \\ & \|P_i - P_j\|^3 & & 1 & P_2 \\ \cdot & \cdot & \cdot & \cdot & \cdot \\ & & & 1 & P_N \\ 1 & 1 & 1 & 0 & 0 \\ P_1^t & P_2^t & P_N^t & 0 & 0 \end{bmatrix} \begin{bmatrix} c_1 \\ c_2 \\ \cdot \\ c_N \\ a \\ b \\ c \\ d \end{bmatrix} = \begin{bmatrix} F_1 \\ F_2 \\ \cdot \\ F_N \\ 0 \\ 0 \\ 0 \\ 0 \end{bmatrix} \tag{3}$$

All that is required to implement this method is a routine to solve a linear system of equations. As long as the points P_i, $i = 1, \ldots, N$, are distinct, the coefficient matrix of Eq. (2) is nonsingular and therefore the system can be solved. But this is a theoretical result and in practical applications there are limits to the value of N, due to the conditioning of the coefficient matrix. Even in the case of nearly uniformly distributed points, the condition number can swamp single precision calculations for data sets of size $N = 300$ to 500. Thus, unless other measures are taken this method is limited to moderate-sized data sets.

Multiquadrics

In many ways the multiquadric method is similar to volume splines. They are both in the category of what are called global basis function methods . Also, both are radial basis function methods (see [Fran90; Niel91b] for more discussion on this).

The general form of the multiquadric modeling function is

$$H(P) = \sum_{i=1}^{N} c_i \sqrt{R^2 + ||P - P_i||^2}$$

The interpolation requirements lead to the system of equations

$$\left[\sqrt{R^2 + ||P_i - P_j||^2} \right] \begin{bmatrix} c_1 \\ c_2 \\ . \\ c_N \end{bmatrix} = \begin{bmatrix} F_1 \\ F_2 \\ . \\ F_N \end{bmatrix} \tag{4}$$

In the case of bivariate data, Carlson and Foley [Carl91] studied the selection of the parameter R^2. For a comparison of different R^2 values on the test functions in the study, discussed later in this paper, see [Dier90; Niel91a]. The default value is $R^2 = 0.1$.

Volumetric Minimum Norm Network

The next technique is a generalization of the Minimum Norm Network (MNN) method [Niel83] for interpolating scattered bivariate data. We briefly describe this bivariate method and indicate how it is extended to the case of volumetric data. There are three steps (see Figure 5):

the convex hull of the points $P_i = (x_i, y_i)$ is decomposed into a collection of triangles;

an interpolating curve network defined over the edges, with certain minimization properties, is computed;

to complete the definition of the modeling function, the curve network is filled in using a C^1 triangular interpolant.

The triangulation of the convex hull of a set of points $P_i = (x_i, y_i)$, $i = 1, \ldots, N$, consists of a list of triple indices, $(i, j, k) \in N_t$. Each triple (i, j, k) represents the triangle T_{ijk} with vertices P_i, P_j, P_k. It is assumed that no two triangles intersect and the union of all triangles is the convex hull. There are

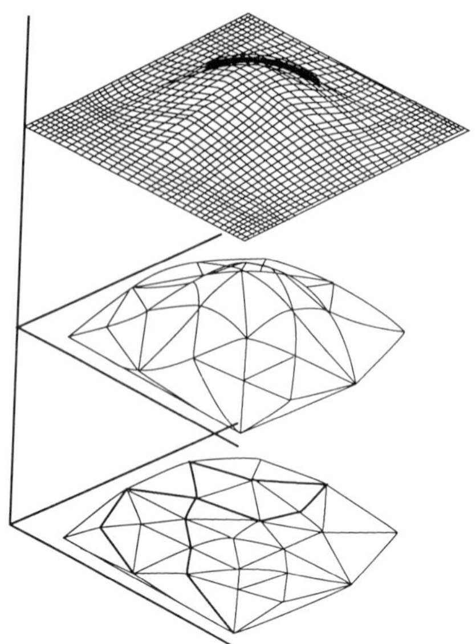

Figure 5. The three steps of the MNN method.

many possible triangulations of the convex hull. Usually some type of optimal triangulation which avoids long skinny triangles is preferred. A popular choice is max-min triangulation, which selects the triangulation with as large a minimum angle as possible. This optimal triangulation has a useful relationship to the Dirichlet tessellation. A Dirichlet tessellation is a partition into regions $R_k, k = 1, \ldots, N$, consisting of all points whose closest point among $P_i, i = 1, \ldots, N$, is P_k. A Dirichlet tessellation is usually illustrated by drawing the boundaries of these regions. An example for planar data is shown in Figure 6a, while Figure 6b shows the max-min triangulation. It is related to the Dirichlet tessellation in that the edges of this optimal triangulation join vertices which share a common region boundary. We also note that this relationship means that T_{ijk} is a triangle of the optimal triangulation, provided the circumcircle of the vertices P_i, P_j, and P_k contains no other points.

While there are more efficient algorithms for computing the decomposition into tetrahedra, they are often not as easy to implement as the less efficient methods mentioned here. The first algorithm is extremely simple to implement, but extremely slow. We refer to this as 'the world's worst algorithm for tetrahedronization':

generate each combination of four points in the data set;

for each set of four points:

find the equation for the sphere uniquely defined for these points;

if no other points in the data set lie within the sphere, these four points are added to the list of tetrahedra.

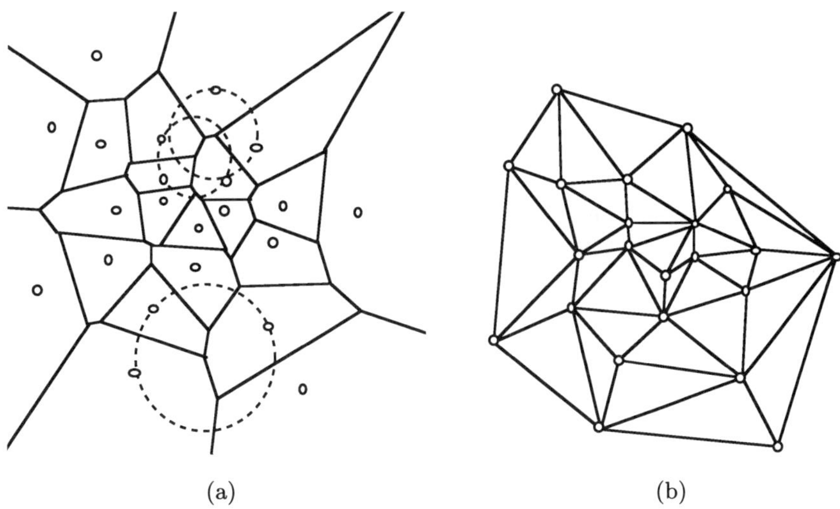

(a)   (b)

Figure 6. The Dirichlet tessellation and its dual triangulation. (a) An example for planar data; (b) max-min triangulation.

The time complexity of this algorithm is $O(N^5)$. This makes the algorithm unusable for data sets of even moderate size. Consequently, a new localized algorithm was implemented. The new algorithm makes use of the fact that each face of a tetrahedron either borders another tetrahedron and is one of its faces, or is an external face of the convex hull. The algorithm is:

    use the first algorithm to find the first tetrahedron

    put this tetrahedron on a list

    for each tetrahedron on this list

        for each face of this tetrahedron

            if this face is not a face of any other tetrahedron on the list

                for each point in the data set (less the three on this face)

                    find the equation for the sphere uniquely defined for this point and the three points on this face

                    if no other points in the data set lie within the sphere these four points are added to the list of tetrahedra

Now consider the second step of this method. In the bivariate MNN a network is defined over the collection of all edges. This network is characterized in a manner similar to the minimum norm characterization of standard cubic interpolating splines. Recall that a cubic spline is the unique minimizer of $\int_a^b \left(F''(x)\right)^2 dx$ subject to interpolation requirements.

In the case of the bivariate MNN, the quantity

$$\sigma(F) = \sum_{ij \in N_e} \int_{e_{ij}} \left(\frac{d^2 F}{d^2 e_{ij}}\right)^2 ds_{ij}$$

is minimized. Here, ds_{ij} represents the element of arc length on the curve consisting of the line segment e_{ij} and $N_e = \{ij$ or ji (but not both): V_i to V_j is an edge of the triangulation$\}$. In the univariate case, when we minimize the integral of the second derivative squared, subject to interpolation requirements, we find that the solution is a piecewise cubic curve and, if the curve is represented in Hermite form, the derivatives are computed as the solution of a linear system of equations. In the bivariate MNN method, the solution of the minimum of $\sigma(F)$ is also piecewise cubic. The minimization process leads to the system of equations

$$\sum_{ij \in N_i} \frac{x_j - x_i}{||e_{ij}||^3} \left[(x_j - x_i)S_x(V_i) + (y_j - y_i)S_y(V_i) \right.$$

$$\left. + \frac{x_j - x_i}{2} S_x(V_j) + \frac{y_j - y_i}{2} S_y(V_j) + \frac{3}{2}(F_i - F_j) \right] = 0$$

$$\sum_{ij \in N_i} \frac{y_j - y_i}{||e_{ij}||^3} \left[(x_j - x_i)S_x(V_i) + (y_j - y_i)S_y(V_i) \right.$$

$$\left. + \frac{x_j - x_i}{2} S_x(V_j) + \frac{y_j - y_i}{2} S_y(V_j) + \frac{3}{2}(F_i - F_j) \right] = 0 \quad (5)$$

where $N_i = \{ij : ij, ji \in N_e\}$. This system is sparse and is easily solved using iterative methods. More discussion on this technique is found in [Niel83]. The ideas easily extend to volumetric data. In this case the system of equations is

$$\sum_{ij \in N_i} \frac{x_j - x_i}{||e_{ij}||^3} \left[(x_j - x_i)S_x(V_i) + (y_j - y_i)S_y(V_i) + (z_j - z_i)S_z(V_i) \right.$$

$$+ \frac{x_j - x_i}{2} S_x(V_j) + \frac{y_j - y_i}{2} S_y(V_j)$$

$$\left. + \frac{z_j - z_i}{2} S_z(V_j) + \frac{3}{2}(F_i - F_j) \right] = 0$$

$$\sum_{ij \in N_i} \frac{y_j - y_i}{||e_{ij}||^3} \left[(x_j - x_i)S_x(V_i) + (y_j - y_i)S_y(V_i) + (z_j - z_i)S_z(V_i) \right.$$

$$+ \frac{x_j - x_i}{2} S_x(V_j) + \frac{y_j - y_i}{2} S_y(V_j)$$

$$\left. + \frac{z_j - z_i}{2} S_z(V_j) + \frac{3}{2}(F_i - F_j) \right] = 0$$

$$\sum_{ij \in N_i} \frac{z_j - z_i}{||e_{ij}||^3} \left[(x_j - x_i)S_x(V_i) + (y_j - y_i)S_y(V_i) + (z_j - z_i)S_z(V_i) \right.$$

$$+ \frac{x_j - x_i}{2} S_x(V_j) + \frac{y_j - y_i}{2} S_y(V_j)$$

$$\left. + \frac{z_j - z_i}{2} S_z(V_j) + \frac{3}{2}(F_i - F_j) \right] = 0 \quad (6)$$

This linear system of equations is completely analogous to those of the original, planar MNN method, and they are solved in a very similar fashion using an iterative method. Once the first-order derivatives at each data site are computed, we fill in the model with a C^1 tetrahedral interpolant. This requires the definition of an interpolant, F, defined on T_{ijkl} that matches given position and derivative information at all four vertices. The method we describe here is a three-dimensional generalization of the side-vertex interpolant described in [Niel79]. It is called the face-vertex method (see Figure 7) [Niel92]. In its transfinite version we assume that position and derivative information is available at all locations on the four faces which make up the boundary of the tetrahedron T_{ijkl}. The basic face-vertex operator is defined as

$$S_i[F](P) = b_i^2(3 - 2b_i)F(V_i) + b_i^2(b_i - 1)F'(V_i) + (1 - b_i)^2(2b_i + 1)F(S_i)$$
$$+ b_i(1 - b_i)^2 F'(S_i) \tag{7}$$

where
$$F'(V_i) = \frac{(x - x_i)F_x(V_i) + (y - y_i)F_y(V_i) + (z - z_i)F_z(V_i)}{1 - b_i}$$

and
$$F'(S_i) = \frac{(x - x_i)F_x(S_i) + (y - y_i)F_y(S_i) + (z - z_i)F_z(V_i)}{1 - b_i}$$

The point S_i is the intersection point of the ray from V_i through $P = (x, y, z)$ and the face opposite V_i. The derivatives are taken in the direction of this same ray. The barycentric coordinates of P are denoted by b_i, b_j, b_k, and b_l.

If we form the convex combination

$$S[F] = \frac{b_j^2 b_k^2 b_l^2 S_i[F] + b_i^2 b_k^2 b_l^2 S_j[F] + b_j^2 b_l^2 b_i^2 S_k[F] + b_j^2 b_k^2 b_i^2 S_l[F]}{b_j^2 b_k^2 b_l^2 + b_i^2 b_k^2 b_l^2 + b_j^2 b_l^2 b_i^2 + b_i^2 b_j^2 b_k^2} \tag{8}$$

then $S[F]$ matches position and derivative values on the entire boundary of T_{ijkl}. When we actually use the face-vertex interpolant in this application, we

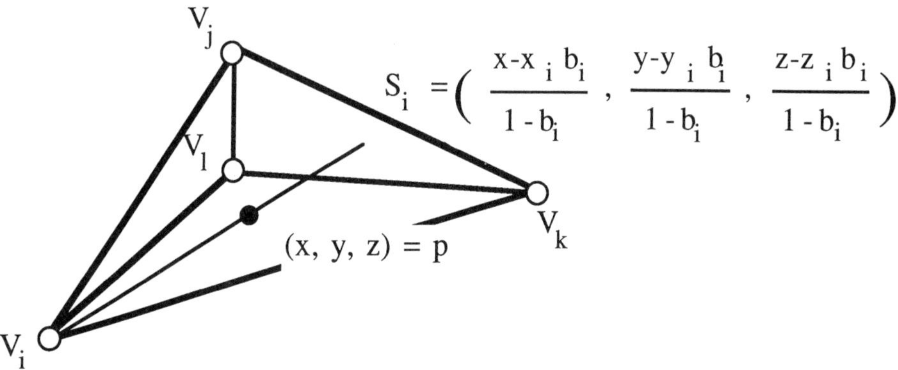

Figure 7. The face-vertex method notation.

only know position and derivative values at the four vertices. In order to apply the operator of Eq. (8), we need to define position and derivatives on the entire boundary of T_{ijkl}. The process of defining the transfinite boundary information from a finite (discrete) amount of data (usually given at the vertices) is called 'discretization'. In the case of the present face-vertex method, first we assume that information is known on all the edges of the tetrahedron, and then we describe how to extend it to the entire boundary. Second, we describe how to discretize the edge information itself.

If we know both position and derivative information on the edges, then we can use any C^1 transfinite planar triangular interpolant to define position values on the interior points of the face triangles. For example, the side-vertex method itself is applicable. Specifying position information on a face also implies some information about the derivatives on the interior of a triangle, namely that all directional derivatives parallel to the face triangle are determined. Thus, in order to completely specify all derivatives, we need only provide a definition for the derivative perpendicular to the face. For this we use the C^0 version of the side-vertex interpolant, which interpolates position data only and not derivatives. Here we apply it to the edge data consisting of derivatives normal to a face. The C^0 side-vertex interpolant has the simple form

$$A[F] = (1-b_i)F(S_i)+(1-b_j)F(S_j)+(1-b_k)F(S_k)-b_iF(V_i)-b_jF(V_j)-b_kF(V_k)$$

The second step of the discretization requires computing edge information when only the point and derivative values are known at the four vertices. For position only on an edge, we simply use univariate cubic Hermite interpolation. This also specifies one directional derivative on the edge, namely $\partial F/\partial e_{ij}$, which varies as a quadratic polynomial. In order to obtain a C^1 join from one tetrahedron to the next, the other two directional derivatives must vary linearly along this edge. This is accomplished by specifying the gradient, ∇F, by the relationship

$$\nabla F_{ij}(p) = (1-t)\nabla F_i + t\nabla F_j + \left\{\frac{\partial F}{\partial e_{ij}}(p) - [(1-t)\nabla F_i + t\nabla F_i, e_{ij}]\right\}e_{ij}$$

where $\nabla F_i = [\, F_x(p_i) \quad F_y(p_i) \quad F_z(p_i)\,]$ and $t = \|p - p_i\|/\|p_j - p_i\|$. This interpolation of the gradient is consistent with the value $\partial F/\partial e_{ij}$ already specified because $(\nabla F_{ij}(p), e_{ij}) = \partial F/de_{ij}$. It also has the property that for $(n, e_{ij}) = 0$

$$\left(\nabla F_{ij}(p), n\right) = (1-t)(\nabla F_i, n) + t(\nabla F_j, n)$$

Thus, we have linear interpolation for any derivative in a direction perpendicular to e_{ij}. This completes the definition of the 16-parameter, C^1 tetrahedron interpolant which is based upon the face-vertex interpolant.

Localized Volume Splines

As mentioned earlier, there are definite limits to the size of the data set for volume splines. Often the problems in scattered volume data exceed these limits. In order to preserve the use of a particular method and apply it to very large data sets, we localize the method. This requires the use of 'localizing' functions which are smooth and have a small region of support. The basic ideas are easily understood by considering the univariate case illustrated in Figure 8. The functions w_k are nonzero only on two intervals and have the property that $\sum w_k(x) = 1$ for any x in the domain. Local scattered data interpolants F_k are computed so that $F_k(x_i) = F_i$ for all data points x_i in the support of w_k. From this, it is easy to see that

$$F(x) = \sum w_k(x) F_k(x)$$

has the property that $F(x_i) = F_i$ for all x_i in the union of the support of w_k, which is arranged to be the entire original domain. In general, any method can be used to obtain the local interpolants F_k. The localizing function w_k is easily constructed with piecewise cubics (bicubics or tricubics). Usually the number and support of the w_k's is selected so that the number of data points per support of w_k is roughly constant.

The particular method of this study uses volume splines and localizing functions which are piecewise (Hermite) tricubics. The overall interpolant is of the form

$$R(P) = \sum_{i=1}^{n_x} \sum_{j=1}^{n_y} \sum_{k=1}^{n_z} W_{ijk}(P) V_{ijk}(P)$$

where n_x, n_y, and n_z determine the number of support regions. There are at most eight nonzero terms in the sum. The weight function is of the form

$$W_{ijk}(x, y, z) = t_i(x) u_j(y) v_k(z) \quad i = 1, \ldots, n_x; \quad j = 1, \ldots, n_y; \quad k = 1, \ldots, n_z$$

where

$$t_1(x) = \begin{cases} 1 & x < q_1 \\ H\left(\dfrac{x - q_1}{q_2 - q_1}\right) & q_1 \leq x < q_2 \\ 0 & x \geq q_2 \end{cases}$$

$$t_i(x) = \begin{cases} 0 & x < q_{i=1} \\ 1 - t_{i-1}(x) & q_{i-1} \leq x < q_i \\ H\left(\dfrac{x - q_1}{q_{i+1} - q_i}\right) & q_i \leq x < q_{i+1} \\ 0 & x \geq q_{i+1} \end{cases} \qquad i = 2, \ldots, h_x - 1$$

$$t_{n_x}(x) = \begin{cases} 0 & x < q_{n_x - 1} \\ 1 - t_{n_x - 1}(x) & q_{n_x - 1} \leq x < q_{n_x} \\ 1 & x \geq q_{n_x} \end{cases}$$

and

$$H(s) = 1 - 3s^2 + 2s^3$$

which is the cubic Hermite satisfying $H(0) = 1$, $H(1) = H'(0) = H'(1) = 0$. The values $q_1 < q_1 \ldots < q_{n_x}$ are user-provided parameters which define the partition

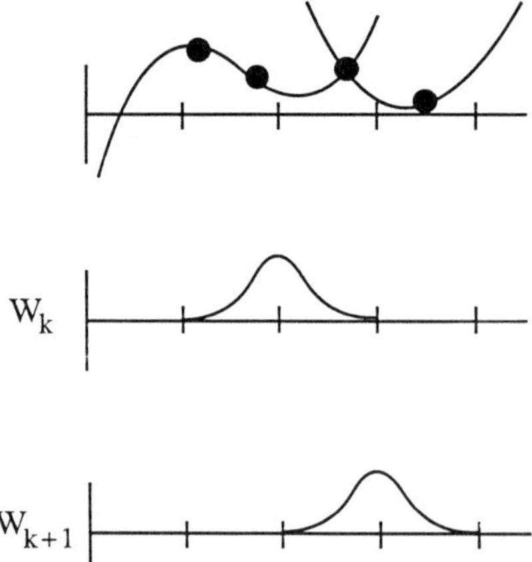

Figure 8. Localizing functions.

of the domain. The $u_j(y)$ and $v_k(z)$ are defined in an analogous manner with point partitioning parameters, $r_1 < r_2 < \ldots < r_{n_y}$ and $s_1 < s_2 < \ldots < s_{n_z}$, respectively. The $Q_{ijk}(x, y, z)$ are just volume spline interpolants solved for each support region R_{ijk}, using only the points from this support region. Also, it is possible to use points covering a larger region than the support region R_{ijk}. A region about 150% larger tends to give a better transition between local approximations. This was not used for the current implementation.

DATA SETS

One of the goals in selecting data sets was to use a small number which are representative of the entire gamut of data sets. A total of six sets was used, three of which were selected to be uniformly placed at random in the unit cube domain, one small, one moderate, and one large. These data sets (see Figure 9) are referred to as R125, R200, and R1000, and they contain 125 points, 200 points, and 1000 points, respectively. The remaining three data sets were selected to represent certain types of data which are likely to occur in real-world situations.

Linear sampling is probably most common in the area of mineral exploration, where it is analogous to taking core samples. The data set, L200, consists of samples taken from a given number of vertical lines which have been randomly perturbed. The perturbation is introduced to reflect imperfections in methods of human measurement.

Planar sampling is another specialized configuration which occurs in real-world situations. This data set consists of scattered samples taken from horizontal planes which have been randomly perturbed. Again, the randomness is introduced to reflect imperfections in the real world. This type of sampling is analogous to samples taken from slices of an object. This data set, consisting of 200 points, is denoted by P200.

Cluster sampling has many analogies to real-world sampling. It is a set of densely sampled areas, with large gaps where no samples are taken. It can

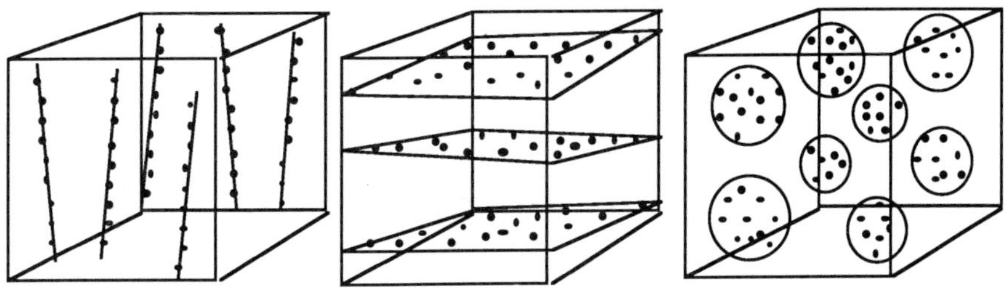

Figure 9. Data set configurations.

be thought of as a collection of random samples. Weather data often comes in the form of cluster sampling. Typically, more numerous measurements of temperature and rainfall are taken in metropolitan areas than in rural areas. This leads to dense clusters of data in metropolitan areas and sparse samples in the rural areas. Another example of cluster sampling occurs when one has some knowledge of the underlying function. Often, dense sampling is taken in areas where rapid change is expected in a function, and fewer samples are taken in areas with less rapid change. This data set, which has 200 points, is denoted by C200.

More details on the data sets and the actual numerical values are found in [Tved91].

TEST FUNCTIONS

The test functions for the current study are extensions to three dimensions of those used by Franke [Fran82], i.e.

$$F_1(x,y,z) = \frac{3}{4} \exp\left[-\frac{(9x-2)^2 + (9y-2)^2 + (9z-2)^2}{4} \right]$$

$$+ \frac{3}{4} \exp\left[-\frac{(9x+1)^2}{49} - \frac{(9y+1)}{10} - \frac{(9z+1)}{10} \right]$$

$$+ \frac{1}{2} \exp\left[-\frac{(9x-7)^2 + (9y-3)^2 + (9z-5)^2}{4} \right]$$

$$- \frac{1}{5} \exp\left[-(9x-4)^2 + (9y-7)^2 - (9z-5)^2 \right]$$

$$F_2(x,y,z) = \frac{\tanh(9z - 9x - 9y) + 1}{9}$$

$$F_3(x,y,z) = \frac{\left[\frac{5}{4} + \cos\left(\frac{27}{5}y\right) \right] \cos(6z)}{6 + 6(3x-1)^2}$$

$$F_4(x,y,z) = \frac{\exp\left\{-\dfrac{81}{16}\left[\left(x-\dfrac{1}{2}\right)^2 + \left(y-\dfrac{1}{2}\right)^2 + \left(z-\dfrac{1}{2}\right)^2\right]\right\}}{3}$$

$$F_5(x,y,z) = \frac{\exp\left\{-\dfrac{81}{4}\left[\left(x-\dfrac{1}{2}\right)^2 + \left(y-\dfrac{1}{2}\right)^2 + \left(z-\dfrac{1}{2}\right)^2\right]\right\}}{3}$$

$$F_6(x,y,z) = \left(64 - 81\frac{\left(x-\dfrac{1}{2}\right)^2 + \left(y-\dfrac{1}{2}\right)^2 + \left(z-\dfrac{1}{2}\right)^2}{9}\right)^{1/2} - \frac{1}{2}$$

The approximate ranges of these test functions over the domain $C = \{(x,y,z):$ $0 \le x \le 1,\ 0 \le y \le 1,\ 0 \le z \le 1\ \}$ are: F_1: $[-0.1, 1.1]$, F_2: $[0.0, 0.22]$, F_3: $[-0.37, 0.37]$, F_4: $[0.007, 0.33]$, F_5: $[0.0, 0.32]$, F_6: $[-0.3, 0.39]$

Results

One of the primary means of comparing methods of approximation applied to a test function is to compare some numerical measure of the error between the test function and the approximation. Here we use the measure of error

$$\text{RMS} = \sqrt{\frac{\displaystyle\sum_{i=1}^{N}\sum_{j=1}^{N}\sum_{k=1}^{N}\left[F\left(\frac{i}{N_i}, \frac{j}{N_j}, \frac{k}{N_k}\right) - A\left(\frac{i}{N_i}, \frac{j}{N_j}, \frac{k}{N_k}\right)\right]^2}{N_i N_j N_k}}$$

where F represents the test function and A represents one of the scattered data interpolants being evaluated. The results given in Tables 1, 2, and 3 use the resolution values for this root mean square error of $N_i = N_j = N_k = 20$.

While numerical error statistics are very useful for comparing scattered data interpolants, they do not allow subjective visual evaluation of the results. Also,

Table 1. RMS error for data sets vs test functions for local volume spline.

	F_1	F_2	F_3	F_4	F_5	F_6
R125	0.026	0.015	0.011	0.001	0.006	0.002
R200	0.013	0.012	0.008	0.001	0.003	0.002
R1000	0.001	0.003	0.001	0.0001	0.0003	0.0005
L200	0.023	0.012	0.006	0.002	0.013	0.001
P200	0.022	0.013	0.007	0.001	0.003	0.001
C200	0.025	0.015	0.016	0.002	0.040	0.001

Table 2. RMS error for method vs test function for data set R200.

	F_1	F_2	F_3	F_4	F_5	F_6
MQS, Q	0.0237	0.0134	0.0127	0.0033	0.0089	0.0012
Volume Splines, V	0.012	0.0014	0.0068	0.0006	0.002	0.0015
Multiquadric, H	0.0109	0.0126	0.0042	0.0003	0.0007	0.0018
Volume MNN, N	0.019	0.0121	0.0128	0.0019	0.0045	0.003
Local Volume Splines, R	0.0131	0.0117	0.0078	0.0008	0.0026	0.0017

error statistics do not convey much information about the local behavior of an approximation; they only provide an overall error estimate. A major component of the current study is an interactive program for the visual evaluation of the performance of various methods. The program allows the user to interactively change the method, data set, or test function. In this way, the user can browse around in order to gain insight into the overall performance of a method and compare it against other methods. The software was written with the idea that the domain was not static. New methods, data sets, or test functions can be added and old ones deleted. We call the program 'Slice Viewer'. A typical screen image is shown in Plate 11.

The slice viewer program allows the user to view slices of the volume with either the x, y, or z value held constant. Across the bottom of the screen are twenty small slices showing the function values of the actual, approximated, and difference functions. At the top of the screen are three enlarged slices chosen by the user from the array below. The user points at slices, and then an enlarged version is displayed in the top portion of the screen. In between the large and small slices is a color map showing the mapping of color values to function values. At the right side of each row of small slices is a range ([lower, upper]) that indicates the numeric values of the lower and upper bounds of the color map. The user can pick which slice to enlarge by simply pointing to a small slice with the mouse and pressing a button. In addition to seeing the entire volume, the user may choose to view only the function values inside the convex hull of the data set used to generate the approximation. All options, other than choosing a slice to enlarge, are available through pop-up menus. The user may show/hide the convex hull, load a new actual function, load a new approximation function, load a new color map, change the joint color mapping of the actual and approximated functions, or change the color mapping of the difference function.

Table 3. RMS error for data set vs method for test function F_1.

	R125	R200	R1000	L200	P200	C200
MQS, Q	0.0293	0.0237	0.015	0.0328	0.0332	0.0454
Volume Splines, V	0.0265	0.012		0.0237	0.0206	0.0268
Multiquadric, H	0.0218	0.0109		0.0177	0.0135	0.0349
Volume MNN, N	0.0327	0.019	0.004	0.0346	0.0257	0.0429
Local Volume Splines, R	0.0259	0.0131	0.0014	0.0235	0.0217	0.0257

We have used the program extensively and found it to be a very valuable aid in learning about the performance of volumetric scattered data interpolants. At this point, it would be nice to invite the reader to 'pop-up' a menu in Plate 11 and begin to play with the program in order to gain some insight which may aid in the selection of a particular method for a particular application. Of course, today this type of capability is not generally available in most publication media, and so at best we can only provide second-hand information. In order to convey some sense of this experience, we have included some assessments made as a result of using the Slice Viewer program. These include our own comments and also those of Professor Richard Franke, who spent a considerable amount of time using the program . We have also included some other overall comparative remarks and assessments.

MQS — Modified Quadratic Shepard Method

The Modified Quadratic Shepard Method is an extension to volume data of a very well-known and very effective bivariate method [Fran80]. It is usually very good at reproducing the qualitative features of the test function. Near the boundaries it is sometimes very bad. It is only C^1 but can be applied to very large data sets and is reasonably fast. In general, the implementation of this method takes more effort than most methods. The user must provide the parameters N_q and N_w or accept the default values.

Volume Splines

Volume splines provide a direct generalization to volumetric data of the univariate cubic interpolating spline when it is represented with distance functions (see [Niel93a]). In most cases the method gives results very similar to the multiquadric method, but at times they are detectably poorer. In the interior of the cube it seems to do better on the hypersphere (test function F_6) than the multiquadric method, but deviates more near the boundaries of the cube. On the random data set, R200 with F_1, it seems to be better than the multiquadric method. The implementation only requires a routine for solving a linear system of equations. The method reproduces linear functions and is C^2. In general, and without modifications, the method is limited to data sets smaller that $N = 300$ to 500. This is the reason why the entry in the second row and third column of Table 3 is missing.

Multiquadric Method

As in the bivariate case, the multiquadric method is generally very good at reproducing the qualitative features of the test function. The implementation consists of solving a linear system of equations. Conditioning of the coefficient matrix limits the size of the data set used. Typically, data sets of 500 or more points yield condition numbers that swamp single precision accuracy. There is a single parameter, R^2, which the user must provide.

LOCAL VOLUME SPLINES

The local volume splines method can be used for very large data sets. Localization sometimes deteriorates the scheme compared with the global method. On the R1000 data set with F_1, it is very good; on the hypersphere, F_6, it seems to be on a par with the multiquadric method. The user must provide the values which partition the domain or accept uniformly spaced default values. This can be a problem in that some subdomain may not have enough points to determine a volume spline. A robust implementation would recognize this situation and take some appropriate evasive action. In general, the implementation is a little more complex than the multiquadric method or volume splines but overall is quite easy. This method is not affine invariant.

VOLUME MNN METHOD

The Volume MNN method is a volumetric generalization of a very efficient and popular bivariate method (see [Niel83]). The generalization is not as straightforward as one would hope. It is more difficult than most other methods to implement. On the positive side, it is a global method that can be applied to extremely large data sets. This is because of the sparsity of Eqs. (6), which yield well to iterative methods. If the tetrahedral decomposition is affine invariant (see [Niel87, 93b]), then the method is also affine invariant. As it is implemented here there are no parameters that the user must provide. The overall qualitative performance of the method is very good.

Acknowledgments. This work was supported by the North Atlantic Treaty Organization under grant RG 0097/88. Karl Sun and Karsten Opitz were very helpful. We also wish to extend our appreciation to Richard Franke for all of the time and effort he has put into this study.

REFERENCES

[Carl91]
Carlson, R., and Foley, T., The parameter R^2 and multiquadric interpolation, *Computers and Math. with Appl.*, Vol. 21, No. 9, pp. 29–42, 1991.

[Dier90]
Dierks, T., "Analysis and Visualization of Scattered Volumetric Data", Master's thesis, Arizona State University, Tempe, AZ, 1990.

[Fran80]
Franke, R., and Nielson, G., Smooth interpolation to large sets of scattered data, *Intern. Jour. Numer. Meth. Engrg.*, Vol. 15, pp. 1691–1704, 1980.

[Fran82]
Franke, R., Scattered data interpolation: Tests of some methods, *Math. Comp.*, Vol. 38, pp. 181–200, 1982.

[Fran90]
Franke, R., and Nielson, G.M., Scattered Data Interpolation and Applications: A Tutorial and Survey, in *Geometric Modelling: Methods and Their Application*, Hagen, H., and Roller, D., Eds., Berlin: Springer-Verlag, 1990.

[Niel79]
Nielson, G.M., The side-vertex method for interpolation in triangles, *Jour. Approx. Theory*, Vol. 25, pp. 318–336, 1979.

[Niel83]
Nielson, G.M., A method for interpolating scattered data based upon a minimum norm network, *Math. Comp.*, Vol. 40, pp. 253–271, 1983.

[Niel87]
Nielson, G.M., Coordinate Free Scattered Data Interpolation, in *Topics in Multivariate Approximation*, Chui, C., Utreras, F., and Schumaker, L., Eds., New York: Academic Press, pp. 175–184, 1987.

[Niel91a]
Nielson, G.M., and Dierks, T., Modelling and Visualization of Scattered Volumetric Data, *SPIE/SPSE Conference Proc. 1459 — Symposium on Electronic Imaging: Science and Technology*, San Jose, CA, February 1991.

[Niel91b]
Nielson, G.M., Foley, T., Hamann, B., and Lane, D., Visualization and modelling of scattered multivariate data, *IEEE Comput. Graph. and Appl.*, Vol. 11, No. 3, pp. 47-55, May 1991.

[Niel92]
Nielson, G.M., and Opitz, K., The face-vertex method for smooth interpolation in tetrahedra, Arizona State University Computer Science Technical Report TR-92-013, 1992.

[Niel93a]
Nielson, G.M., Modeling and visualizing volumetric and surface-on-surface data, to appear in *Focus on Scientific Visualization*, Hagen, H., Mueller, H., and Nielson, G., Eds., Berlin: Spinger-Verlag, 1993.

[Niel93b]
Nielson, G.M., A characterization of an affine invariant triangulation, accepted for publication, *Computing*, 1993.

[Tved91]
Tvedt, J., "A Software System for Comparison of Trivariate Scattered Data Interpolation Methods", Master's thesis, Arizona State University, December 1991.

[Wixo78]
Wixom, J., and Gordon, W.J., On Shepard's method of metric interpolation to scattered bivariate and multivariate data, *Math. Comp.*, Vol. 32, pp. 253–264, 1978.

2 Modeling

Abstraction, Context, and Constraint

Roy Hall and Mimi Bussan

Abstract

The design process and the assembly of thousands of components can only be supported by systems that use a variety of presentational abstractions to reduce screen complexity. Reduction of screen complexity is required to allow the designer to focus on important detail, provide uncluttered overviews, reveal relationships, and facilitate interactive manipulation. Providing a wide selection of presentational abstractions to reduce screen complexity introduces a specification, management, and control challenge and often has the side effect of hiding features and context that are necessary in specifying or visualizing interrelationships. We explore strategies for managing abstraction, context, and constraint to minimize ambiguity in interaction and presentation.

Introduction

This paper discusses experiments, experiences, and future directions in managing complexity through abstraction, context, and constraint within what we believe to be a representative interactive modeling application. Two years ago, at the State of the Art in Computer Graphics Summer Institute in Edinburgh, we described the design of a software architecture for a modeling system that we hoped would support complex design tasks [Hall91a]. At that stage, the system was largely prototypical. A year later we reported further on this system as it had been introduced into an architectural CAD studio and also used as a testbed for continuing research [Hall91b]. Backed by significant system use and user feedback, we now comment on the success of this system and outline a plan for future research.

Modeler Use in the CAD Studio

The modeling system has been in use for six semesters in a fourth-year architecture design studio which is part of the five-year professional degree program in the Department of Architecture at Cornell University. During the Spring 1992 semester, students had access to significantly faster hardware and increased software functionality. We found that the complexity of their models overwhelms the existing abstraction, context, and constraint mechanisms.

COMPLETED PROJECTS

Plates 12 and 13 show models typical of those being created by students during design investigations in a one-semester design studio. These were generated in the Spring 1992 studio taught by Val Warke and Don Greenberg. The modeler was run on Hewlett-Packard graphic workstations, and the rendering was done using Hewlett-Packard rendering software.

We observed that the complexity of the model never reaches that desired by the user. Instead, the speed of interaction with the model limits the complexity of the models created. In short, the scope of a project grows until the limitations of the system become too frustrating to allow continued growth.

PROJECT STATISTICS

In our system, a model is a hierarchical network of procedures. We are finding that it is not unusual for a hierarchy to be more than 13 levels deep and for completed models to include over 3000 procedure nodes. When the procedure network is traversed to build the geometry, the result is often in excess of 200,000 polygons.

Statistics are gathered throughout every interactive session. The results help us evaluate and improve the system. An analysis of the statistics from the Spring 1991 semester indicated that the system was waiting for user input for approximately 48% of each session. We believe that high values for system wait time are good, because it means the user is not waiting for system response. Approximately 39% of each session was spent in menu operations, 8% in interactive editing of the graphic representation, and 5% in adjusting the view. By operation count, 45% were menu operations, 25% viewport manipulation, and 30% camera manipulation.

With improved software and faster hardware during the Spring 1992 semester, the time distribution was 70% wait, 18% menu, 7% in viewing, and 5% in graphic interaction. The operation distribution was 37% in menu operations, 44% in viewing operations, and 19% in graphic interaction. The low percentage of time spent in interactively editing on the graphic display was disappointing. Most of the interaction occurred through menu manipulations.

IMPACT OF HARDWARE IMPROVEMENTS

We expected hardware improvements to have a significant impact on the complexity of the work done on the modeling system. We did not expect this work to be so complex that it would completely overwhelm the editing facilities provided. Increased hardware speed does not solve the modeling problem. On the other hand, until models of very high complexity are used for testing it is difficult to appreciate the importance of sophisticated abstraction tools.

A System Overview

This section provides an overview of the modeling system goals and the structure of the software implemented in striving to reach those goals. This overview is brief so as not to be redundant with previously published material (see [Hall91a, 91b]).

The main goal was to provide an interactive graphic tool that would be useful from the initial explorations through final specification for complex design problems. The properties we associate with complex design are:

> the problem is generally ill-defined;
>
> the database of commercially available products is huge;
>
> the database of items comprising the final product is huge;
>
> the range of scale in the final product is huge;
>
> the design problem is resolved by repeated schema revision and performance evaluation;
>
> several schema may be under consideration simultaneously;
>
> multiple disparate systems with different schematic abstractions must be addressed simultaneously.

These properties are discussed in greater detail in [Hall91a]).

The modeling software has a layered architecture which separates the modeling application software; an interface management tool library; and a device-independent graphic library, which maps into the hardware specific graphics library. The application is partitioned in an object-oriented fashion. This partitioning allows extensibility and simulates a 'typical' product fabrication hierarchy consisting of parts, subassemblies, and final assembly.

THE PROCEDURAL DATABASE

Most man-made objects can be represented by a description of the steps or procedures that are carried out to shape and assemble the parts into the whole. These procedures are carried out with a purpose or intent. We speculate that keeping the description of the design as a sequence of procedures is a step towards embodying design intentions within the description of the model. We further speculate that access to this description will facilitate exploration of alternatives.

To describe a single step, we use a procedural node (see Figure 1). Local data describes parameters that control the procedure and the sources of procedural input data. The specification of procedural input is by procedure type and the name of the local data file that the procedure will use. The procedure can be invoked to provide an interactive graphic editor for its local data, to produce

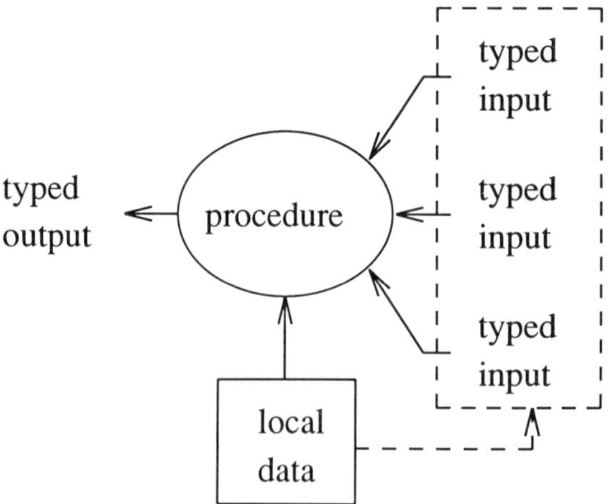

Figure 1. Procedural node.

geometric output, or to draw 2D and 3D representations of itself. The interactive editor can also pass editing control to any of its input procedures.

A model is simply a network of procedures. More specifically, a model is a procedure that collects geometry from other procedures (including models) and positions that geometry with respect to a local axis system. The modeling system is an interactive graphic editor and management system for all of these data files, and a policy enforcer that dictates a consistent structure for the addition of new modeling procedures.

MANAGING DISPLAY COMPLEXITY

Next we discuss techniques for reducing display complexity. A general observation is that all of these techniques are successful on a small scale. However, when models assume the complexity of real products (buildings, automobiles, appliances, etc.) the initial implementation of these techniques has proven to be inadequate.

Within a node in the model hierarchy the user has control over the presentational style, level of detail, and visibility of all child nodes. The user may also elect to view parent nodes as context. Graphic display types include a literal 3D representation, 3D abstractions, and a 2D schematic representation.

Editing Arenas and Context

Traversal of the part/process hierarchy leads to the concept of an editing arena. The graphical editor associated with a procedural node allows manipulation of local data and graphic selection of children nodes to which editing control can be passed (see Figure 2). When editing control is passed to a child, editing in the parent arena is suspended until the user has finished working in the child arena and editing control is returned to the parent. An assembly procedure facilitates the building of a subassembly hierarchy.

When editing control is passed to a child node, a context drawing callback is pushed onto a context stack before editing control is transferred. That context draw routine is popped when editing control is returned. Through this mechanism, the current editing arena has access to the draw routine for the context of any editing arena closer to the root of the hierarchy. Unfortunately, the context stack seldom gives the user access to the most desirable amount of contextual information. Too little information impairs the editing process; too much can either obscure detail or degrade interactive performance.

This structuring of encapsulated process nodes, edit-control passing, and context inheritance provides intuitive graphic movement through the structure of the model. However, it becomes necessary to move through the levels of the model hierarchy to reach a particular instance of a leaf node in context for editing. Movement through the hierarchy can be both tedious and visually disorienting as the user pages through the editors for each node to allow selection of the next child node, or pages back through these editors in returning to the top level.

Nodes are named, making it possible to go directly to a node. However, context is lost since there can be many paths to the same node. Previous researchers (for example, Mitchell [Mitc77], Eastman [East85], van Emmerik [vanE91] and others) have suggested that multiple views into a database through various abstractions provide more opportunities for meaningful interaction and feedback. We are currently testing a schematic representation (see the section in this paper on this topic), which shows promise in addressing these problems.

Alternate 3D Representations

Multiple levels of detail for part and assembly display, wireframe and rendered presentation styles, and visibility control are provided to help the user control display complexity. Multiple levels of detail are provided by every procedural

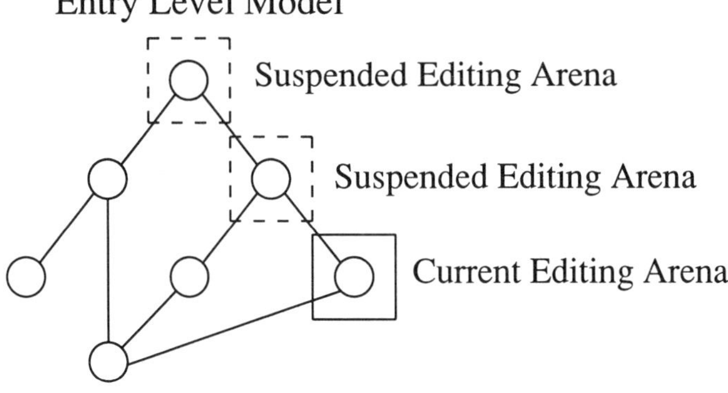

Figure 2. Hierarchy and editing arena.

node in the hierarchy. The lower levels of detail are used primarily to reduce line density on the display and to improve the interactive speed for complex models. The lowest level of detail is always a bounding box (see Figures 3 and 4). Note that while the components of a model can be displayed at any level of shape accuracy when the model is the editing arena, the shape accuracy choices are extremely limited when the model is included as a submodel.

Presentation style includes wireframe or rendered control on a part-by-part basis for assembly nodes.

Children of the current editing arena can be made visible or invisible in the graphic display. In addition to reducing screen complexity, the visibility options introduce a method to manage the existence of several simultaneous schema during design exploration. While this option is extremely powerful, the management of what is visible and not visible, especially for multiple schema exploration in complex models, requires great user effort.

Schematic Representations

In addition to the literal 3D geometric representation common to all interactive modelers, we provide a 2D or schematic representation of the structure of a model. The schematic provides a visual program for model construction.

A schematic representation has proven to be more useful than originally expected. Users often find this representation less ambiguous and faster for picking and data evaluation. Additionally, this representation often reveals information about the state and structure of the model that could otherwise only be obtained by traversing the geometric hierarchy (see Plate 14). In this plate, the schematic is in the main viewing window. The leftmost box represents the current editing arena, which is an assembly procedure. The local data is the list of objects contained in this assembly. The current object is highlighted in green; instances of this object are boxed, and invisible objects are shown in red. The circle to the

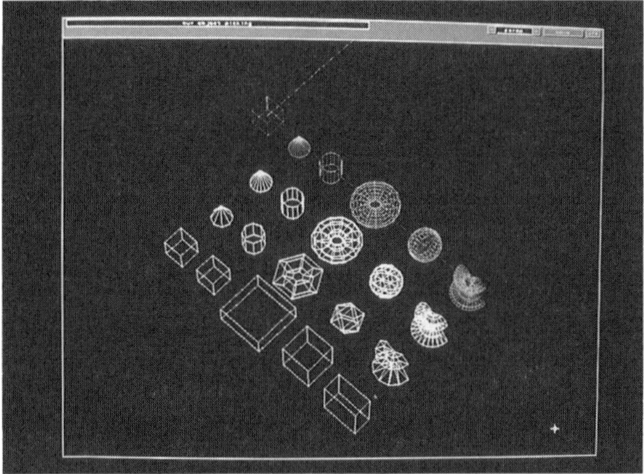

Figure 3. A model with a breakdown of possible shape accuracy for each component.

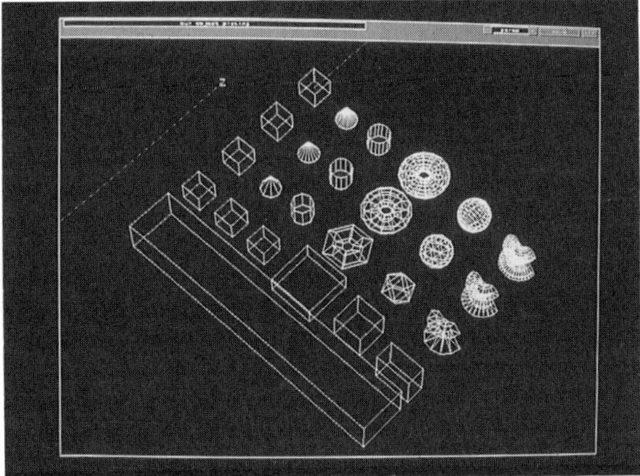

Figure 4. The shape accuracies of a model used as a submodel.

left of each object name is selected to expand the object. The expanded object, really a listing of local data for the object, is in one of the boxes to the right.

System Deficiencies

Deficiencies in the system can generally be attributed to one of three causes: failure to provide a sufficiently rich collection of procedure types; inadequacy of the underlying procedure network to represent design intent; or failure of the interface and data management mechanisms to reveal structure of and allow navigation through the procedure network.

We can identify many areas where the procedure library is insufficient. However, all of the identified deficiencies can be addressed by implementing known techniques within the existing modeling framework. In the interests of research, we instead elected to concentrate our efforts on addressing the interface and underlying representation problems.

Managing Database Complexity

The original implementation of our techniques for managing display complexity detracted from our original database design intentions. Instead of structuring models in a fashion that reflects construction sequences or other functional groupings, users often structure models to take advantage of side-effects of the display management techniques. The procedural node for assembly is often used to improve interactive editing response by isolating a small context to gain control over visibility and rendering style. While the resourcefulness of our users is commendable, this subversion of the hierarchical procedure network is indicative of either poor interface to the display management techniques or inadequacies in the underlying procedure network structure.

The breakdown of these methods can usually be traced to:

the lack of a generalized grouping mechanism to help users manage display techniques when automatic methods are inadequate;

the lack of a control mechanism that can reach outside the local editing arena;

the lack of an encapsulation mechanism for creating 'super objects'.

The extent of these inadequacies becomes increasingly evident as the complexity of models exceeds several hundred parts.

GENERALIZED GROUPING

The original implementation of the modeler provided some very specific grouping mechanisms for move groups (a collection of objects that can be moved as a group), and visibility groups (a collection of objects that can be made visible/invisible as a group). These groupings were specified and revealed in the 3D representation only and could not be overlapping. Picking an object also picked the group the object belonged to.

An effort to correct some of the problems of the first grouping mechanism was to add a scope for visibility, presentation style, and level of detail operations. The scope could be set to the current object, all instances of the current object, picked objects (i.e., interactive picking until the operation is terminated), all but the current object, and all objects. In effect, this was a set of predefined groups.

The 2D schematic representation provides an opportunity to improve the grouping mechanism. We are investigating the presentation of the structure of the model as a matrix, with a parts list on one axis and the group list on the second axis (see Figure 5). Note that this display allows immediate access to object selection, group selection, object expansion and subsequent editing, and group inclusion editing. In addition, color is used to indicate current object, current group, visibility, and instancing.

The scope of move operations is extended to allow 'current object' and 'current group'. The scope of presentation operations is extended to add 'current group' and 'everything but current group'.

A shortcoming with this system is the lack of extension of the grouping mechanism across levels in the hierarchy. The structural decision to keep all local data files and their editors independent does not readily permit mechanisms that link across the hierarchy.

CATALOGUES

Without an organizing strategy specifically suggested and supported by the modeler, the part database became overwhelming. There was no way for a user to keep track of parts even though they were all named by the user. After a semester of work, it was not unusual for a user to have created over 1,500 local data files for procedures; some users have exceeded 4,000. A solution under trial is a catalogue

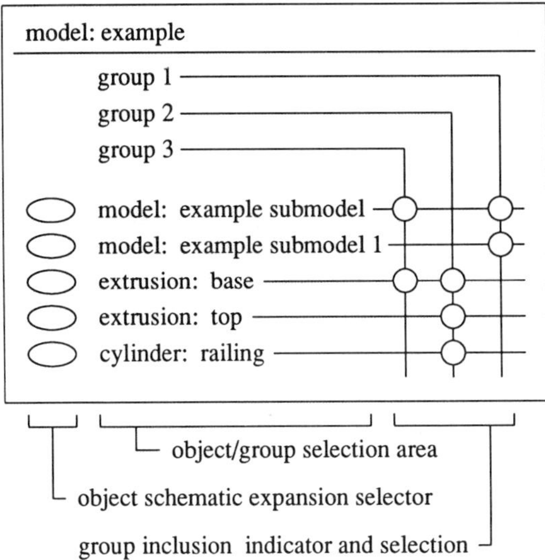

Figure 5. Schematic display, including grouping.

encapsulation method, which allows subassemblies or parts created in one data area to be revealed to other data areas through a read-only catalogue reference.

While working in a catalogue data area, the user specifies parts or assemblies that are revealed as catalogue items and assigns each an item name. Each catalogue data area is given a catalogue name. Catalogue items are selected by catalogue name and item name within the catalogue.

This mechanism provides standard parts catalogues, whose components have the level of autonomy that is expected in the 'real' world. The structure of the catalogue item is completely hidden from the current model, so that undue complication is not presented to the user. The user makes a personal unique copy of the catalogue item for customization. A catalogue hierarchy has not been implemented, but it is an extension we expect to need in the future.

INHERITANCE MECHANISMS

The lack of inheritance mechanisms for level of detail and rendering modes has occasionally been a cause for user complaint. We realize the lack of inheritance mechanisms is an inconvenience that requires attention. However, the low level of user feedback has led us to defer action in this area to a later date.

Constraints and Relationships

A model that is represented as a hierarchy of independent processes captures a sequence of construction, but it does not capture design intent and explicit relationships. Two efforts are in progress to attempt to improve this situation.

The first is a parameter management mechanism, and the second is persistent constraints. Visual programming techniques are being explored as a tool for exposing and editing these relationships.

Parameter Management

All local data is specified through a parameter management mechanism. This mechanism supports a parameter stack. Any procedure node can push parameters onto this stack before passing editing control to, or making a request of, a child procedure, and pop them when editing control returns or the request has been answered. The parameter stack is used in parameter interpretation for constructing local data for any procedural node.

When local data is first created, all data is defaulted to be local in scope, named, and constant in value (which is how local data currently works). Local data elements can be edited to be of a type that is exported or pushed onto the stack before invoking a child. Local data elements can be edited to be of a type with a default value that is replaced by the stack value if there is an identically named parameter on the stack. Additionally, data elements can be defined through expressions of other parameters.

While a parameter mechanism is conceptually simple for small models, we have found it difficult to reveal all of the explicit and implicit relationships in a complex model for effective and predictable editing.

Persistent Constraints

Direct manipulation is currently supported with constraints that last for the duration of the editing session only. The independent nature of the data makes it impossible to insure that low-level objects have not been changed in a way that invalidates constraints previously set on an inactive high-level model. Additionally, the current constraint and direct manipulation methods are specified relative to face, edge, and vertex geometry of the objects at the currently displayed level of detail. Changing level of detail, object editing, or object substitution generally invalidates the constraint, because the geometry on which the constraint was based cannot be correlated to geometry of the new object. We will explore named features as a method of identifying specific geometry across different objects, across different levels of detail, and after object editing. We expect named features to be especially valuable with catalogue items. A catalogue item will have a collection of features that would be common to similar items in the catalogue. For example, the features 'length', 'diameter', 'bearing surface', and 'centerline' might be common for all bolts.

Visual Programming

Figure 6 illustrates the mechanism for expanding information in the schematic view of a model (assembly) node. In the condensed state only the name of each object appears. The object name is a handle to both local data in the model pertaining to that object and to the local data of the object. The button at the left of the object name is used to request expansion.

Van Emmerik [vanE91] uses a schematic display as a 'program' for model construction, and offers both the 3D graphic display and the schematic display for editing. We currently use the schematic display only for picking and as a more informative presentation of model structure. Our current plans call for allowing selection of any local data element for editing. Edits made in either the 3D display or the schematic display are reflected on both.

Although the schematic display is textual, users often work with the display at a scale where the text is unreadable. Color and spatial organization of the schematic are often sufficient to allow a user to interact with the schematic without accessing the specific information contained in the text. This suggests that even greater abstraction in schematic representations may be useful in providing immediate access to the structure of a model.

Interface Issues

We believe the main interaction with the model should be through the graphic display. The layered software structure of this application imposes interface challenges in realizing this goal.

IMPROVING INTERACTION WITH GRAPHIC REPRESENTATIONS

Graphic display is successful for interaction only if display rates are maintained. We are examining strategies for maintaining speed in the face of continued growth in model complexity. While the technique described here was implemented for examination only, it should also be extended to model manipulation.

Our system includes several viewing windows on the 2D or 3D graphic representations. The interface software layer controls examination of these abstractions (i.e., moving the camera relative to the abstraction). The application software layer controls the editing (i.e., picking, object positioning, adding objects, etc.) and provides the 2D and/or 3D drawing routines. During examination the interface interprets the user's gesture, repositions the camera accordingly, sets up display windows and viewports, and requests the application to redraw itself. During manipulation, the application notifies the interface that an update of the displays is required. The interface then sets up display windows and viewports, and requests the application to redraw itself.

The technique we explore is based on the work of Bergman et al. [Berg86]. The display is automatically simplified if the interactive speed target is not met. The original display is restored when interaction stops. Implementing this technique in our layered system raises two issues: first, only the application knows what abstractions are appropriate, how to derive them, and when to display them; second, only the interface knows when the user is trying to perform an interactive task and things are going too slowly.

condensed schematic:

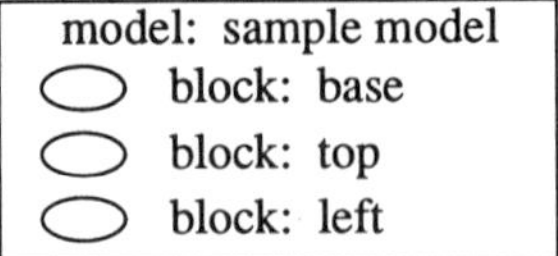

expanded schematic:

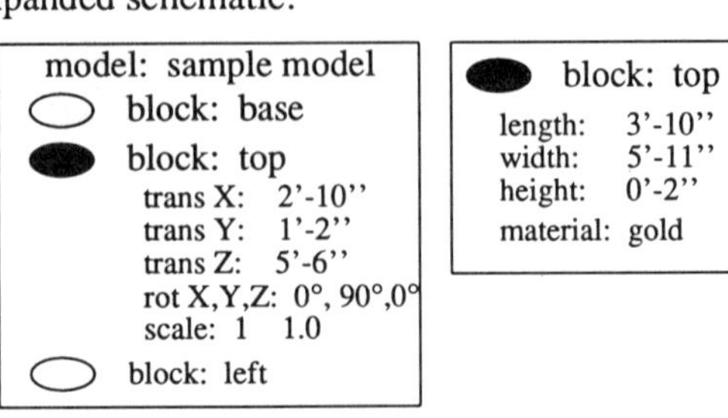

Figure 6. Schematic display condensed and expanded.

We are currently exploring the dialogue between interface and application. The interface signals the application that things are going too slowly. The application may elect to respond with a faster drawing method. Alternatively, the application can specify several different-speed drawing routines, and the interface selects the appropriate redraw based upon current update speed.

The interface window control pseudocode is:

```
IF (in EXAMINATION mode) THEN
  WHILE (pen down) DO
    revise camera position
    CALL application redraw
    IF (too slow) THEN
      CALL notify(draw faster)
      switch to faster redraw
    ELSE IF (faster than required) THEN
      CALL notify(draw more detail)
      switch to more refined redraw
    END IF
  END DO
  CALL notify(done interacting)
  switch back to normal redraw
  CALL application redraw
ELSE
  condition graphics input
  CALL application view action
END IF
```

Minimum and maximum frame rates control notification. Examination starts at the same level of detail as last used, and the detail does not increase if it has already decreased during this examination. While users generally feel this increases productivity, there is great dissent about what should be displayed in simplified drawing. Users also express a need for the option to disable the simplification.

SAVING AND RESTORING STATE

When a user returns to an editing session, the state of the model should be as it was left. The same is true for the editing tool and the presentation of the model. Specifically, this means all modes, cameras, tool placements, colors, display states, groupings, display expansions, etc., should be saved and restored between sessions.

While this need for saving and restoring state is obvious, we have found that the coordination of this activity is nontrivial. Problems arise for several reasons:

> the application, interface, and graphics are very independent in their layering;
>
> different graphic hardware with varying capabilities may be used for the next editing session;
>
> multiple users work in the same data area;
>
> one user may be running multiple editors into the same data area;
>
> any submodel can be selected as an entry point for editing;
>
> different editors could be working with any piece of data (we commonly have three or four versions available).

ADVANCED RENDERING

We originally included high-level rendering display in the modeler but soon discovered that the unpredictable rendering time left displays hung in rendering mode for intolerable lengths of time. Rendering is now performed by spawning batch rendering jobs that save results in files for subsequent viewing.

Conclusions

Many challenges face the designers of complex interactive systems. These challenges are addressed in part by abstraction, context, and constraint mechanisms. However, effective interaction techniques for using these tools must be provided before their full potential can be realized. Generalized grouping mechanisms, parameter management mechanisms, visual editing on schematic displays, and carefully constructed dialogue between interface and application are steps towards this goal.

Evaluating the success of tools to help in representing and editing complex models can only be tested with complex models. Schemes that work well in simple cases cannot be expected to extend to complex cases. The results are often both unexpected and counter-intuitive. Lastly, user feedback must involve both user suggestion and extensive observation of editing sessions with a great deal of questioning. User feedback often deals only with the symptoms, not the real problems, and is often biased by what the user believes might be possible or easy to implement, not what is required.

Acknowledgments. The authors acknowledge the work of Leonard Wanger, Priamos Georghiades, Paul Wanuga, Mark Reichert, Kathy Kershaw, Mike Monks, Greg Spencer, and Rick Pasetto in implementing the Cornell modeling system. We thank Hewlett-Packard for the generous grants to the Program of Computer Graphics that provided the equipment on which this work was performed, and also the National Science Foundation for long-term support of the research at the Program of Computer Graphics. A portion of this work was funded through National Science Foundation Grants DCR8203979 and ASC8715478. The Program of Computer Graphics is a member of the newly formed NSF Science and Technology Center for Computer Graphics and Scientific Visualization. And, last but not least, we recognize the patience and contributions of some 70 architecture students who have continually pushed the modeling system beyond its capabilities.

REFERENCES

[Berg86]
Bergman, L., Fuchs, H., Grant, E., and Spach, S., Image rendering by adaptive refinement, *Comput. Graph.*, Vol. 20, pp. 29–37, 1986 (SIGGRAPH 86).

[East85]
Eastman, C., Abstraction: A conceptual approach for structuring interaction with integrated CAD systems, *Comput. and Graph.*, Vol. 9, No. 2, pp. 97–105, 1985.

[Hall91a]
Hall, R., Supporting Complexity and Conceptual Design in Modeling, in *State of the Art in Computer Graphics: Visualization and Modeling* (State of the Art in Computer Graphics Summer Institute, Edinburgh, UK, July 1990), Rogers, D.F., and Earnshaw, R.A., Eds., New York: Springer-Verlag, pp. 153–183, 1991.

[Hall91b]
Hall, R., Bussan, M., Georgiades, P., and Greenberg, D.P., A testbed for architectural modeling, *Proc. Eurographics '91*, Vienna, September 2–6, 1991.

[Mitc77]
Mitchell, W., *Computer Aided Architectural Design*, New York: Petrocelli/Charter, 1977.

[vanE91]
van Emmerik, M.J.G.M., Interactive design of 3D models with geometric constraints, *The Visual Computer*, Vol. 7, pp. 305–325, 1991.

Topological Modeling of Phenomena for a Visual Computer

Tosiyasu L. Kunii

Abstract

Visualization models are diverse because their application areas are wide and varied. Examples of attempts to integrate the models occur in the areas of fractals and finite elements. However, little has been done to integrate visualization models based on more general and abstract characteristics derived from differential or topological considerations. Higher-order abstraction modeling allows us to link computer vision with computer graphics in a visual computer. In scientific, industrial, and medical applications, it is increasingly important to be able to compare the model with the observed images. Visualizing complexity requires higher-order abstraction modeling.

Introduction

WHAT IS A VISUAL COMPUTER?

A visual computer is capable of directly processing visual objects. It inputs and identifies visual objects through computer vision, directly computes visual algorithms such as machinery assembly sequences, design processes, and drafting instructions on visual processors, and outputs the results of visual computation on a computer graphics display. Direct appeal to human vision is a major reason for the popularity of a visual computer and for the severe competition in its development.

REQUIREMENTS FOR A VISUAL COMPUTER

Visual computation is an art requiring both broad and high-level research for its advancement. The complexity and the multidisciplinary nature of visual computation are only two of the reasons for this requirement. We human beings are accustomed to seeing motion pictures. It is also necessary to advance knowledge of the human visual interface, including GUI (graphical user interface) for motion pictures. It helps in efficiently designing and implementing motion sequences of visual objects. Visual processor designers are competing vigorously for improved records in computation speed, in computed object size, and in functional richness.

Visual Object Algorithms

Computer science is one of the most advanced and fastest growing scientific and technical disciplines. It is the major discipline dedicated to the study of designing and implementing sequences of computational motion. A sequence of computational motions is called an algorithm. Algorithms were originally for numerical computation, and then evolved to cover sequences of file processing and database management. Recently, algorithms have reached the level of computing sequences of the motion of visual objects. The visual objects computed now include such complex multibodied objects as human bodies. We can compute visual object movement directly and develop visual object algorithms. The computation also includes the movement and setting of visual computer devices, facilities, and environments.

Thus, a visual computer computes visual algorithms directly, and presents the results in an immediately comprehensible visual form. Visual computing continues to provide excellent essential research themes to computer science.

Massively Parallel

Visual algorithms, and hence visual computation, are massively parallel in nature. To understand why, let us look at an example of visual objects. In machinery, all the machine components basically work concurrently and in parallel. In design, all the elements of a design plan and design equipment used work in parallel. Visual computation is conducted most effectively by having a visual computer as a massively parallel computer. Right now our prototype design of a parallel computer employs 64 units of i860 processors. The expected performance is around four gigaflops. The visual computation cases we have covered so far are diverse, opening up a whole new world of visual algorithms and visual computation.

How Visual Object Computation Looks

To show how visual computation looks, we consider a case of athletic computation. An athlete's body is modeled as a multibody consisting of 50 segments. A recent extension added more segments, in particular of hands. Now the multibody has 82 segments. From a sequence of athlete images obtained through computer vision, we compute the power change between the segments based on inverse dynamics. Six Lagrangian equations specify the dynamics of each segment. Computing the power vector change of a multibody with 82 segments requires solving close to 15 thousand ($6 \times 82 \times 30$) Lagrangian equations. We also compute the power change exerted from one person to another by the same method. The computed powers are displayed as vectors. Athletic instructors are finding the results very useful in diagnosing athletic movements, and also in designing improved training programs. Sports medicine doctors show strong interest in applying the method to rehabilitation programs.

BREAKING THROUGH HARDWARE LIMITATIONS CAUSED BY MODELING COMPLEXITY

Visual computing is reaching a new phase through exploding application development supported by drastic hardware speed-up. A short list includes more gates on a chip through submicron technology, and massive parallelism through network-oriented architecture. Now one can visualize extremely complex objects and phenomena. With this possibility, the limit of the hardware capability is clear. While the hardware speed-up is only proportional to the number of processors, the required computation power is a combination of the number of elements in the visual object computed. This phenomenon is well known as the combinatorial explosion in computation. A visualization model helps to eliminate improbable combinations. Conventionally used visualization models are based on simple geometric models or rendering models. They cannot help much in preventing the combinatorial explosion. Models with higher-order abstraction power are required. For example, it is well known that modeling the beginning of the universe requires theoretical singularity modeling. A human body is another highly complex object with numerous attributes which is sometimes called a small universe. Particularly, its internal organs require more than geometric models, such as the models based on algebraic topology, which includes singularity theory and homotopy theory. The features presented here are a part of new approaches to complexity modeling. As the case to model, eventually the small universe — a human body — appears as the main theme in this paper.

The following two sections sketch a few possible directions for future complexity modeling and explain why.

THEORIES BEHIND ⋯ BIFURCATION THEORY AND SINGULARITY MODELING

One observation easily made is the increasing demand to model a situation where the continuity of an object or a phenomenon breaks down. Hence we lose the basis to continue working along the same line of thinking. The point where the situation loses continuity and becomes singular [Golu88] is often a bifurcation point [Arno87]. For example, with machines becoming so complex we need a design model which extracts and describes the process of component cracking or breaking. When a machine component vibrates or receives pressure, there arises a bifurcation point where the component branches out either to continue to deform or to start to crack or break. Looking at the human walk, each step serves as a bifurcation point where the next step either succeeds or fails. That is why it takes so long for a baby to learn to walk and it is so difficult to realize a two-legged walking machine. In modeling garment wrinkling, there are also bifurcation points where the garment cloth either continues to bend or starts to create a fold or a cusp at each point. Plate 15 shows a sequence for a garment sleeve wrinkling at an elbow [Kuni90]. When a tropical rain forest grows many bifurcation points appear, at each of which the trees either continue to grow or start to die. Plate 16 shows two scenes from the 250 year simulation of the formation of a tropical rain forest [Kuni91]. In economics there is a bifurcation point where the economic situation either improves or gets worse [Puu91].

LINKING COMPUTER GRAPHICS WITH COMPUTER VISION IN A VISUAL COMPUTER

Higher-order abstraction modeling allows us to link computer vision with computer graphics in a visual computer. For example, in scientific, industrial, medical, and topographical observation or inspection of complex objects or phenomena, the models allow us to determine in advance, and extract, particular features out of many factors. We must pay attention and navigate using computer vision while we are watching the displayed computer graphics images to confirm the observed or inspected results. Through the models, the observed and displayed images can be matched to verify their validity. One example is the Great Walls of stars in the universe which seem to favor the idea of its beginning concurrently at multiple places instead of at one place as suggested by the big bang theory. Much medical diagnosis through computed tomography and X-ray imagery belong to this category. In addition, the homotopy model for differentiable surface generation from a series of outlines goes beyond the triangulated surface model. It allows us to extract surface characteristics such as the peaks, pits, and passes to easily identify a scene in maps which contain complicated topographical shapes. Diseased spots in a human organ can be extracted in a similar manner. An example of the internal structure of a human ear reconstructed from slices by using the homotopy model is shown in Plate 17a.

Higher-order Abstraction Models

DIVERSITY AND REMEDY IN MODELING

Visualization models are diverse because their application areas are very wide and varied. People have been trying to integrate them into a small set of handy models, for example, the fractal model and the finite element method. Little has been done, however, to integrate visualization models based on more general, abstract, and versatile abstraction framework derived from topological and differential characteristics, such as the critical points of the modeled objects, to capture commonly observable features. For example, we recognize the terrain by its critical points, that is, the peaks, pits, and saddle points (see Figure 1). When we consider the energy potential surface, the peaks, pits, and saddle points represent the equilibrium states. As can be seen from these examples, the critical points play significant roles when we characterize the object.

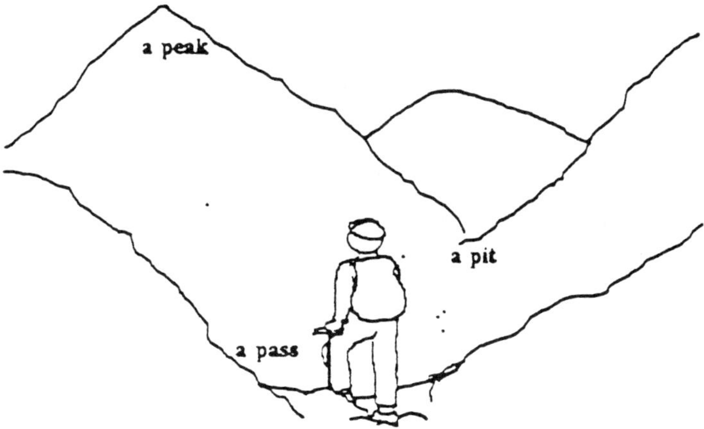

Figure 1. Characterization of a terrain.

MODEL VISUAL: AN INTEGRATED VISUALIZATION MODEL

Our visualization model, Model Visual, has an abstraction hierarchy of incrementally modular data structure based on differential characteristics. It is self-visualizing, which makes it self-explanatory to users.

We look at varieties of areas which seem unrelated and explain how they can be visualized by Model Visual. The application models integrated into Model Visual are three: the homotopy model as applied to medical imagery, the singularity model as applied to garment wrinkling, and the bifurcation model. The bifurcation model is shown only to illustrate how we abstract it from an application-oriented model, for example the tree model applied to tropical rain forest growth.

The Homotopy Model

The first example is the homotopy model, which reconstructs an object surface from a given series of planar contours on cross sections, for example CT images. This is a high demand area, particularly in geographical mapping. It is also of great use in the medical field, where reconstructing the entire shape of a human organ from a set of cross sections is of great significance. It is difficult to envision the three-dimensional structure of the organ by viewing individual CT slices.

There are two typical ways to do this. The triangular tile technique (see Figure 2) first approximates the contours using linear line segments, and then generates triangular patches between contours on adjacent cross-sectional planes. The spline method first uses a spline curve to approximate contours and then reconstructs surfaces with a spline approximation between adjacent contours.

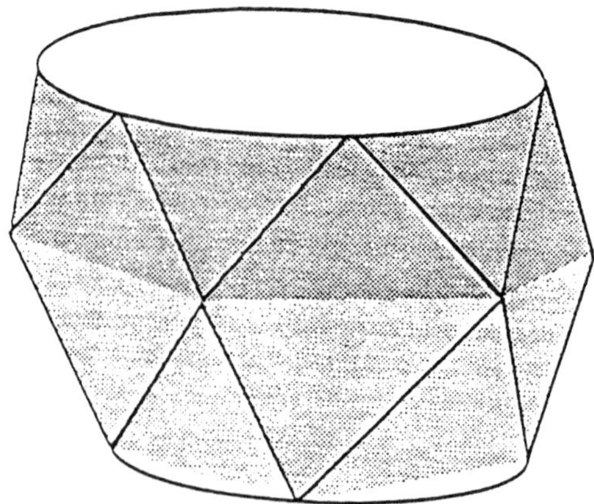

Figure 2. Triangular tile technique.

The triangular tile technique suffers from defective triangles. To reconstruct the surface this technique generates triangular patches between adjacent contours. The triangular tile technique and the spline approximation technique generate surfaces that are not smooth when the shapes of consecutive contours change greatly. When triangular patches are to be generated between such contours, the surface normal at point A (see Figure 3) is the same as the surface normal at point C, which is far from point A. On the other hand, the surface normal at point B is very different. The resulting surface is not smooth.

The homotopy model integrates these two surface models and remedies their deficiencies. In the homotopy model each contour is represented by a shape function. The surface generated between contours is the locus of the transformation of one contour to the other. This transformation is represented by a homotopy, which is the general concept of transforming one function to another (see Figure 4). The homotopy model uses a graph called the continuous toroidal graph to express the correspondence between the points on adjacent contours (see Figure 5).

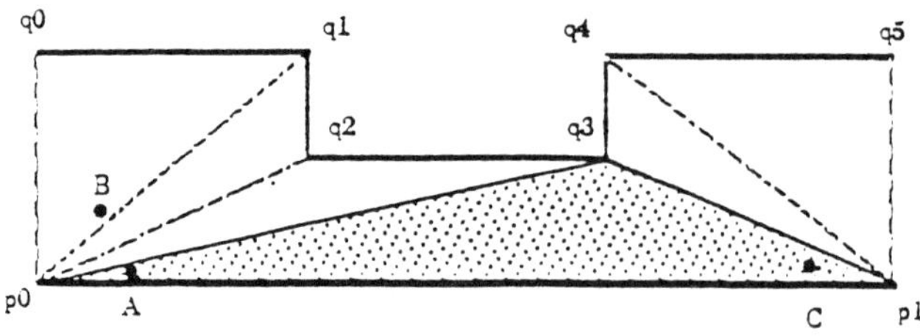

Figure 3. Defective triangles that are inevitable when the triangulation method is used.

The Homotopy Model and the Continuous Toroidal Graph

First, assume that the lower and upper contours are represented by the shape functions $f(x)$ and $g(y)$. We take the parameter x on the x-axis and the parameter y on the y-axis. Suppose a path passes through the point (x, y) on the continuous toroidal graph. This means that the points $f(x)$ and $g(y)$ are connected by the homotopy.

Generally a surface is represented by a path drawn as a solid line, as shown in Figure 5. The toroidal graph that represents the triangular tile technique is expressed as the step function which is a poor approximation of the real path. The spline approximation method is represented by the function $y = x$, which still poorly approximates the real path. When the real path is very complex, the approximation is not good enough and the surface generated becomes distorted. Thus, the continuous toroidal graph abstractly models the basic key feature of these typical approximation models.

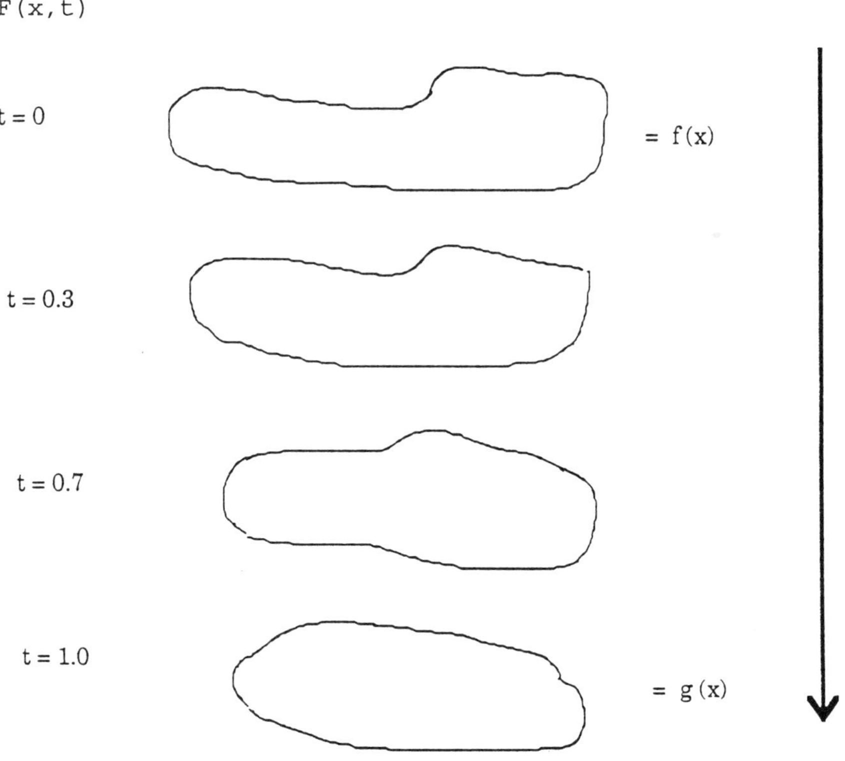

Figure 4. Surface generation using a homotopy.

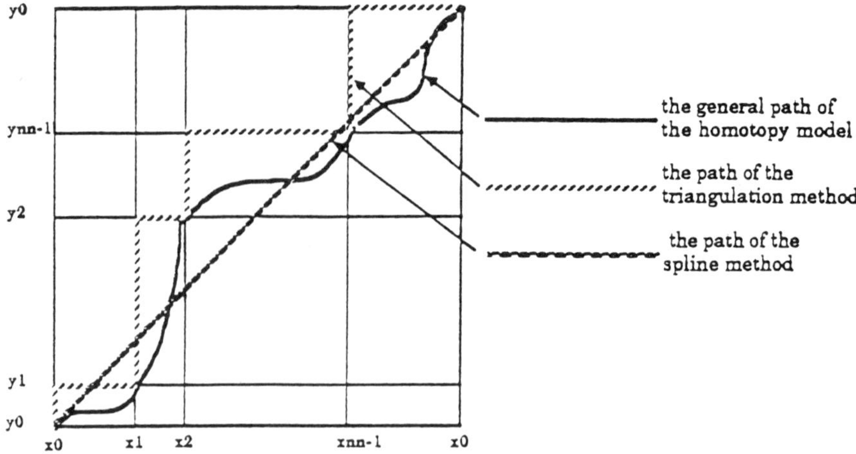

Figure 5. Acceptable paths on the continuous toroidal graph.

The homotopy model is more than the generalization of typical surface approximation models. By carefully specifying a set of toroidal graphs, such essential surface operations as taking the first-, second- and higher-order derivatives of the surface to identify the surface properties can be defined on the surface generated by the homotopy model. The homotopy model is thus convenient to use as the basic model. Properties, including the peaks, pits, and saddles of the surface, are more easily reconstructed. Plate 17a shows three human auditory ossicles (malleus, incus, and stapes) reconstructed using the homotopy model. The reconstructed surface is smooth enough to take derivatives. Plate 17b shows the same objects reconstructed by Christiansen's triangulation method, displayed with Gouraud shading. The shape looks ambiguous because the surface normals of the triangles are different from the real surface normals.

The Singularity Model

Modeling Garment Wrinkling and Singularity

The second model proposed and tested uses theoretical singularity modeling as applied to modeling of the garment wrinkle formation processes. When we started to talk about garment wrinkling the immediate questions were: Why wrinkling? Why not something of more scientific or industrial merit? However, it serves as a good example of model complexity, both scientifically and industrially. For scientific merit we could, of course, choose the whole universe. The advantage of using garment wrinkling as an example is in its handiness, along with sufficient complexity, for example the requirement to consider singularities in order to understand it.

One of the main concerns of cosmology is to model the beginning and evolution of the universe as a whole. Singularity theory plays a central role in this.

Look at the initial creation of matter in the universe from the state of homogeneous energy distribution in space. Since the energy is equal to the mass of matter multiplied by twice the speed of light, there is a possibility of modeling the creation of mass as the creation of a wrinkle in energy space, where the homogeneous energy distribution was broken and high energy concentration is taking place at locations where matter exists. The birth of matter is modeled by the birth of a singularity.

In our visualization model, Model Visual, garment wrinkle creation can possibly be modeled the same way simply by replacing the word 'energy' by 'cloth' and changing the scale factors. Whether this can actually be done or not is an open problem; one of the largest challenges and temptations is testing the wrinkle modeling of the creation of the universe against a computer graphics four-dimensional visualization of astronomical observations. Responding to the challenge of open problems is the privilege of scientists, who are essentially volunteers in discovering something new.

Let us now turn to the question of the industrial merit of studying garment wrinkling. In the fashion industry, garment wrinkling is actually considered an important key factor in garment design, especially at the highest level of design. Fashion designers try to get the most out of anything that constitutes a garment. In particular, they try to exploit the physical characteristics of the fabric of garments. Wrinkling occupies a major position in fashion design, for example to give a relaxed and casual atmosphere to garments when worn. The design process has a number of stages, including the initial sketch by fashion designers and the extraction of patterns from the initial sketch by pattern making experts. The extracted patterns, when assembled, are expected to match the original image of the fashion designers. The traditional tools of designers have long been limited to crayons and paper. Recently, several CAD systems were proposed to assist designers with graphical editing and 3D previewing tools. But little has been done to fulfill the requirement of simulating the wrinkling behavior of garments. Before explaining our model in detail, let us look at three frames of a wrinkle formation animation (see Plate 15).

WRINKLING AS GLOBAL INFORMATION

To model the shapes of garment wrinkles, we use global information to reduce the amount of computation for large numbers of components. When a garment is deformed, wrinkles are formed or extinguished. Shape changes are mainly observed around wrinkles, while other parts of the garment remain unchanged. In fact, the geometry of the wrinkles and of the other parts are different: at the wrinkles both the metric and the curvature change, whereas at the other parts the metric is preserved and only the curvature changes. This observation implies a potential key hypothesis for wrinkles as the indexes of global shape change.

The hypothesis that the wrinkles are the indexes is used to construct a model of garment wrinkling by employing a mathematical method known as singularity theory. The basic idea of singularity theory is to consider a singular set of surface-to-surface mappings.

Typical Signs

When we take a projection of a surface, there are three typical types of projections. Singularity theory shows that the shapes depicted in Figure 6 are, in general, the only stable patterns. The other types of patterns are unstable. If we project from a slightly different direction, the pattern is decomposed into some combinations of the patterns shown in Figure 6. These patterns are cusps, folds, and crossing lines. Further, crossing lines can be represented as the combination of two folds. Hence, we can use the two stable patterns, cusps and folds, as the indexes of surface shape.

Where p+ +c Singularity Emerges

There are special instances where other types of patterns emerge by changing the viewing direction of a given shape. Figure 7 shows a situation where (a) a cusp and a fold approach each other; (b) the cusp and fold merge; and (c) the cusp and fold finally separate. The merged state (b) is classified as a 'p+ +c' singularity, which describes the structure of branching and vanishing.

Modeling Primitives

Branching and vanishing are complementary to each other. A point on a surface can be a branching point when it is viewed from one side, and when viewed from the other side it can be a vanishing point (see Figure 8). Since this singularity is very rare, the behavior of the points corresponding to this type of singularity can serve as a far greater constraint than the behavior of the other points. Such p+ +c singular points are the characteristic points of garment wrinkles. They serve as the primary indexes of global shape change. By extracting the p+ +c

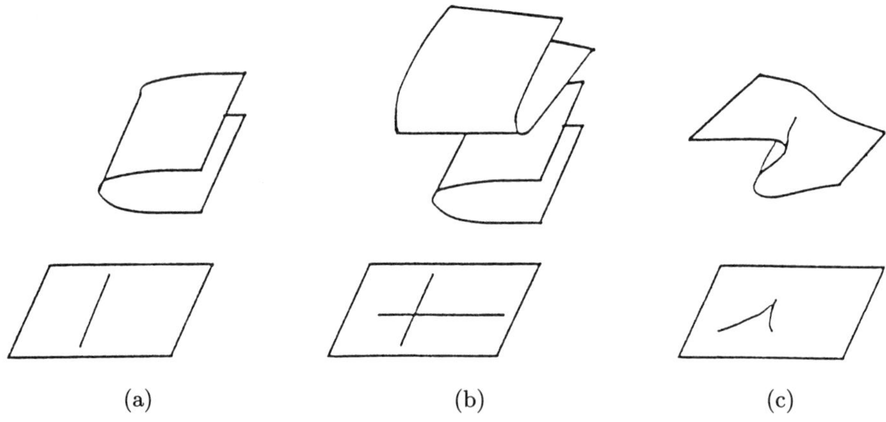

(a)   (b)   (c)

Figure 6. Typical surface shapes after projection. (a) Fold; (b) crossing lines; (c) cusp.

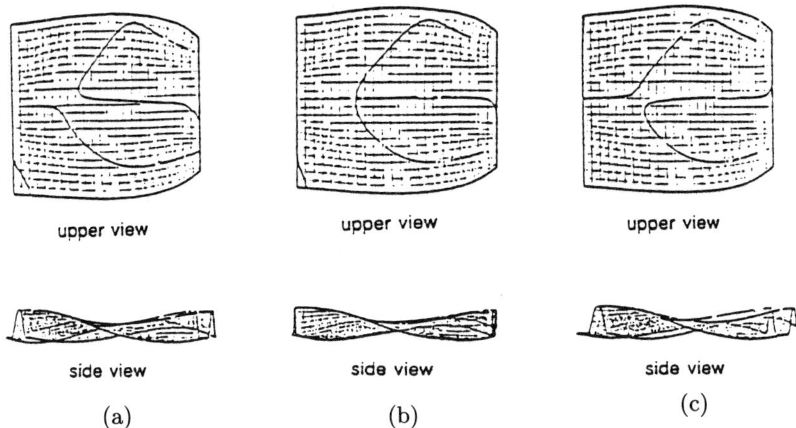

Figure 7. A case where p+ +c singularity emerges. (a) fold and cusp; (b) p+ +c singularity emerges; (c) fold and cusp.

singular points and the cusps and folds incident to them, we can limit the number of possible wrinkle shapes. The other parts of the surface can be reconstructed by interpolating the coordinate values of the cusps and folds.

WRINKLE MODELING PRIMITIVES AS AN INSTANCE OF REEB GRAPH

The distribution of the p+ +c singular points and the folds and cusps is described in a graph called a wrinkle graph, as shown in Figure 9. The vertices correspond to the p+ +c singular points, and the edges correspond to the folds and cusps. These primitives represent critical points and play important roles in our Model

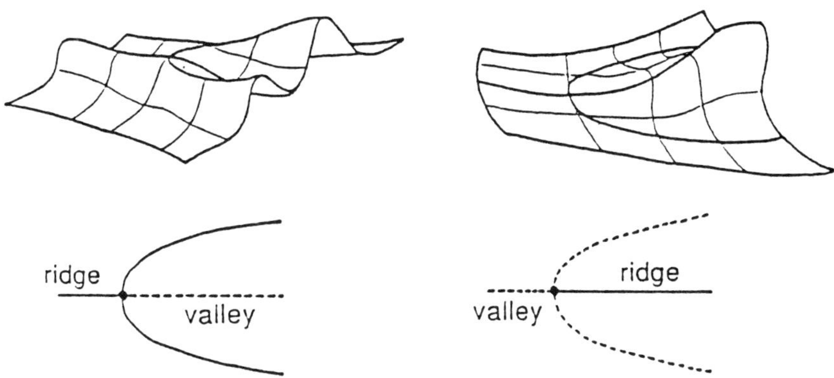

Figure 8. Wrinkle modeling primitives.

Visual. We created a wrinkling algorithm based on this model. In this simulation, we assumed that no p+ +c singular point is newly created or destroyed during the process of wrinkle formation. The animated result approximates the visual reality.

Bifurcation and Forest Growth Modeling

FOREST GROWTH MODELING

The third model of higher-order abstraction is the bifurcation model. We illustrate it through forest growth modeling.

In a forest a tree is interacting with other trees and the environment, including other vegetation and animals. In forestry, the process by which vegetation invades a large and bare area and grows into a stable state is called the 'primary succession'. Clements [Clem16] called the stable state the 'climax'. The process whereby a tree cannot live out its lifetime because of accidents or disease is called the 'secondary succession'. Forestry considers succession the main feature of a forest.

In a forest the trees, other life forms, and the environment interacting with each other form an ecological system, or an 'ecosystem.' Thus, modeling the forest ecosystem means modeling the forest succession.

TREE INTERACTION MODELING

Among the internal properties of trees, the sunlight-photosynthesis relation dominates the production rate of trees. Mutual shading is the dominant interaction

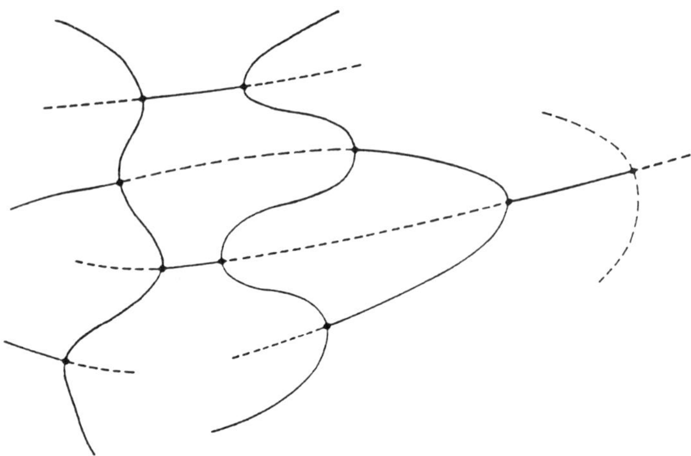

Figure 9. A wrinkle graph of modeling primitives as an instance of the Reeb graph.

among trees that controls forest growth. This means that the model should be able to specify the growth of trees by utilizing the sunlight-photosynthesis relation. To model tree growth, we used a tree growth model we had developed previously, called the A-system.

The A-system allows interactive tree image generation, and produces a three-dimensional geometrical model of most kinds of higher-order trees from a few parameters, e.g., the divergence angle d, the branching angles $h1$, $h2$, and the contraction ratios $r1$, $r2$ (see Figure 10). The A-system has enough facilities for tree image generation. It also has the capability to compute the total area of all the leaves of a tree, the effective total leaf area that receives sunlight, and the production rate (growth) of the tree from the sunlight-photosynthesis relation.

We modeled and visualized the tropical rain forest formation processes for 250 years at yearly intervals. Interestingly enough, the 'bifurcations' of the forest growth observed in the tropical rain forest in Pasoh on the Malay peninsula was also observed in this animation. This type of singularity observed on the animation screen is not just fun to watch. It is a key to understanding the nature of bifurcation and also the forest ecosystem. In a way, to model it using Model Visual yields results common to other complex phenomena, such as the formation of the universe and garment wrinkling.

BIFURCATION IN FOREST GROWTH

Tree interaction through mutual shading results in either the further growth or the diminution of trees at various locations in a forest. Such locations are the branching points of forest growth and become saddle points of the growth function. A saddle point is a critical point and plays an important role in our Model Visual. Branching information is associated with each saddle point.

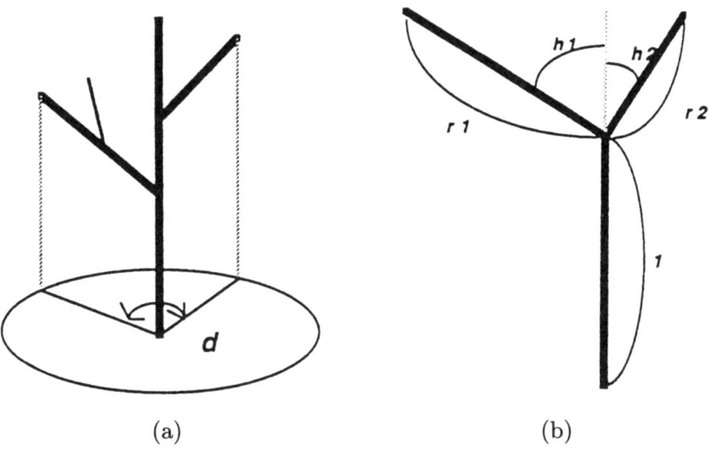

Figure 10. The A-system for interactive tree image generation. (a) Divergence angle d; (b) branching angles $h1$, $h2$, and contraction ratios $r1$, $r2$.

Model Visual

A Visual Computer as a Common Visualization Platform

The common structure made into hardware is a visual computer serving as the common hardware platform. What are a few basic structures governing the diversity of visualization? We have seen three examples which seem unrelated to each other. Diversity in the appearance of phenomena and objects does not necessarily mean diversity in the structures governing them. Common structures are sometimes called models, or theories. Then, what are a few basic structures abstractly representing the diversity of visualization? To see this, we first think of the structure common to the appearances of diverse phenomena and objects. It is a type of abstract data structure, hierarchically organized for modularity. Any evolution in the structure must be added without affecting the existing structure. Such an incrementally modular visual structure can be built by using topology at the most abstract layer of the hierarchy, geometry at the next layer by adding the coordinate system and appropriate metrics to the top layer, and nonstructural information, such as colors and mass, as the bottom layer. The data structure thus defined serves as the basic visualization model and is named Model Visual.

Operators as Abstract Machine Instructions

If we consider Model Visual as an abstract visual object machine, then machine instructions are the operators of Model Visual. Model Visual has two kinds of operators. Layer-specific operators consist of the topological, geometrical, and other attribute operators. Global operators include the view, recognition, display, and database operators. In other words, operators can be grouped into intralayer operators and interlayer operators. There are eight categories of functions: define, transform, update, delete, search, recognize, select, and display.

Model Visual as a Self-visualizing Machine

Model Visual is a self-visualizing machine. Let us briefly sketch a small core concept for making it self-visualizing. The basic computational methods of generating itself are known in different areas. For example, Von Neumann proposed the theory of self-reproducing automata. Compiler–compiler tools such as yacc and lex are another example. To the best of our knowledge, however, a self-visualizing visualization model to build a self-visualizing machine is not yet known.

Let us first confirm that to visualize is natural for a human being. Then the notion of the self-visualizing visualization model means that the model contains display information on all the structures, operators, and their relationships, so that the model displays itself for a human being to recognize. The human being can, at least partially but hardly fully, delegate the recognition and selection operations to the model. That is why the model always prompts, on the display screen, the course and results of the operations for further human interaction.

THE SELF-VISUALIZATION MECHANISM

The self-visualization mechanism consists of the self-visualization administrator, the human interface and the model interface used to interact with the rest of the model, the self-visualizing symbol depository, and the self-visualizing operators. The human interface is based on our early work on a menu generator [Shir89]. Provision is also made for supporting visualization data sharing, prototyping, and history management through a visualization database management system.

THE TOPOLOGICAL LAYER

For the topological layer, the main feature of Model Visual is in its use of surface topology, which can go beyond graph theoretical and combination topology. To represent the topology of objects, existing methods use the vertices, edges, and faces of the surface. In other words, the control points of such methods are the vertices. In the case of natural objects, such as those found in biology or medicine, a shape can have a large number of degrees of freedom. We must seek for other methods to represent their topology. In Model Visual the control points are the critical points, such as the peaks, pits, and saddle points of the surface.

Advanced three-dimensional modelers favor the Euler-Poincaré characteristic in terms of the number of vertices, edges, faces, holes, and rings of the surface used to maintain the topological integrity of the surface. We intend to go beyond that level. The mountaineer's equation provides us with the necessity. It is based on Morse theory. The mountaineer's equation states that a similar relationship with the Euler-Poincaré characteristics holds concerning the number of peaks, pits, and saddle points.

WHY CRITICAL POINTS AS THE CONTROL POINTS? — OBSERVABLE CHARACTERISTIC POINTS OF OBJECTS AND PHENOMENA

Let us explain why we use the critical points as the control points. When we recognize an object surface, we often recognize its shape by looking at its peaks, pits, and saddle points. For example, when we go mountaineering we recognize the topography of the terrain by such critical points. When we see a tree in a forest, we recognize the species through its peaks and saddle points. The critical points of a potential surface represent the equilibrium states.

The relation among the critical points is represented by a Reeb graph. The incremental modularity of the abstraction hierarchy allows all the information to be attached freely to the core information of the model, which is in the topology layer. To represent the topological information of objects, a Reeb graph is used in our approach, and other information is attached to this graph. The Reeb graph plays the role of the generalized topological 'skeleton' of the three-dimensional surface structure of the object or phenomenon being visualized.

The Reeb Graph

The Reeb graph represents how the critical points are connected to each other. George Reeb first introduced this graph in his thesis [Reeb46]. Formally, a Reeb graph is defined on a manifold, but we do not discuss it in detail here. For simplicity, let us think of the height function, $h(x, y, z)$, that gives the height of the points on the object surface. If two points, $(x1, y1, z)$ and $(x2, y2, z)$, which are at the same height, are in the same connected component on the cross section of the surface at the height z, these points are identified on the Reeb graph. In other words, a cross-sectional contour is represented as a point on a Reeb graph.

As a simple example, we show the Reeb graph of the height function of a torus (see Figure 11). This is easy to see when we consider the cross-sectional planes. All the contours on each plane are represented as a node of the Reeb graph.

Integrating Geometric Modelers into Model Visual

Having a Reeb graph as the top topological layer of Model Visual, we now show how the example phenomena discussed previously are integrated into this model. Now the master of the scene is the Reeb graph; the scene is the second geometrical layer of the model.

What we are actually showing is how different types of geometrical information can be modularly and incrementally associated with the Reeb graph in the first layer to form the second layer. With a Reeb graph it is simple. It is done by associating any geometrical information with the nodes on the Reeb graph. In the following, the diverse cases of geometrical information integrated into Model Visual are listed:

Case 1. Surface reconstruction from the contours

In the first case, where an object surface is reconstructed from cross-sectional contours, a point on the Reeb graph is associated with a contour of the object. The advantage of the hierarchical modular structure of Model Visual becomes prominent by separately storing the small key information in the top layer as the Reeb graph in the primary memory, and very large geometrical information attached to it in the geometry layer in the secondary memory.

Case 2. Volume rendering

In the second case, a point on the Reeb graph is associated with the interior image of a contour. The interior image can be a cross-sectional image, such as a CT image. This representation finds good application in volume rendering. Medical imagery favors volume rendering techniques in reconstructing a solid object from a given series of CT images.

Case 3. Singularity theory, critical points, and bifurcation

In the case of the theoretical singularity modeling of the garment wrinkle formation process, we used the p+ +c singular points and the cusps and folds as the primitives. For this application, a point on the Reeb graph is associated with the coordinate values of the p+ +c singular points and the points on the cusps and folds (see Figure 12).

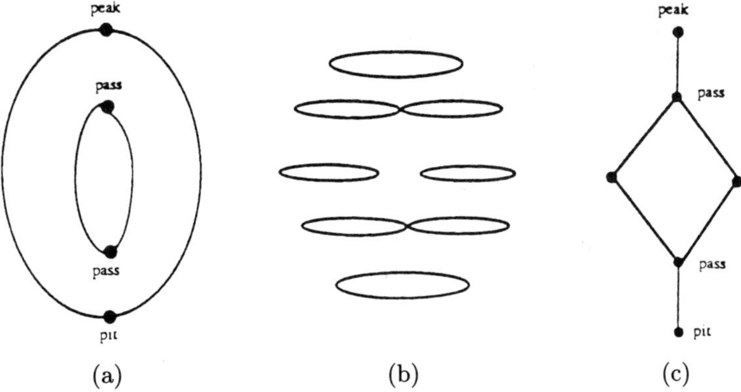

Figure 11. A torus. (a) The critical points; (b) the cross sections; (c) the Reeb graph.

Case 4. Walk-through animation

In this case, a point on the Reeb graph is associated with a location inside the contour. That is, when a viewpoint moves along the Reeb graph we can walk through and observe the inside of the object we are visualizing. Such animations are useful for simulating gastroscopes and a guided tour of a building, particularly of museums.

Case 5. Forest growth

For botanical tree- and forest-growth visualization, as shown previously a Reeb graph can represent the skeletons of the trees and also the pattern of forest formation processes. In this application, the critical points, particularly saddle points, also called passes, of the Reeb

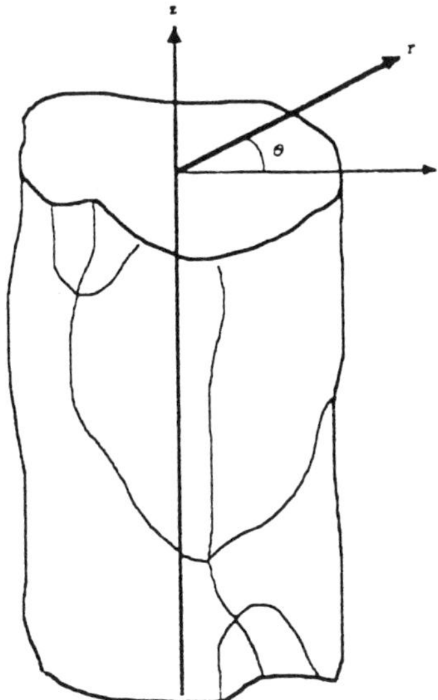

Figure 12. The cylindrical coordinate system.

graph are significant. In modeling tree growth, the passes correspond to the branching points, and the peaks and pits to the tips of the branches growing upward and downward, respectively. In modeling forest growth, the tree interaction through mutual shading results in either the further growth or the diminution of the trees at the various locations of a forest. Such locations are the branching points of the forest growth and become the saddle points of the Reeb graph when we use the growth function for each tree instead of the height function. The nodes that are not critical can be interpolated from the critical points. For this reason, they are derivative and can be neglected. With each saddle point, branching information is associated and stored in the second geometrical layer of Model Visual.

Information Locality and Computer Architecture

Visualization requires heavy computations and in many cases is too slow to run on currently available hardware. In hardware, computational speed gain is achieved by holding the information locally in both time and space as the basic principle. The evolution of computer architecture can be discussed either from the viewpoint of the evolution of the devices used or from the evolution of the objects processed. The former can be safely named the EE (electrical and electronic) view to computer architecture and the latter the CS (computer science) view.

Looking at the evolution of computers from the CS point of view, particularly from the principle of locality, the first generation architecture, named the Von Neumann architecture, was for numerical computation. Its unit of locality was one word, equivalent to a few bytes. When data processing became important and databases came into existence, many pages of business files were stored in secondary memory space. Then, second generation computer architecture, called virtual storage architecture, assumed the size of the unit of locality of a few to several hundred bytes.

Now we are talking about visualization. What we have to do first is to estimate the unit of locality in visualization aiming at the third generation architecture, named visual computer architecture. The unit of locality is in the range of a few kilo- to megabytes.

The locality has been turned into an actual hardware speed-up through addressing schemes which exploit locality. For numerical computation with a locality unit of one word, a word address counter, called the program counter, which pointed at a word in the main memory space, served well supported by an automatic counter increment mechanism. For files, the virtual storage architecture added a file page counter, usually simply called the page counter, with an automatic consecutive page roll-in/out mechanism in between the main and secondary memory.

For visualization, Model Visual has the potential to localize visual information using a Reeb graph in the top layer as the addressing scheme, with the support

Table 1. Memory necessary to store information associated with a point on a Reeb graph.

Case	Unit
Case 1. Homotopy model	roughly 2 kilobytes
Case 2. Volume rendering	3 megabytes
Case 3. Singularity theory	3 megabytes
Case 4. Walk-through animation	3 megabytes
Case 5. Forest growth	in the order of 1 kilobyte

of a graph tracer driven by the search operator of Model Visual; a node counter; an automatic counter incrementer; and a lower-layer roll-in/out mechanism. The size of the memory necessary to store unit information attached to a point on the Reeb graph is now enumerated as shown in Table 1.

Conclusions

Through a few quite diverse case studies, we have shown that Model Visual can cover and integrate diverse applications of visualization. In this model the Reeb graph served as the core of the top layer. The model also revealed the potential capability to serve as the foundation of designing visual computer architecture. The principle of information locality is finding the best match with the Reeb graph to implement the 'addressing scheme' of the visual computer.

REFERENCES

[Arno87]
Arnold, V.I., Gusein-Zade, S.M., and Varchenko, A.N., *Singularities of Differentiable Maps*, Boston: Birkhaeuser, Vol. 1, 1985, Vol. 2, 1987.

[Clem16]
Clements, F.E., Plant succession: An analysis of the development of vegetation, Carnegie Institute Pub. 242, Washington, DC, 1916.

[Golu88]
Golubitsky, M., Stewart, I., and Schaeffer, D.G., *Singularities and Groups in Bifurcation Theory*, New York: Springer-Verlag, Vol. 1, 1985, Vol. 2, 1988.

[Kuni90]
Kunii, T.L., and Gotoda, H., Singularity theoretical modeling and animation of garment wrinkle formation processes, *The Visual Computer*, Vol. 6, pp. 326–336, 1990.

[Kuni91]
Kunii, T.L., and Enomoto, H., Forest: An Interacting Tree Model for Visualizing Forest Formation Processes by Algorithmic Computer Animation — A Case Study of a Tropical Rain Forest, in *Computer Animation '91*, Thalmann, N.M., and Thalmann, D., Eds., Tokyo: Springer-Verlag, pp. 199–213, 1991.

[Puu91]

Puu, T., *Nonlinear Economic Dynamics*, 2nd ed., Berlin: Springer-Verlag, 1991.

[Reeb46]

Reeb, G., Sur les points singuliers d'une forme de Pfaff completement integrable ou d'une fonction numerique [On the singular points of a completely integrable Pfaff form or of a numerical function], *Comptes Rendus Acad. Sciences Paris*, Vol. 222, pp. 847–849, 1946.

[Shin91]

Shinagawa, Y., and Kunii, T.L., The homotopy model: A generalized model for smooth surface generation from cross sectional data, *The Visual Computer*, Vol. 7, pp. 72–86, 1991.

[Shir89]

Shirota, Y., and Kunii, T.L., Automatic Generator for Enhanced Menu Based Software — Program-Specifications-by-Examples, in *Designing and Using Human-Computer Interfaces and Knowledge Based Systems (Proc. Third International Conf. on Human-Computer Interface)*, Salvendy, G., and Smith, M.J., Eds., Amsterdam: Elsevier, pp. 829–836, 1989.

Color
Plates

Plates 1 and 2 can be found on the frontispiece.

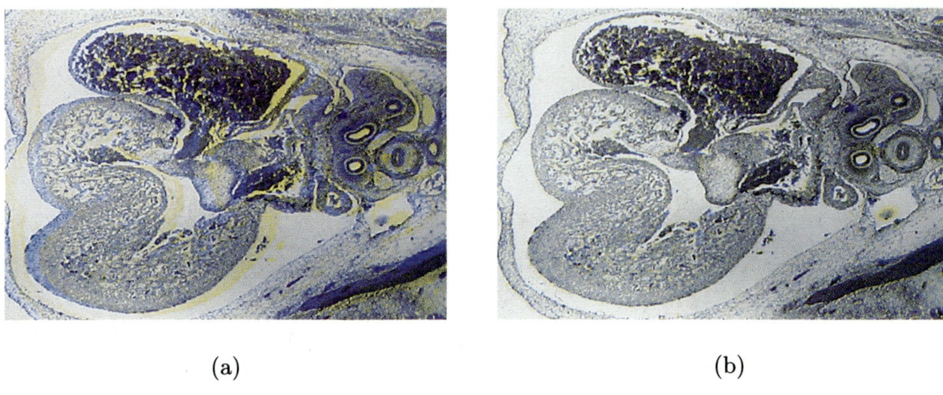

(a)   (b)

Plate 3. Two serial sections of an embryo heart. (a) Before registration; (b) after registration using color merging. (Images courtesy Gudrun Klinker, Digital Equipment Corporation. Data courtesy Michael Doyle, University of Illinois at Chicago.)

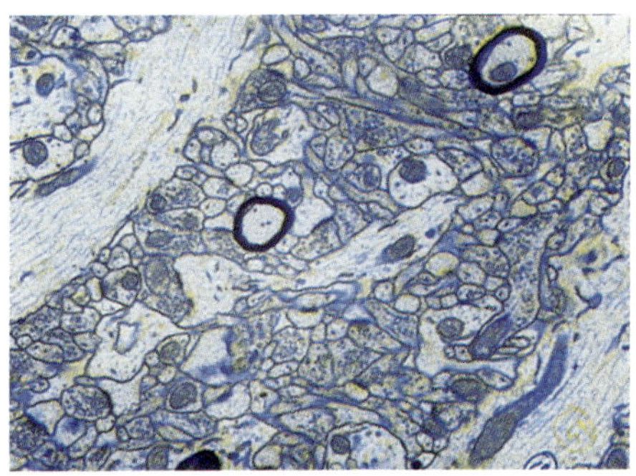

Plate 4. Two serial sections of a neuronal dendrite registered using color merging. (Image courtesy Gudrun Klinker, Digital Equipment Corporation. Data courtesy Kristen Harris, The Children's Hospital, Boston.)

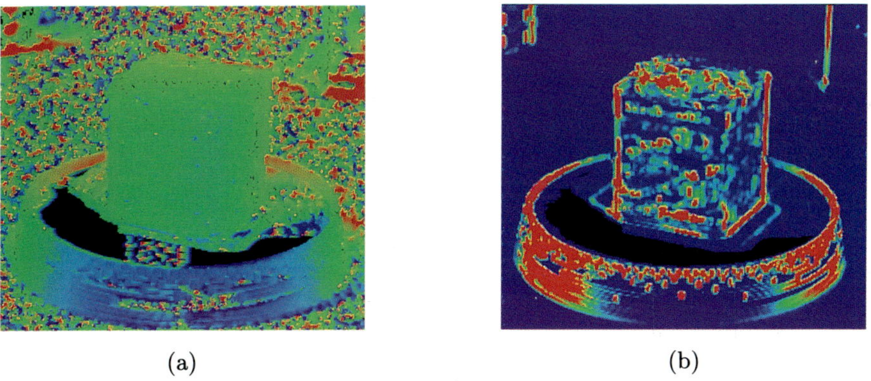

(a)   (b)

Plate 5. Object reconstruction from optical flow. (a) Local flow estimates (blue in front and red in back); (b) certainty in flow estimates (red denotes highest certainty). (Courtesy Richard Szeliski, Digital Equipment Corporation.)

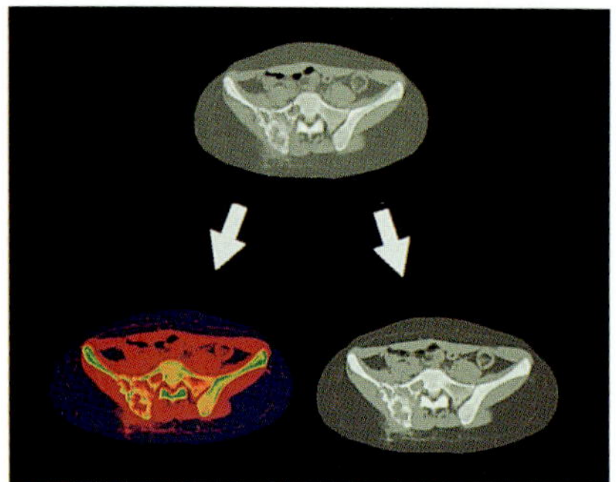

Plate 6. Classification of one CT slice. (Reproduced from [Ney90] ©1990 IEEE.)

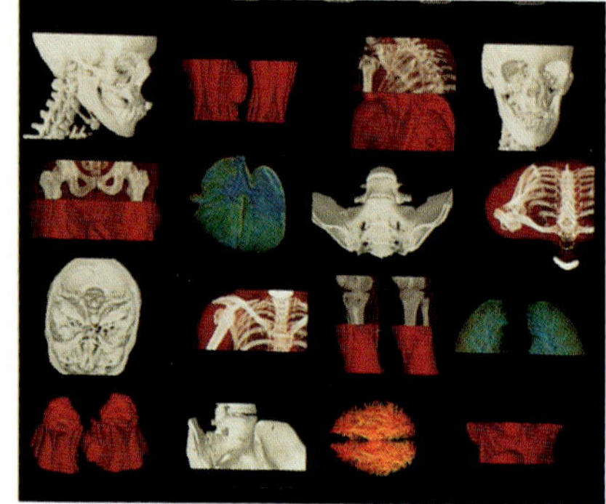

Plate 7. Collage of CT data. (Courtesy Derek Ney and Elliot Fishman, The John Hopkins Medical Institutions.)

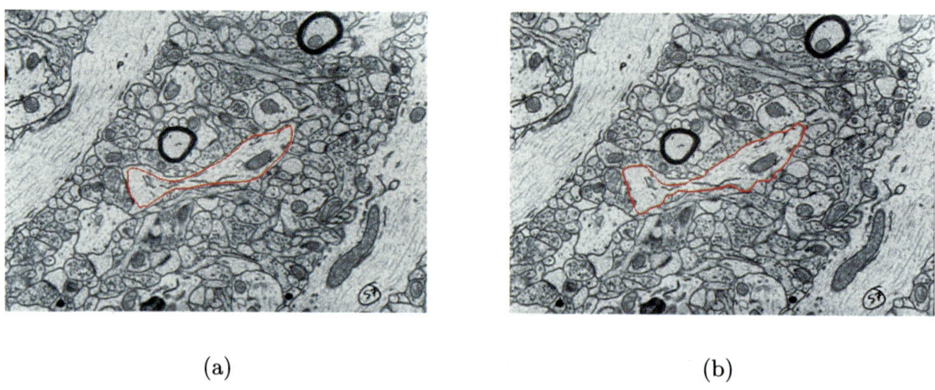

(a)   (b)

Plate 8. Segmentation of a neuronal dendrite using a deformable contour. (a) Initial sketched contour; (b) initial equilibrium; (c) manipulating the contour with interactive springs (green lines); (d) final profile. (Reproduced from [Carl91].)

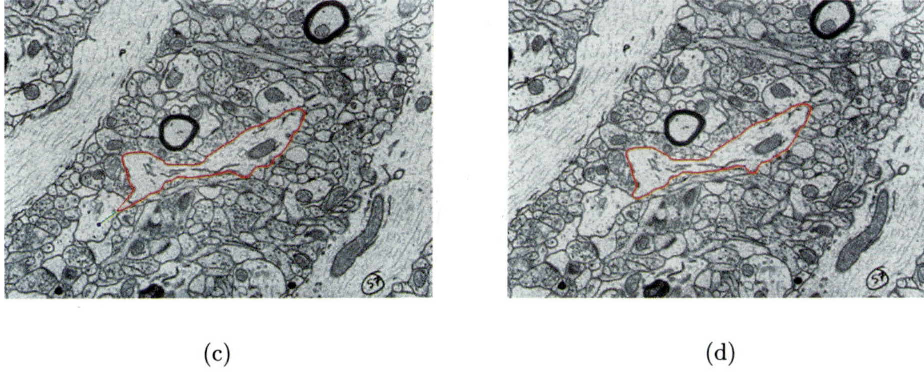

(c)

(d)

Plate 8. (Cont.)

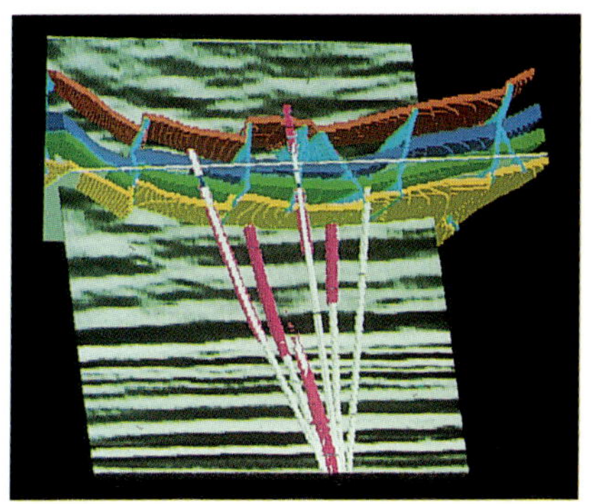

Plate 9. A combination of volume data (sands), image data (seismic section), surface data (fault surfaces, oil-to-water contact surface), and curve data (wells and well logs). (Reproduced from [Sabe89] ©1989 IEEE.)

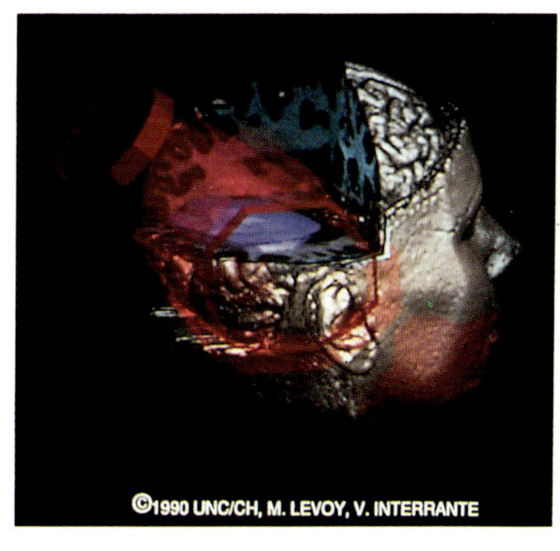

Plate 10. MR data from a live subject. (Reproduced from [Levo90b] ©1990 IEEE.)

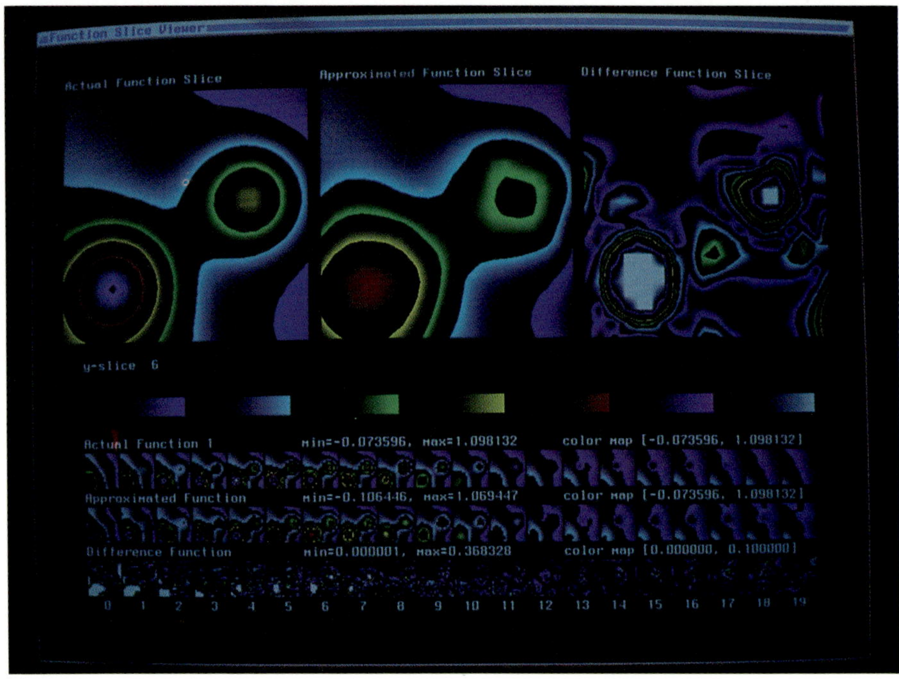

Plate 11. Typical Screen Image of 'Slice Viewer.'

Plate 12. Theater design model,
by Matthew Bannister and Charles D'Autremont.

Plate 13. Theater set model, by Matthew Bannister.

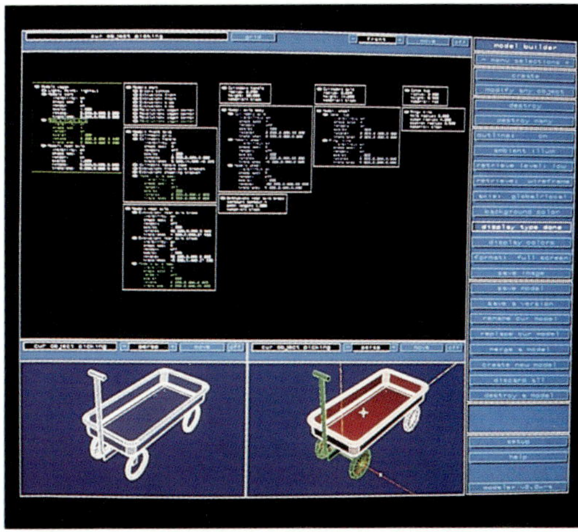

Plate 14. Expanded schematic representation for a simple model. Note that the structure of assembly, instancing, visibility and other details are revealed in the schematic representation, but hidden in the graphic display.

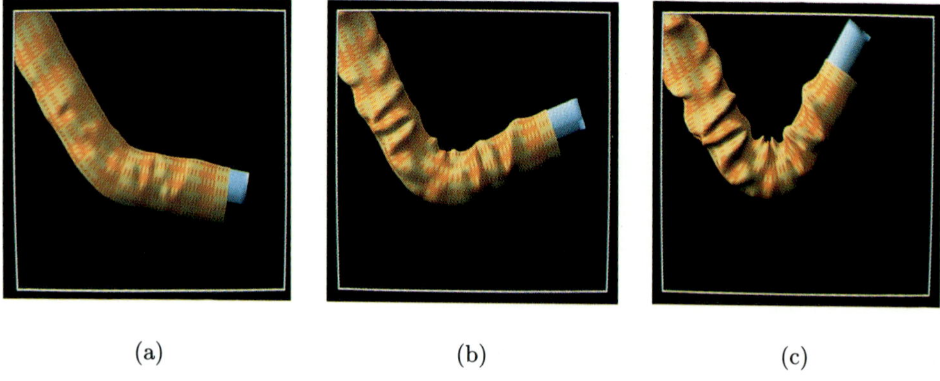

(a)   (b)   (c)

Plate 15. A garment sleeve wrinkling at an elbow.

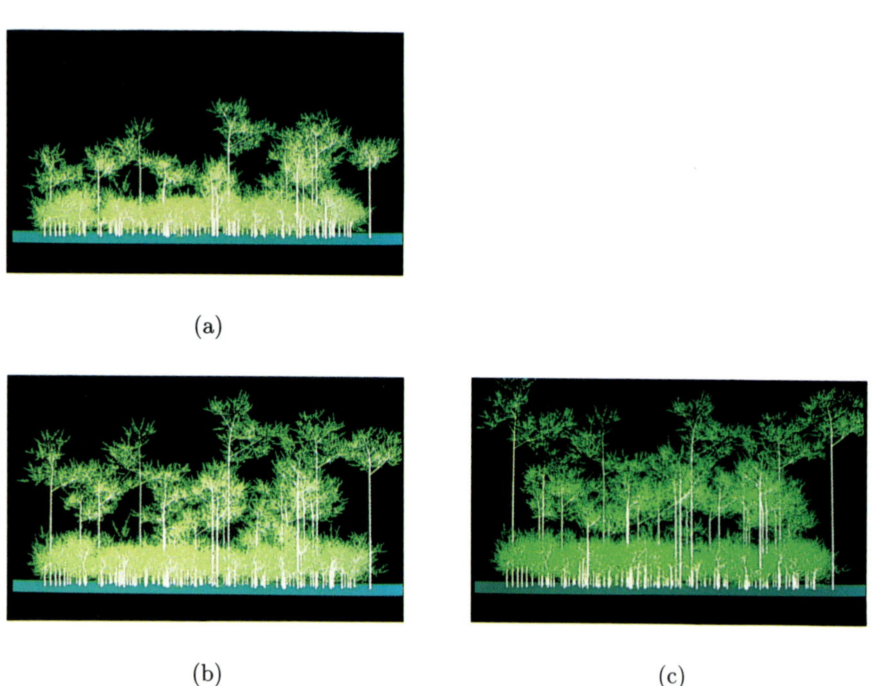

(a)

(b)   (c)

Plate 16. A tropical rain forest formation process.

(a)   (b)

Plate 17. Reconstructed human auditory ossicles using (a) the homotopy model [Shin91]; (b) Christiansen's triangulation method.

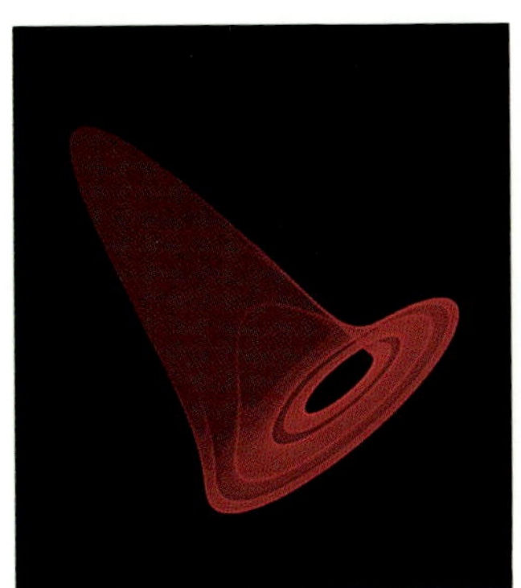

Plate 18. A depth-cued image of the invariant measure of the Rössler attractor. Voxels on the attractor are rendered as point light sources, with intensities according to the corresponding measure.

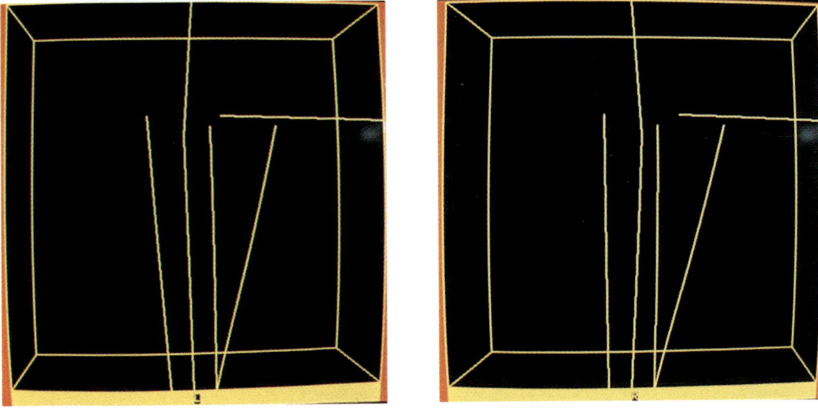

Plate 19. Left and right stereo views illustrating the picket fence problem.

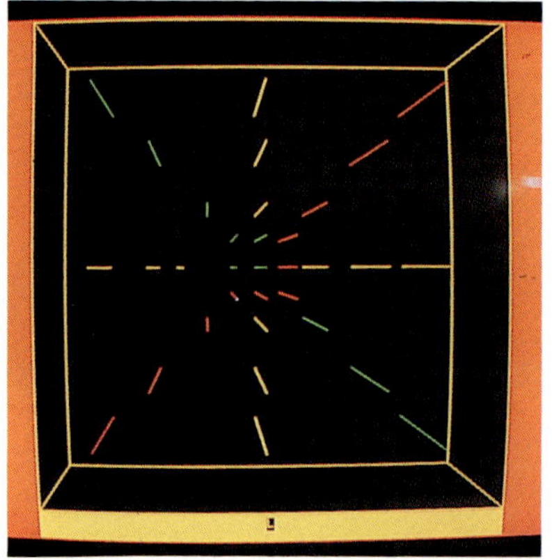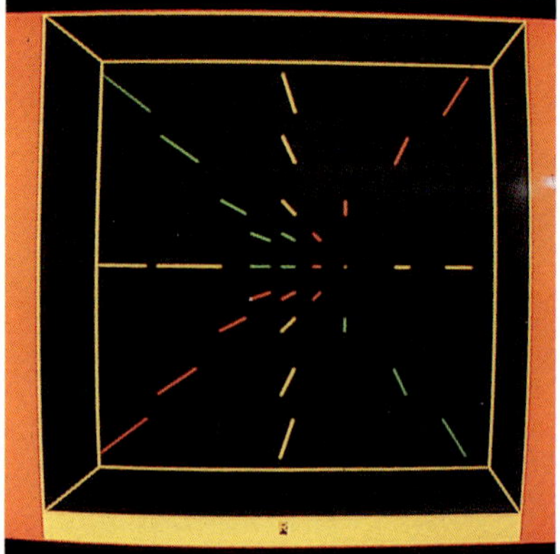

Plate 20. Left and right stereo views illustrating the double image problem.

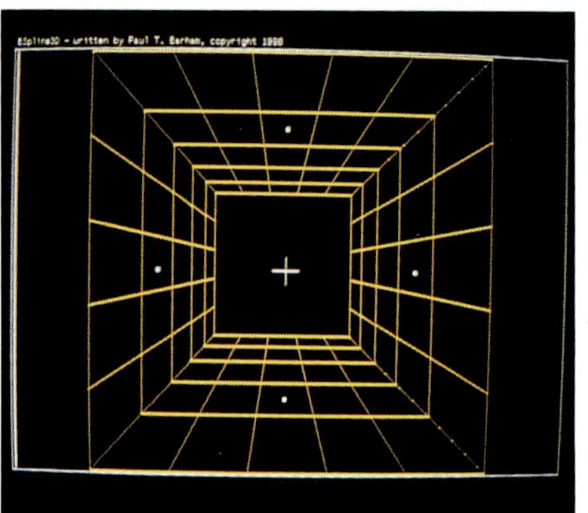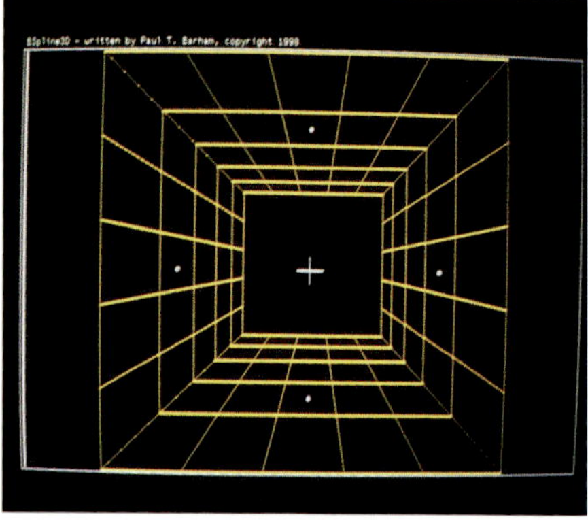

Plate 21. Left and right stereo views using ghost points and a grid reference cube to help determine absolute position.

Plate 22. Left and right stereo views with supersampling.

Volume Rendering Strange Attractors

Dietmar Saupe and Wayne Tvedt

Abstract

We consider approximation and rendering techniques for strange attractors that arise in the study of chaotic dynamical systems. We propose that the ideal representation of a strange attractor is a volume rendering of its invariant probability measure, and provide efficient data structures and convergence criteria for the task.

Introduction

The primary task of complex visualization in mathematics is creating meaningful images of objects which defy intuition. It is more than an issue of approximation, because one has not only to define what quantities can be visualized, but to be conscious of their topological properties.

One of the most confounding topological structures to come into currency is that of the strange attractor. Guided by mathematical development, physicists and mathematicians were led to believe that the long term behavior of dynamical systems would always run into simple patterns of motion, such as a rest point or a limit cycle. The discovery of strange attractors by the meteorologist Edward N. Lorenz in 1962 disproved this belief. Strange attractors are those patterns which characterize the final state of dynamical systems that are highly complex and show all the signs of chaos. They are indeed strange, and yet they are now proven to be all around us. Moreover, strange attractors are the point where chaos and fractals meet in an unavoidable and most natural fashion: as geometrical patterns strange attractors are fractals; as dynamical objects strange attractors are chaotic. Researchers in the natural sciences became aware of the subject and concentrated on the irregular patterns of processes which they had previously dismissed as misfits. There is now a whole new experimental and theoretical industry dealing with strange attractors and their reconstruction from experimental data. Scientists hope to be able to crack the mysteries of our planet's climate as well as the secrets of turbulence or human brain activity through the metaphor of strange attractors.[†]

[†] For an introduction to the topic of chaos and strange attractors for the nonspecialist, see [Peit92].

In this paper we discuss methods for rendering strange attractors of continuous systems in three-dimensional phase space. The methods can also be adapted to other systems, which may be discrete or may live in a higher-dimensional space.

For the purposes of this paper, we present an intuitive and working definition of a strange attractor for continuous or discrete dynamical systems in Euclidean spaces (given by differential or difference equations of motion). The final mathematical definition which provides the 'correct' way to deal with attractors is still outstanding.[†] A set, A, is considered a strange attractor if the following four conditions are satisfied:

> there is a neighborhood R of A such that R is a trapping region, i.e., each trajectory started in R remains in R for all time; moreover, the orbit becomes close to A and stays as close to it as we desire. Thus, A is an *attractor*;
>
> orbits started in R exhibit sensitive dependence on initial conditions; this makes A a *chaotic attractor*;
>
> the attractor has a fractal structure and is thus called a *strange attractor*;
>
> A cannot be split into two different attractors; there is an initial point in R such that the corresponding trajectory gets arbitrarily close to any point of the attractor A.

In the usual way to draw a strange attractor we begin by computing a trajectory that starts in the trapping region, discarding the transient phase needed to get sufficiently close to the attractor. It then lets that orbit run along the attractor until we have a satisfactory image. Though perhaps good suggestions as to the general shape of the attractor, such pictures are misleading, for the best you can come up with is a spotty, skeleton-like cover without any depth cues. They are not truthful pictures, by the obvious fact that you get a different skeleton when a different initial point is picked. And, letting the trajectory run for a longer time does not improve things: it starts to fill up the silhouette as a solid and we lose all internal detail. For example, the continuation of the trajectory from the Rössler attractor shown in Figure 1 would just be seen from above as a solid disk with a hole in the center.

The trajectory technique also falls short of actually showing the real structure of the attractor, with all its bends and folds, the bandedness (or lack thereof) of the distribution of trajectories on the attractor and the spatial texture, smooth in some directions but fractally distributed in others. For instance, we found that the attractors of Lorenz and Rössler, which seem to have the same texture with the trajectory method, are actually quite different in texture.

In short, two ideals of adaptive data rendering are missed:

> the final image should be some kind of precise, meaningful statement about the object — a quantity to look at;
>
> even if we can never get a 'true' image and must settle for some series of approximations, we should be able to buy more quality of image (that is,

---

[†]See, for example, the discussion in [Guck83], pp. 255–259.

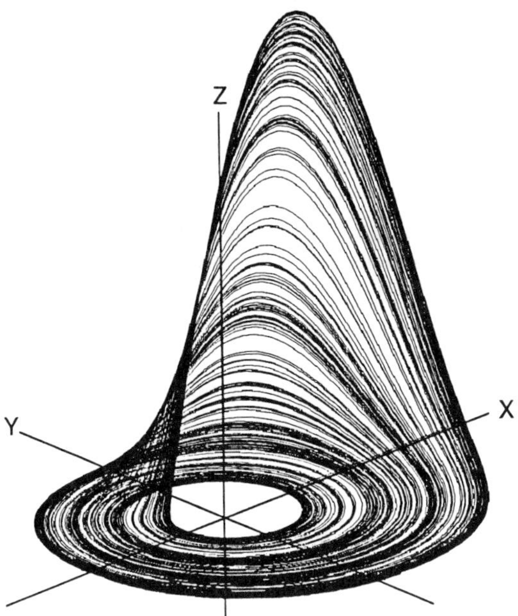

Figure 1. A trajectory of the Rössler system plotted in three-dimensional phase space as a first picture of the Rössler attractor.

convergence of the image with the 'true' object) with time, and we should have some idea as to how fast the quality improves with time.

We seek the same order of confidence in rendering strange attractors. The most natural quantity to look at is the attractor's *natural measure*. Roughly, this measure of a region represents the portion of time that a trajectory, moving chaotically over the strange attractor, spends in that region. For example, let us assume that a given trajectory $X(t), t \geq 0$ generates the attractor. Then the measure μ of a cube C in phase space is the fraction of time the solution $X(t)$ passes through the cube

$$\mu(C) = \lim_{T \to \infty} \frac{1}{T} \int_0^T \mathbf{1}_C\big(X(t)\big) dt \tag{1}$$

where $\mathbf{1}_C$ is the indicator function having value 1 in C, and 0 otherwise.

There is an analogy here to physics. One way to think about an electron of, for example, a hydrogen atom is in terms of a particle having a certain location and impulse at each point in time. In other words, we can imagine an electron as a particle rapidly spinning around on a shell about the nucleus of the atom. However, a view which is more appropriate in many respects is that of the electron as a charge distribution on the entire shell. The older, mechanical type of interpretation corresponds to that of representing strange attractors as portions of short or moderately long trajectories, while the other has similarities to the natural measure on strange attractors.[†]

Actually, the first oscilloscope traces of strange attractors, looked at by the first explorers in the field, were decent approximations of their natural measures. The output of one or more variables of an electronic circuit representing the equations of motion is plugged into a standard laboratory oscilloscope. The 'deposited' trajectories are always fading away, but slowly. If the sweep/fadeout rate is tuned right, one can capture the high-density regions and show the smooth connecting 'tissue' in between. However, these images are not quantitatively correct — the trajectories are weighted according to how recently they were deposited, with a bright spot at the leading point — and are always shimmering and hard to photograph.

By recording a histogram of trajectories numerically, we hope to achieve the same smoothness, but with measurable precision and manipulation capability.

Computing Strange Attractors

We consider a chaotic flow moving (depositing its measure) around a regular Cartesian lattice of mesh size ε and aim at representing the attractor as the set of cubes (voxels) having nonempty intersection with the set. By a 'chaotic flow' we mean a system of differential equations in $\mathbb{R}^3$ with a strange attractor. For example, the Rössler system is given by the equations

$$\dot{x} = -(y + z) \quad \dot{y} = x + \frac{y}{5} \quad \dot{z} = \frac{1}{5} + (x - c)z \tag{2}$$

which yields the chaotic Rössler attractor for the parameter $c = 5.7$.

We consider a trajectory started on or very close to the attractor and determine all cubes C that the trajectory passes through at some time. Ideally we would want to accumulate the time spent by the trajectory in each cube, but a numerical 'trajectory' is actually a sequence of points $X_0, X_1, X_2, ...$, tolerably close to the mathematical trajectory, computed by some integration scheme. Rather than interpolating between points and measuring voxel intersections, we increment a counter at each voxel that is hit by the discrete orbit, which statistically should yield the same result. The integral in Eq. (1) can be approximated in this case by the sum

$$\mu(C) \approx \frac{1}{n} \sum_{0}^{n-1} \mathbf{1}_C(X_i) \tag{3}$$

If we let $n \to \infty$, then equality holds.

A note should be made about the choice of step length h in the integration scheme. Our approach here is to sample the solution such that at all times

---

[†] However, the natural measure of a strange attractor is different in the sense that its support is a fractal and it does not allow a density function; it is a singular measure.

the distance of two subsequent points is on the order of half the mesh size ε or less. In practice, though, maintaining the same step size h for the entire process is impractical, because the speed of the trajectory can vary greatly over the attractor. It is more economical to reparameterize the differential equation using arc length. Then we can set $h = \varepsilon/2$, and the trajectory will be sampled at the constant rate of twice the mesh size. The samples must be appropriately weighted according to speed corresponding to the original equation.

Voxel techniques are always brutal memory consumers; but fortunately we can take advantage of the fractal distribution of the actual data set in a very concrete way. If the object is said to have dimension near 2.1, then we expect the number of cubes needed to span the object to scale as $\varepsilon^{-2.1}$ rather than ε^{-3}, which means that at high resolutions that data is closer to planar size (N^2) than spatial (N^3). Actual data structures always have pointer overhead, and in the case of octrees, the fact that you need to cover the lower leaves (at small mesh sizes where you reap the advantages of having a low fractal dimension) with parent nodes (at scales where you do not) means your savings are not quite so astronomical. But it is still necessary to keep the data structure manageable in a workstation environment. Running on an SGI Indigo with 16 Mb and all the window system overhead in the background, we were able do our stats on a $512 \times 512 \times 512$ octree. Pointer overhead counted for about a third against the actual number of leaves storing histogram values.

One needs to store the histogram not only to capture the measure but also to know when to stop the computation. A standard procedure which is often used to compare images is derived from root-mean-square (rms) differences. It is straightforward to adapt the method to quantify differences between approximations of measures of the attractor. Not knowing the true measure of the attractor, we generate two measures simultaneously in the same octree, or rather two overlapping ones, and take the rms difference. This (almost) doubles the memory needed — 'almost', because although leaves are duplicated most of the parent nodes are shared.

Our empirical tests for the Rössler attractor show that the relative rms difference decreases by a factor of about 0.7 when the number of sample points is doubled. The computation can be stopped when this rms difference drops below a specified threshold, or when the allotted computing time is used up. At a final stage the rms difference yields an indication of the quality achieved by the approximation. We then average the two measures to get a slightly better fit, and project the result onto the viewing plane.

Rendering the Natural Measure

In principle we can proceed using standard methods of volume rendering. Here we only point out a few but important differences. It is uncommon in volume rendering to deal with high resolution but sparse data sets. In other words, we need to consider volumes of, say, 512^3 voxels, most of which carry a zero measure.

There are several possible ways to project the data. For us it was sufficient to project each nonzero voxel as a light source with intensity corresponding to the measure it carries, applying common histogram equalization and gamma correction to improve contrast.

Alternatively, we can interpret a data point as representing a partially opaque object in space, which reflects light from one or more external light sources. For the purpose of computing the reflected light, normal vectors need to be supplied. In volume rendering, normal vectors are usually obtained from gradients computed by central difference schemes. In the case of strange attractors, however, there is a more appropriate way to arrive at normal vectors. At every point of a trajectory there is also a maximal spreading direction, which indicates in which direction nearby trajectories of the attractor are most strongly repelled from the given one. In other words, the velocity vector at a point, together with the vector for the maximal spreading direction, gives us a tangential plane, from which we readily obtain a normal vector. These maximal spreading directions are related to the so-called Ljapunov exponents and can be conveniently computed along with the trajectory of the original system (see, e.g., [Peit92]).

As a first result of this research, we present two images for the invariant measure of the Rössler attractor (see Figure 2 and Plate 18). They are based on approximately four million points.

Open Problems and Extensions

The rms test is an experimental and intuitive one, and in some sense an arbitrary choice. Are there more suitable tests? Does the addition of noise in the maximal spreading direction perpendicular to the trajectory help to achieve a faster convergence toward a 'fuzzy' rendition by sacrificing a little detail in resolution? We can even go one step further and replace the trajectory points that enter the data structure by small line segments centered at the points and oriented in the maximal spreading direction. This amounts to drawing the attractor using a calligraphic pen with its fat edge along the spreading direction.

An alternative approach to the direct computation of the measure in state space is to consider only the measure in a transverse two-dimensional cross-section of the attractor, called a Poincaré section. Its computation is more accessible in two regards. We save in storage by using a planar lattice rather than a spatial one. Moreover, the integration of the differential equation can make full use of adaptive step-size methods. Thus, one can expect that convergence of the approximations of the natural measure associated with the Poincaré map can be achieved more rapidly. Additionally, methods can be devised to extend this measure to the full three-dimensional state space.

The final observation to be made is that, as with computing the digits of π to arbitrary precision, there is an inherent amount of work to be done in order to describe a complex object to the human senses. The order of 'work' needed — convergence time, memory requirements, program complexity — is an essential

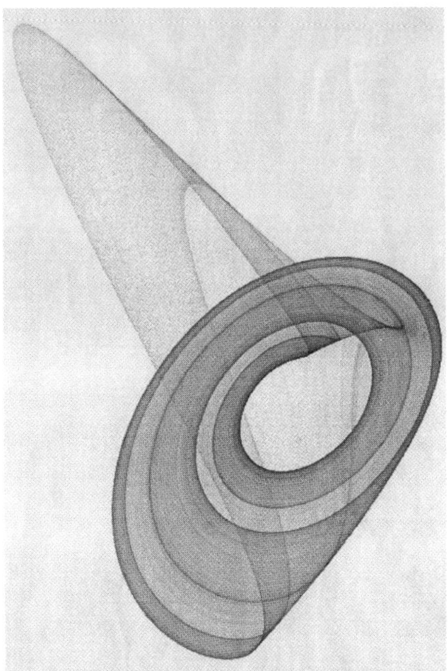

Figure 2. The invariant measure of the Rössler attractor; darker parts indicate regions of high measure. The picture is based on 4 million points with a normed rms quality factor 0.04.

property of that object. In the case of strange attractors, perhaps the order of work can be tied to the objects' information dimension, or used to define a taxonomy of attractors according to their complexity.

Acknowledgments. This paper was inspired by some renderings of a natural measure as a (projected, two-dimensional) histogram done by Scott Hotton as part of a class project at the University of California, Santa Cruz, in the study of driven oscillators. We also thank Carl Evertsz for useful discussions on the convergence of fractal measures.

REFERENCES

[Guck83]
Guckenheimer, J., and Holmes, P., *Nonlinear Oscillations, Dynamical Systems, and Bifurcations of Vector Fields,* New York: Springer-Verlag, 1983.

[Peit92]
Peitgen, H.-O., Jürgens, H., and Saupe, D., *Chaos and Fractals,* New York: Springer-Verlag, 1992.

3 Virtual Reality Techniques

Stereo Computer Graphics

David F. McAllister

Abstract

Stereo computer graphics is rapidly becoming an important part of computer aided geometric design, visualization, virtual reality systems, and many other applications of computer graphics. The improvements in speed, resolution, and economy in graphics workstations, as well as the development of liquid crystal polarizing shutters and parallax barrier methods, help make interactive stereo an important and useful capability. We discuss perception and implementation issues as well as some recent research in algorithm and graphics user interface design for stereo applications in a workstation environment.

Introduction

Over the past several years and since the publication of Okoshi's work [Okos76], there has been rapid advancement in 3D techniques and technologies. The improvements in speed, resolution, and economy in computer graphics, as well as the development of liquid crystal polarizing shutters and liquid crystal parallax barrier methods, make interactive stereo an important and useful capability. True 3D is rapidly becoming an important part of computer graphics, visualization, and virtual reality systems. In addition, the improvement of high resolution color printing has made 3D hardcopy more available and useful for archiving and transportation of 3D images.

Graphics algorithms which work well for producing single frame images do not necessarily extend easily to rendering stereo pairs. Also, the work required to render a left and right eye stereo view is not necessarily twice that required to render a single eye view. Research in the area of computer generated stereo animation has only recently begun and has produced many interesting research questions. We treat some of these issues below. Our emphasis is on CRT or projected images. See [Robi91] for a discussion of stereo issues in head mounted displays.

We first review the common visual depth cues and how they interrelate. We later use them to distinguish between salient 3D technologies.

Depth Cues

There are several depth cues which the human visual system uses to determine the relative positions of objects in a 3D scene. These cues are divided into two categories, physiological and psychological.

Physiological Depth Cues

Accommodation is the change in focal length of the lens within the eye as it focuses on specific regions of a 3D scene. The lens changes thickness due to a change in tension from the ciliary muscle. This depth cue is normally used by the visual system in tandem with convergence, binocular disparity, and motion parallax.

Convergence or *vergence* is the rotation of the eyes inward to converge on objects as they move closer to the observer. If the eyes rotate outward beyond the normal parallel position for observing objects in the distance, we call this phenomenon wall-eyed. Stereo images which are not correctly registered or computed may force the viewer to look at the image wall-eyed, which can introduce eye strain and subsequent headaches.

Binocular disparity is the difference in the images which project on the left and right eyes when viewing a 3D scene. It is the salient depth cue, which is used by the visual system to produce the sensation of depth or stereopsis.

Motion parallax provides differences in views of a scene by moving the scene or the viewer. Consider looking at a cloud of discrete points in space. Assume all points are the same color and approximately the same size. Because there are no other cues to use to determine the relative depths of the points, we move our head from side to side to get several different views of the scene; this is called 'looking around'. We determine relative depths by noticing how much two points move relative to each other: as we move our head from left to right or up and down the points closer to us appear to move more than do points further away.

Psychological Depth Cues

Psychological depth cues include linear perspective, shading and shadowing, aerial perspective, interposition, texture gradient, and color.

> *Linear perspective* is the property that the size of the image of an object on the retina changes in inverse proportion to its change in distance;

> *Shading and shadowing* are standard graphics techniques used to help the user determine depth relationships. Faces of an object which are further from the light source are darker, giving cues of both depth and shape. Shadows cast by one object on another also give clues as to relative position and size;

> Objects which are further away tend to become less distinct, appearing cloudy or hazy. Blue, having a shorter wavelength, penetrates the atmosphere more easily; hence distant objects sometimes appear bluish. This phenomenon is called *aerial perspective*;

> If one object occludes, hides, or overlaps another, we assume that the object doing the hiding is closer. This is called *interposition*;

> *Texture gradient* is the property by which texture becomes blurred as objects become more distant;

> We use *color* in several ways. The fluids in the eye cause some refraction

to take place; the fluids refract different wave lengths at different angles. Hence, often objects of the same shape and size and the same distance from the viewer appear to be at different depths because of differences in color. In addition, light-colored objects appear closer than dark colored objects.

The human visual system uses all of these depth cues when determining relative depths in a scene. The cues are usually additive. However, in certain situations some of the cues are more powerful than others, which can produce conflicting depth information.

A Technology Taxonomy

Okoshi [Okos76] and Tilton [Tilt87] present an excellent history of 3D technologies. In addition, a useful reference which summarizes many 3D patents in the area of 3D technologies is found in [STAR91]. Most 3D displays fit into one or more of three broad categories: holographic, multiplanar, or stereo pair. In general, holographic and multiplanar images produce 'real' or 'solid' images in which binocular parallax, accommodation, and convergence are consistent with the apparent depth in the image. They require no special viewing devices and hence are called autostereoscopic.

Autostereoscopic Technologies

Holography is an autostereoscopic technology, but it is beyond our scope. Holograms can be used to store multiple stereo pairs in strips, creating what is called a holographic stereogram [Mcal93].

Multiplanar methods are similar to volumetric methods in computer graphics, where the image is subdivided into voxels, or three-dimensional cubes. The varifocal mirror technique divides a 3D scene into thousands of planes, and a point-plotting electrostatic CRT plots a single point from each plane. A circular mirror vibrating at 30 Hz reflects these points while changing their apparent distance from the viewer. The points combine to produce a real image. There are also rotating mirrors which are embedded with LEDs, and those which reflect beams of laser light. In all cases the image is transparent (see [Mcal92b] for a more detailed discussion).

The third technology type, the subject of this paper, is the stereo pair.

Stereo Pairs

The production of stereoscopic photographs (stereo pairs, or stereographs) began in the early 1850s. Stereo pairs simulate the binocular disparity depth cue by projecting distinct flat images to each eye, one for the left eye and one for the right. There are many techniques for viewing stereo pairs, depending on their format (e.g., recall the device for viewing the View-Master™ reel).

Terminology

Horizontal parallax is the distance between the left and right eye view of a point in the scene when projected on a plane perpendicular to the observer's line of sight, called the stereo window. Positive parallax occurs if the object is behind the stereo window, the left eye view being to the left of the right eye view (see Figure 1). Zero parallax occurs if the point is at the same depth as the stereo window, and negative parallax occurs if the point lies in front of the stereo window. Normally the stereo window is in the plane of the viewing screen, but it need not be.

Free Viewing Stereo Pairs

The concepts and technologies described in this paper are illustrated using computer generated stereographs. The color plates (Plates 19–22) are arranged for parallel or uncrossed viewing. For parallel viewing the leftmost image is a left eye view and the rightmost image is a right eye view. For parallel stereo viewing, place a piece of paper between the two images so the right eye cannot see the left eye view and vice versa (Figure 2). For crossed viewing the right eye view is on the left and the left eye view is on the right (Figure 3). For crossed eye viewing stare at the region between the two images and gently cross your eyes until the two images merge in the center. You will still be able to see the right and left eye images on the periphery, but concentrate on the center image. After a few seconds, most people are able to perceive depth in the image. You must hold the images parallel with your eyes or you will not be able to merge the left and right eye views. This technique for viewing stereo images is also called free or transverse viewing (Figure 3). If you parallel view images designed for crossed

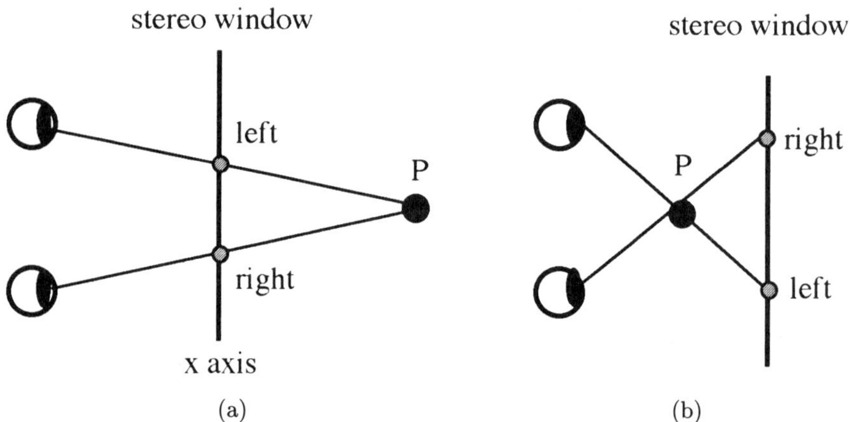

Figure 1. Horizontal parallax. (a) Positive parallax; (b) negative parallax.

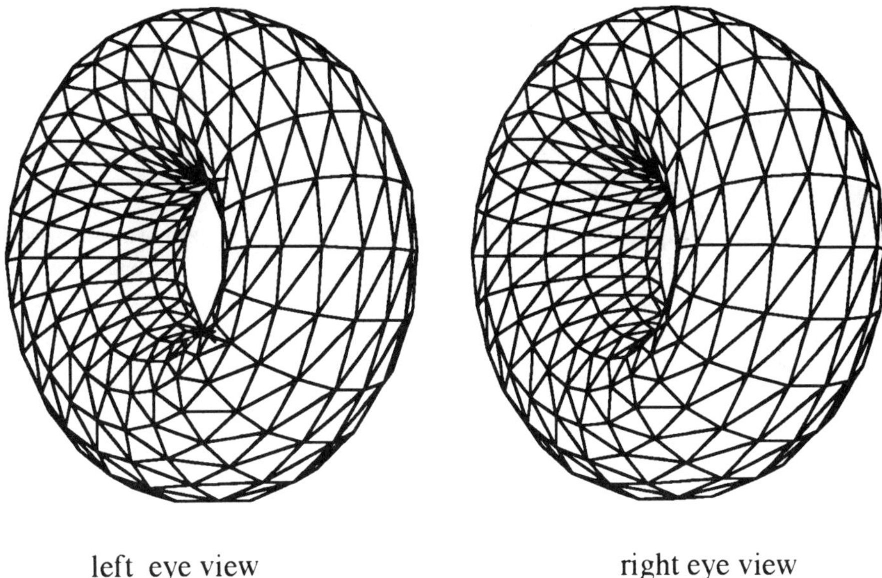

left eye view   right eye view

Figure 2. Stereo images arranged for parallel viewing.

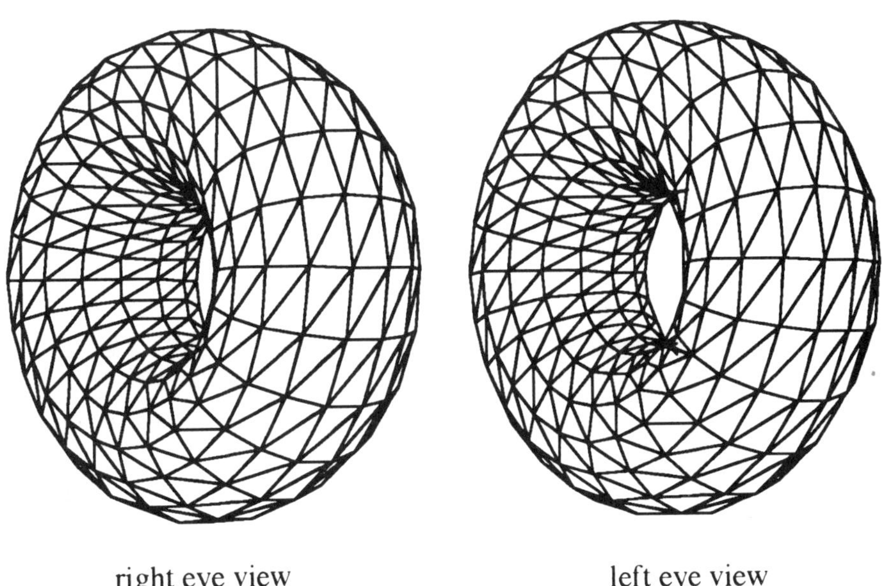

right eye view   left eye view

Figure 3. Stereo images arranged for crossed viewing.

eye viewing, then the left eye is viewing the right eye image and vice versa. The depth in the image is reversed. In this case we have what is called pseudostereo.

Figure 4 is a random dot autostereogram of $\sin(x^2+y^2)$, which requires crossed viewing. There are no depth cues other than binocular parallax. Merge the two dots beneath the image to view the functional surface. Crossing your eyes even further produces other images.

Computation of Stereo Pairs

Several ways to compute stereo pairs have been proposed. There are perception issues which eliminate some techniques from consideration. Vertical displacement occurs when the left and right eye views of a given point (called homologous points, see Figure 5) on a 3D scene differ vertically (that is, do not lie on a horizontal line parallel with the viewers eyes); this produces vertical parallax. Prolonged viewing of images which have vertical displacement can produce headaches, eye strain, and other uncomfortable physical symptoms. Rotation of an object followed by perspective projection can cause vertical displacement (Figures 6a and b). Hence, this technique is not recommended for computing stereo pairs. Hodges [Hodg90] discusses this in more detail.

In addition to vertical parallax, linear perspective is important for depth relationships and object shapes to be maintained. Although parallel projection does not produce vertical displacement, the absence of linear perspective can create a 'reverse' perspective as the result of a perceptual phenomenon known as Emmert's law: objects which do not obey linear perspective can appear to get larger as the distance from the observer increases. The preferred method for computing stereo pairs is to use two off-axis centers of perspective projection (the position of the left and right eyes) which simulates the optics of a stereo camera where both lenses are parallel. See Hodges [Hodg92] for a discussion of this.

Stereo Output Technologies

We divide the technologies into two broad groups, those which present both eye views simultaneously or time parallel, and those which present the left and right eye images in sequence using optical techniques to occlude the right eye when the left eye view is being presented, etc. This latter is called field sequential, or time multiplexed [Hodg87].

Time Parallel

3D movies traditionally used the old analglyph method which required the user to wear glasses with red and green or red and blue filters. Both images were presented on the screen simultaneously. Hence, it was a time parallel method. Many observers had headaches when leaving the theater, thus giving 3D, in particular stereo, a bad reputation. A phenomenon called ghosting, or cross talk, was a significant problem. The filters did not completely eliminate the opposite

Figure 4. A random dot autostereogram.

eye view, and hence the left eye saw not only its image but sometimes part of the right eye image as well. The stereo pairs in this paper present both eye views simultaneously, and hence use a time parallel method. This technique can also be used in computer graphics. There are hand-held viewing devices which permit the adjustment of one eye view to register the left and right eye views so they can be viewed in parallel. Viewing static images in this way is straightforward, but it can be difficult and tiring when viewing animation. The most popular way for viewing stereo on graphics workstations is the field sequential technique.

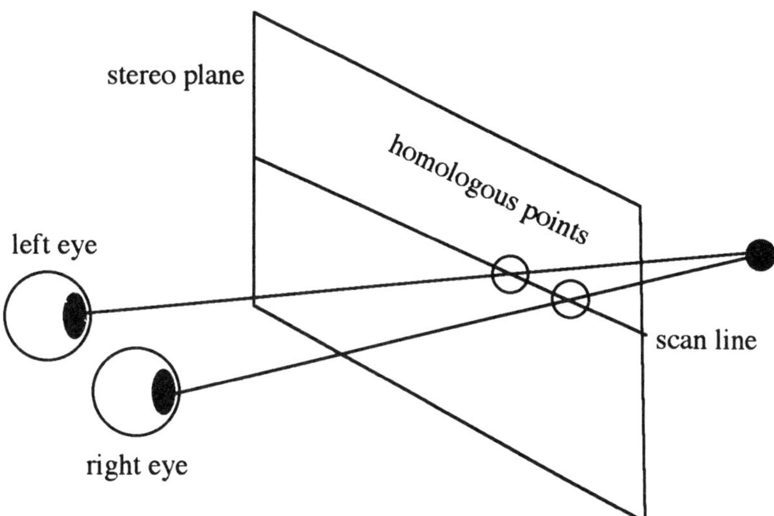

Figure 5. Homologous points.

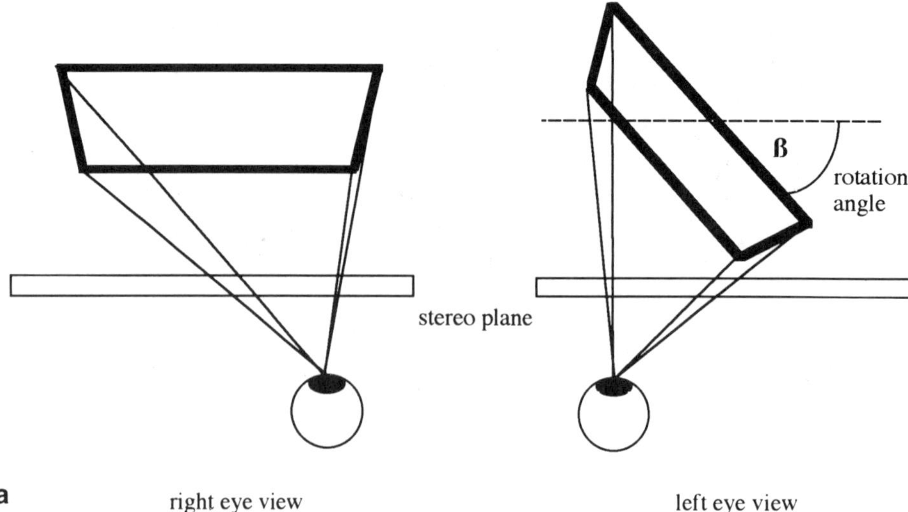

Figure 6. Vertical disparity. (a) Left and right eye views computed by rotation and perspective projection; (b) disparity in homologous points.

FIELD SEQUENTIAL

The field sequential technique presents the left and right eye images alternately. While the right eye view is viewable, the left eye is blocked using a mechanical or electro-optical shuttering device. Similarly, when the left eye view is viewable, the right eye is blocked. Early mechanical devices were used to occlude the appropriate eye during CRT refresh. A comparison of many of these devices is found in [Lips89].

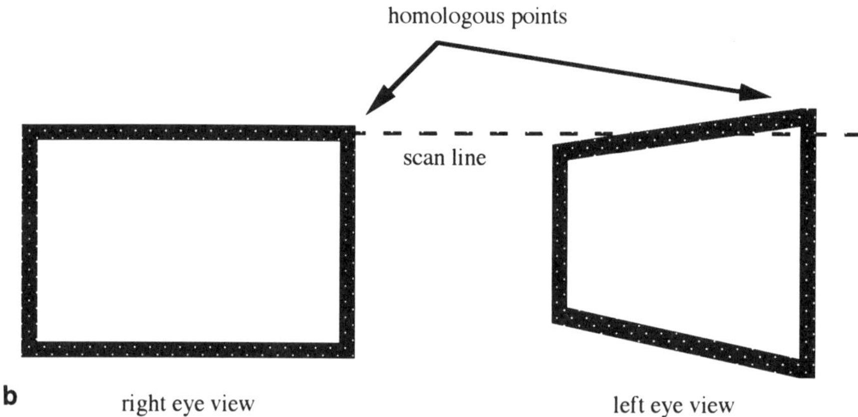

Figure 6. (*Continued.*)

Currently, the most common way to show stereo pairs on a workstation uses LCD shutters such as those manufactured by StereoGraphics and Tektronix. Monitor refresh rates should be at least 120 Hz to preclude flicker. The shutter fits over the face of the CRT and polarizes the light circularly in opposite directions during each refresh. In this case, the user wears passive circularly polarized glasses. When the light from the screen is polarized in one direction, the eye with polarization in the opposite direction is occluded. Active glasses operate in a similar manner except the switching mechanism is produced by an infrared signal from a driving device which mounts on the CRT. The glasses are powered by a battery. The technology of these devices is described in more detail in [Mcal92a, 93].

Some Design Issues

DISTORTION

There is an optimal position for an observer to view a stereo image. A point can appear further in depth as a viewer moves away from the screen, with no change in parallax. Similarly, the image appears to 'follow' the viewer as one moves the head from side to side (Figure 7). Both motions cause distortion in the image and can affect judgment of absolute relationships. Gogel discusses the psychological and perceptual aspects of this phenomenon (see [Goge90]).

VIEW VOLUME

When possible, the view volume should be restricted to the region which is viewable by both eyes. Since the perspective projection to each eye results in

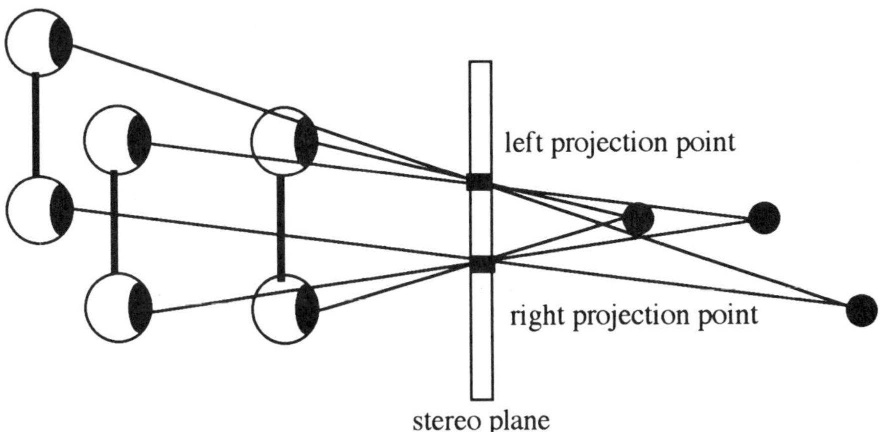

Figure 7. Distortion caused by head movement.

different truncated pyramid shapes at the left and right boundaries of the view volumes for each eye, it is possible to have an object that the left eye views and the right eye does not, and vice versa. A possibility exists, in the extreme case, that each eye sees an object the other eye does not, and that these objects are so similar that they are merged as one. As shown in Figure 8, the objects fuse in front of the stereo window. Objects which are placed in these nonoverlapping areas have no depth information. These objects are distracting, cause eye strain, and make the scene difficult to fuse.

In [Butt88] an interactive paint program is described which was implemented on a field sequential 60 Hz LCD shutter system. Several interesting stereo phenomena were manifested.

INDUCED Z SHIFT

The field sequential method can produce an interesting result, a change in apparent object depth caused by horizontal motion. Movement to the right causes an apparent decrease in depth, while movement to the left causes an apparent increase, with correct depth returning as soon as motion ceases. This phenomenon is caused by a combination of the rendering speed of the system, the image

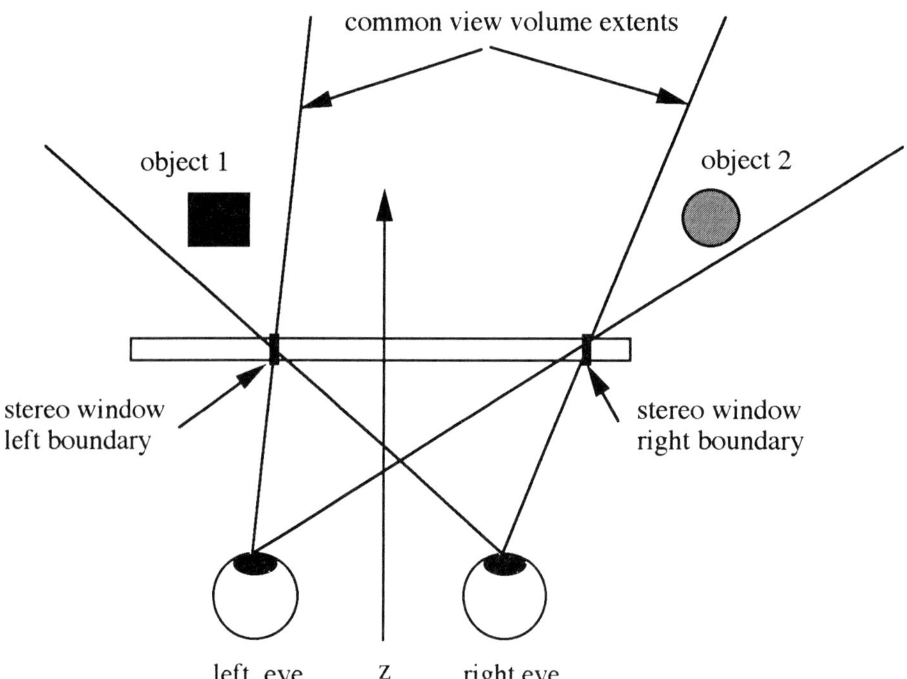

Figure 8. Objects outside common view volume.

display sequence, the phosphor decay rates, and the user's short term visual memory. To illustrate, suppose the parallax of the left and right eye image of an object as it moves from left to right is fixed at 10 pixels. Suppose the speed of the object is such that it moves in five-pixel increments, and it begins to move after the left eye view is refreshed. Hence, the first left/right pair (Ll/R1) occurs 15 pixels apart. On the next refresh, the left eye view 'catches up' and is 10 pixels to the left of the previous right eye view. When the new right eye view, R2, is displayed the parallax is 15 pixels once again. As a result, while in motion to the right the object parallax alternates between 15 and 10 pixels. The visual system tends to average these depths, giving an apparent depth of $(10 + 15)/2 = 12.5$ pixels. This results in an apparent increase in depth solely as a result of horizontal motion.

Erasing in Stereo

In normal 2D paint programs, part of an object can be removed by overpainting it with another object in the background color. In stereo, if the user only desires to partially erase the underlying object, then the parallax at the edges of the background colored object may be discernible. Thus, the object may appear as a solid and at a different depth than the erased object. Attempts to erase an object when the cursor is not exactly at that object's depth do not result in erasure, but rather produce a new 'object' in the background color at the new depth. Hence, to treat this case knowledge is required of the depth and color of the object immediately behind the region being erased, or the eraser must implicitly identify a subarea of the object which becomes transparent or is deleted.

Rubber Band Vectors

The rubber band vector mode works well if vectors can be drawn within the refresh speed of the frame buffer. This prevents buffer switching on the same retrace pulse as the shutters, with the result that both eyes see the same image. With workstations or graphics boards which are 'stereo ready' this is not a problem, since quad-buffering is supported.

Often, as the vector length increases the stereo sensation remains, but with a noticeable flicker or cross talk between left and right eye images. If the vector requires too much drawing time, proper synchronization can occur, but only on alternate signals. In this case, each eye is presented with one of the opposite eye's images for every two of its own. Despite its limitations, effective drawing can be accomplished using the rubber band vector mode, since the flicker or cross-talk conditions are usually short in duration.

Picket Fence Problem

Raster technology produces another perceptual problem that is most noticeable in the rubber band vector mode. This problem is called the picket fence problem since, as a vector that is oblique in Z moves through the vertical, the vector is partitioned into a series of vertical pickets staggered behind each other. This phenomenon only occurs when the vertical segments of the diagonals in each left and right image are closely matched in length. This means that the vectors in each left and right image must be nearly mirror images of each other. The problem is most noticeable when a vector has approximately a 45° slant in Z and is within 10–20° of the vertical in X and Y. Beyond these vertical parameters in X and Y, sufficient differences in left and right segment lengths exist, so that the visual system tends to blend them together and mask the problem. Plate 19 illustrates both aspects of this phenomenon, which is usually not bothersome since it is restricted to a fairly narrow range of parameters. When it does appear, it does not degrade stereo perception significantly. Higher resolution and antialiasing reduce the effect.

PERCEPTUAL ZOOMING

If we render an object using parallel vs. perspective projection, translating the object away from the viewer can cause the object size to appear to increase rather than decrease. The phrases 'size constancy' or 'perceptual zooming' describe this phenomenon. Emmert's Law states that as the convergence angle decreases (i.e., objects become more distant), objects within about one meter of the viewer are perceived as increasing rather than decreasing in size. Size constancy arises from the fact that as an object moves away and appears to grow larger in accordance with this law, its actual retinal image decreases in size. This results in a roughly constant perceived size within this one meter range [Jule71].

However, even though stereoscopic objects appear to move away from the viewer when the convergence angle decreases, they are in reality still fixed at the distance of the monitor from the viewer. Thus, there is no decrease in retinal image size to compensate for the perceived increase in size, hence the term 'perceptual zooming'. When rendering stereo cursors it may be more efficient to do a table look-up of cursor size based on parallax.

DOUBLE IMAGES

A more annoying and distracting phenomenon is the problem of double images. This is most obvious with long, slender objects parallel to the z-axis, and manifests itself as an inability to fuse the left and right eye images throughout the object's length. Plate 20 illustrates this case.

If the eyes are focused on either end of a long rod, double images are perceived at the other end. A further difficulty occurs when there is no point object or feature to maintain the viewer's visual attention, so that the point of convergence is unstable. Consequently, the eyes tend to wander back and forth along the rod. Also note that lines which recede from the viewer parallel to the z-axis and originate on the x-axis have no discernible parallax and appear as colored segments on the x-axis. [Mcal93] presents a more detailed discussion of this problem.

Research Topics

We present a brief survey of some of the research directions which have recently been described in the literature. First we consider the problem of minimizing total parallax in a scene. We then examine some stereo applications which allow the user to interactively modify a scene while in stereo, by drawing new objects, selecting and moving objects, and deleting or erasing objects. These descriptions motivate interface issues and perceptual problems. We discuss ways to reduce the cost of rendering by using information from one eye view to help reduce the computation required in rendering the other eye image. We also give examples to show that some algorithms which work well in monoscopic environments may be difficult to extend to stereo.

Minimizing Absolute Parallax

There have been suggestions as to how to place objects in a scene so that viewing is least fatiguing and most pleasant. The common measurement of parallax is the subtended angle which makes the measurement independent of viewer distance. For comfortable viewing, Valyes [Valy82] recommends a maximum angle of 1.6 degrees uncrossed. Yeh and Silverstein [Yeh90] suggest a maximum of 27 min arc (interocular distance $= .008d$) crossed and 24 min arc (interocular distance $= .007d$) uncrossed, where d is the distance from the viewer to the stereo plane. Hodges [Hodg92] recommends 1.5 degrees (interocular distance $= .028d$) crossed or uncrossed.

Another rule of thumb that has been mentioned is that negative parallax is in general not to exceed 30% of the distance between the stereo window and the observer, although animators have found that most viewers can fuse images with negative parallax which brings the apparent position of the object to within 80% of this distance. Lipton [Lipt82] recommends that if a scene contains a single object it be placed so that the center of the object is in the plane of the stereo window. He also states that no points in the scene should have parallax equal to the interocular distance, since prolonged viewing can cause fatigue.

In [Mcal92b] the author studied the mathematical relationships of minimizing parallax. Using two off-axis projections and taking the difference of the x coordinates, the parallax of a point P with coordinates (x, y, z) becomes $ez/(z - d)$. Note that when $z = d$, i.e., a point is on the z-axis between the two eye points, the parallax becomes arbitrarily small (large negatively), as expected. Also, as z approaches infinity the parallax converges to e, as expected. Hence, the problem is interesting only if we consider the absolute value of parallax. If a point is hidden it is ignored, since it does not contribute to the visual properties of the scene.

If we graph the parallax function $f(v) = |v/(v - d)|$ for $d = -1$, we get the picture in Figure 9. If we expand the function $v/(v - d)$ about the origin, we get the series

$$-\sum_{k=1}^{\infty} \left(\frac{v}{d}\right)^k$$

which is alternating, since $d < 0$. For values of $|v|$ less than $|d|$ the series converges rapidly, and the function can be well approximated by the first term $-v/d$. Hence, the parallax function can be approximated by $|v/d|$ for small v.

Let $D = \{P_j = (x_j, y_j, z_j),\ 1 \le j \le N\}$ a finite set of visible points in a stereo scene. To minimize the total parallax we must assume that a value of z_j can occur multiple times in an image. Hence, we minimize a weighted sum $S_w(v)$ of translated parallax functions, where the weights w_j are positive integers which count the number of occurrences of the depth z_j

$$S_w(v) = \sum_{j=1}^{N} w_j \left| \frac{z_j + v}{z_j + v - d} \right|$$

The inclusion of the weight w_j in the function $S_w(v)$ multiplies the slopes of the jth parallax function by the weight w_j. If there are i roots less than a point v^* (which is not a root) and $N - i$ roots greater than v^*, then an approximation to the slope at v^* is

$$\frac{\sum_{j=1}^{i} w_j - \sum_{j=i+1}^{N} w_j}{d}$$

The left term in the numerator is increasing and the right term is decreasing as i increases from 1 to N. Let k be the index where the quantity is zero and does not change sign, or the index such that the quantity is negative for k and positive for $k + 1$. In general, the true minimum occurred at a root $-z_i \ge -z_k$. The difference of the weight sums ignores the distribution of the values of the parallax roots, and hence the estimate decreases in accuracy if the spread of the roots is large. The author restricted all roots to lie in an interval of width $|d|$.

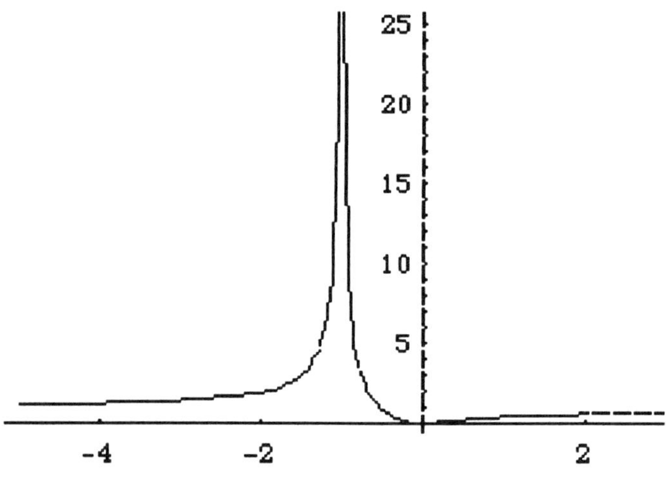

Figure 9. The parallax function $|v/(v - d)|$, $d = -1$.

To illustrate, let $z_i = i$, $1 \le i \le 30$; compute the location of the true minimum vs. the approximation minimum for different weight functions w_i. The results are given in Table 1.

In most cases, the approximation gives a reasonable estimate of the minimum. When $w_i = i^4$, the translation value moves the point closest to the viewer to -24, which is 80% of d. Hence, if the scene becomes more complicated as the depth increases, some points may require large negative parallax to minimize the weighted parallax sum. It is not known if there are cases when $S_w(v)$ does not have a unique minimum or if the minimum ever occurs at a point other than a root.

STEREO CURSOR DESIGN

Interactive input techniques for three-dimensional computer graphic systems have been widely researched for the past two decades. Most of this research was conducted using some type of two-dimensional input device to manipulate either a two- or three-dimensional cursor in a 3D scene [Roge80; Levk84; Bier86; Niel86; Butt88]. Unfortunately, the mapping between the two-dimensional input device control and the three-dimensional cursor movement is not intuitive.

With the introduction of six degree-of-freedom input devices in the early 1980s, researchers were able to supply the user a one-to-one correspondence between the device control movements and the cursor's movements. Since the 3D scene was usually rendered on a two-dimensional screen, researchers found that the user was still unable to manipulate and position the cursor in an intuitive manner, due to the lack of depth perception [Roge80; Badl86]. However, Lipscomb [Lips79] found that users can learn to position rapidly in three dimensions using a monoscopic display by positioning first in 2D with a view parallel to the XY plane, then rotating to a view parallel with the YZ plane and positioning horizontally across the screen, along the former z-axis. Biochemists using this method constructed several molecules of several thousand atoms each about as fast as those who used stereo. This manipulation technique is called 'motion decomposition' [Kilp76].

Stereo systems are now being used in conjunction with six degree-of-freedom input devices to yield true three-dimensional input and output [Schm83; Wald86;

Table 1. Location of estimated vs. true minima for $z_i = i$, $1 \le i \le 30$.

w_i	true min	estimated min
1	-9	-15
i	-16	-21
$31 - i$	-6	-9
i^2	-21	-23
$(31 - i)^2$	-5	-6
$i(31 - i)$	-12	-13
i^3	-23	-25
i^4	-25	-27

Beat87; Beat88; Burt88]. Interfaces for these systems are now important areas of research [Brid87; Mosh88; Wixs88; Wixs90]. An early such stereo cursor system developed by Richard DeHoff and Peter Hildebrandt of Tektronix, Inc. [Deho89] had a pointer symbol tethered to a reference symbol on screen, so the cursor had the effect of rubber-banding out of the center of the view volume. The reference symbol was defined as a '+' and was attached by a straight line to an 'x' which was the pointer symbol. The reference symbol had zero parallax, and the pointer symbol had parallax proportional to its position in the view volume. The parallax of the tether line varied from zero, at the reference end, to its maximum, at the pointer end. One of the interface issues not considered in the above system is the type of stereo cursor to use for particular applications. For example, standard 2D cursors are acceptable for text manipulation, while cursors which communicate depth in a stereo environment must be chosen for the particular application.

Barham and McAllister [Barh91] describe an interactive stereo system which allows a user to construct, draw, and modify B-spline space curves. Their system used a Spatial Systems Spaceball™ to control the stereo cursor, while a mouse was used to manipulate a 2D cursor for menu selection. The toggling back and forth between the mouse and the Spaceball was annoying, since the user was required to move his attention from the screen to the particular input device and then back to the screen.

Cursor Types

Several two-dimensional and three-dimensional cursor types are described in previous research (see [Roge80; Bier86; Niel86; Butt88; Beat88]). The two-dimensional cursor shapes included the circle, triangle, crosshair, and full-space crosshair. The three-dimensional cursors included the sphere, pyramid, jack, full-space jack, cube, and tri-axis. The full-space crosshair, jack, and tri-axis cursors are shown bounded by the view volume in Figure 10.

The point on the cursor used to select a given point or create a new point is referred to as the hotpoint. The hotpoint of the circle, square, sphere, and cube is at the center of the object. The hotpoint of the triangle, pyramid, and arrowhead is at the apex of the object. The hotpoint of the crosshair, full-space crosshair, tri-axis, jack, and full-space jack is the intersection of the vector components of the objects.

The hotpoint can be projected onto the side walls of the reference cube as a cue to the cursor location in the view volume. These projected points are referred to as the cursor's ghost points. The use of ghost points in Plate 21, in conjunction with the grid reference cube, gives an indication of absolute position of the cursor within the view volume.

Cursor Selection and Placement

Several subjects participated in an experiment to select and move all the control points for a test curve using a Spaceball™ as an input device. The subjects used

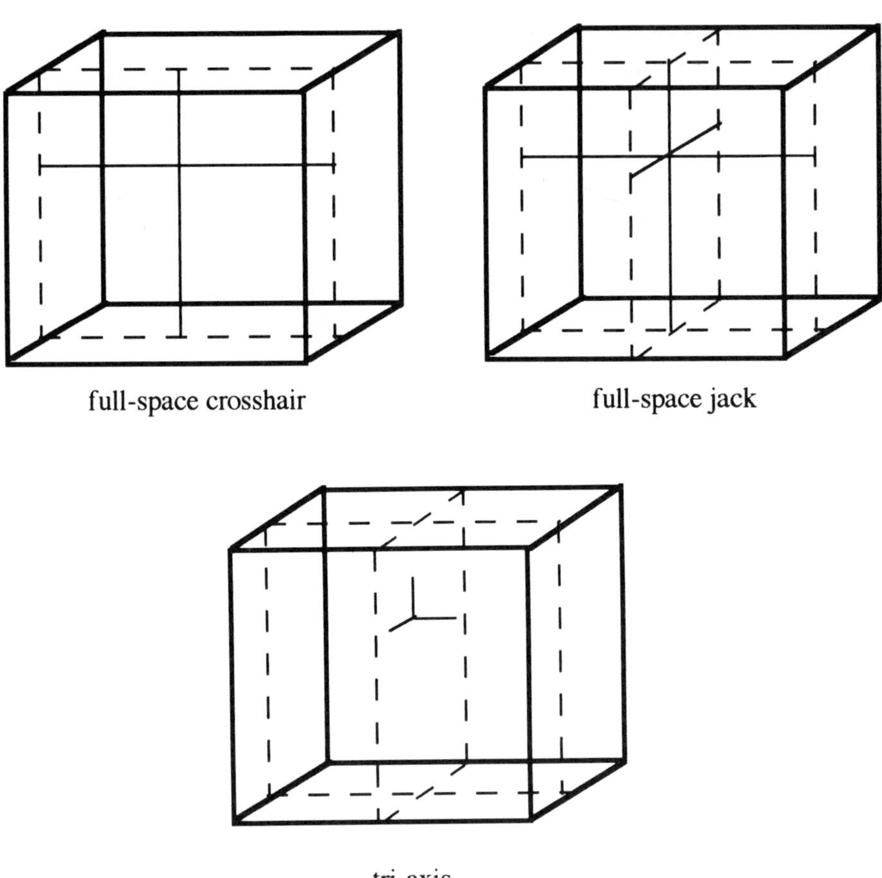

full-space crosshair   full-space jack

tri-axis

Figure 10. Examples of full-space and tri-axis cursors.

stereopsis for a rapid initial placement of the cursor near the control point. Once near the control point, interposition was used almost entirely for fine placement of the cursor on the control point. Thus, the cursors that were most effective are the ones that give good disparity cues and ones that are easy to use for interposition. The additive nature of depth cues seemed to apply, since cursors which only provided one of the cues were consistently ranked lower than those providing both [Wick90]. A gravity feature is extremely convenient if it can be toggled on and off with ease.

Drawing New Curves

The task for the second experiment was for the subject to reproduce an existing curve as accurately as possible. Interposition was not allowed. Hence, other cues became important for the drawing task. Full-space cursors were frequently chosen due to their ability to deliver position within the view volume. When the full-space cursors were not chosen, users always chose to use the ghost points for the extra sense of location they provided. The grid was always preferred on the reference cube for its sense of scale and the extra sense of texture reference. Visual enhancements play an important role in stereoscopic tracking tasks [Kim89].

Full-space jacks and crosshairs give a good sense of location within the view volume. Regular jacks and crosshairs combined with the use of ghost points are also effective indicators of position. Combining a small circle cursor at the origin of a jack or crosshair yields sufficient parallax information and excellent interposition cues due to its flatness. When drawing using the cursor, rubber banding is important. Depending on the application, the rubber band should start from a logical and useful point that does not interfere with the rest of the scene. When selecting points with the cursor, a gravity feature should be an option. A cube with a grid texture surrounding the view volume supplies a needed reference.

Perceptual Problems

The horizontal and vertical lines of the full-space crosshair and jack cursors do not appear to be at the same depth. This perceptual phenomenon can be caused by the fact that the hotpoint is the center of attention and the horizontal line of the full-space crosshair does not present any parallax near this point. All parallax for the horizontal is in the peripheral vision and does not yield as strong an effect as foveal attention [Ande90]. Placing a small circle at the origin of the crosshair appears to bring the depth of the horizontal and vertical lines together. This may be a grouping effect due to the identical color, parallax, and proximity of the objects [Naka89]. Another factor that may influence the crosshair line separation is line width. The built-in line drawing algorithm does not take into account the aspect ratio or addressability of the monitor. This can cause horizontal lines to be wider than vertical lines. Since relative size is a depth cue, the differing line widths may contribute to the perceived depths of the lines of the crosshair [Rein90]. Antialiasing should be applied to all lines to create uniform line widths and to prevent differing amounts of aliasing for the same line in the different eye views.

Identifying the appropriate cursors for application types was not investigated. There may be better ways to create and select objects in a stereo environment.

Stereo Interface Issues

As suggested, a considerable amount of attention has been devoted to interface development for the creation and manipulation of 3D objects, and to techniques for understanding depth relationships in a $2\frac{1}{2}$ D environment. Much of this information is not applicable in a stereo environment. Visualization of multidimensional data has also made stereo an important partner in computer graphics. We consider some of the efforts to define an interface for use in a stereo environment.

Menu Design

In Carver and McAllister [Carv91] the development of an interactive object-oriented drawing program is described. The effort raised several issues about the design of a stereo interface and the features which should be present in an operating system to facilitate the development of stereo applications.

It is difficult for most stereo users to fuse abrupt changes in parallax. For example, if a cursor makes discontinuous changes in depth quickly, the visual system often requires time to adjust to the different position of the cursor and to fuse the left and right eye images. A rapid change in negative parallax normally requires a few seconds to fuse.

Stereo software systems should be designed to produce output in one or more stereo windows. These stereo windows are part of the 2D windowing system of the workstation. The left and right eye views of the windowing system menus and window boundaries are identical and have zero parallax; hence they appear in the plane of the display surface. If the user wishes to access services from the 2D menus, windows of the 2D windowing system, or another stereo window while working in a stereo window, the visual system must adjust to the discontinuous change in parallax caused by viewing an object in stereo to viewing, e.g., text with zero parallax. This can be very disconcerting and annoying and can cause fatigue. A possible solution is to allow the operator to signal that an abbreviated (tear-off) menu should appear at the same approximate depth as the cursor. The user then selects actions from the menu while continuing to focus at the same depth. This technique has been used in virtual reality applications.

Fusing problems also result if there are multiple stereo windows. For example, consider overlapped windows where there is only negative parallax in one window and positive parallax in the other. Possible solutions to the multiple stereo window problem include permitting the user to disable stereo in a particular window. Most windowing and application systems do not permit multiple active stereo windows. Solutions have not been proposed to treat these cases. There are no standards.

Text

If text is to obey linear perspective under translation, then the operating system utilities must be able to produce text of arbitrary font sizes. Text represented by bitmaps can be scaled from a finite set of installed fonts which can produce unsatisfactory text shape and considerable aliasing. To retain maximum image resolution, an outline font handler is used to generate any fractional text height from the outline font representations.

When a text object is moved within depth, its projected height is updated to maintain its consistent virtual height (string width is scaled automatically by using the appropriate font size). Normally, the font size after translation in depth is stored in a table as a function of its size at zero parallax (at the depth of the stereo window) and its current depth.

Text handlers normally assume that the text is to be generated in a plane parallel to the viewing screen. If rotational transformations are to be applied to text, then text handling becomes much more complicated. Modifying the outline definition of a font to handle rotation and linear perspective is not currently available in existing text handlers such as Postscript. Outline fonts are often described using Bézier or Hermite splines. Neither of these splines is invariant under projection [Roge90]. This implies that the entire curve must be drawn, rotated in 3D, and then projected. Nonuniform Rational B-splines (NURBS) are invariant under projection [Roge90], which implies that rotation and projection need be applied only to the control points and the resulting curve drawn from the transformed control points. An alternative is to place a bounding rectangle around text and apply the transformations to the rectangle. The equivalent 2D transformation (after projection) is then applied to the text in the rectangle. Bitmapped fonts suffer from considerable aliasing using this approach. Obviously, these problems do not arise if text is restricted to be parallel to the stereo window. Solutions to handling text in stereo are lacking.

OBJECT CREATION AND MANIPULATION

Stereo makes it possible to manipulate implicit and parametric surfaces quickly and accurately. The investigation of stereo interfaces for creation and modification of these surfaces has only just begun.

In [Deva91] the authors describe the stereo rendering of implicitly defined surfaces of the form $f(x, y, z) = 0$, where f is Lipshitz. Using stereo, manipulation of tensor product surfaces becomes considerably more straightforward. Wright and McAllister [WRIG92] describe an interface for the creation and manipulation of rational Bézier tensor product surfaces. A three button mouse is used for control point manipulation and specification of affine transformations. Sliders are used to change control point weights.

Applying affine transformations to objects becomes easier, since a cursor can be manipulated in depth. The third button of a three button mouse can be used to produce a pop-up menu at the depth of the cursor for selecting the type of transformation (rotation, scale, translation). The cursor can then be used to select and drag a point on the object to imply the axis of rotation or direction of translation. Bounding boxes can be used for scaling an object in the same way that draw programs use it to scale 2D objects.

INPUT DEVICES

There are many devices for 3D input, such as mice, digitizers, graphics tablets, acoustic devices, magnetic field devices, force and torque converters, etc. (see [Mcal93] for a discussion of 3D input devices). There are no devices which permit 3D animators to draw in space over long periods of time. This is an important product design problem which is yet to be solved.

In monocular or $2^{1}/_{2}$ D graphics, requiring the user to manipulate multiple input devices increases the chance for error. This problem is exacerbated by stereo, since the user must re-fuse the image each time he returns to view the screen. Better and more flexible input devices must be designed to allow rapid and error-free 3D input of vectors, curves, text, 3D objects, etc., without requiring the user to move between various input devices.

Stereo Algorithms

Rendering of left and right eye views need not require twice the time of rendering a single frame. There are simplifications which can be exploited to reduce the required rendering time in certain cases. It is often the case that much of the work done independently for each eye view is redundant. Adelson et al. [Adel91] describe ways to recognize and exploit this redundancy, thereby increasing efficiency. Several of the modifications exploit the fact that homologous points lie on the same scanline (that is, have common y values); others use the interocular distance and the depth to compute parallax (see the earlier section on minimizing absolute parallax). An example of the latter is the pixel shifting algorithm described below.

PIXEL SHIFTING

The pixel shiing algorithm was originally designed to produce many stereo pairs quickly for approximation of the images in a holographic stereogram [Mcal93]. Once a left eye image is computed, the right eye image is quickly approximated. The strategy uses linear interpolation to shift pixel values to approximate different perspective images [Love90]. If the x coordinate is given for one eye and the depth is known (say from a z-buffer computation), then the coordinate of the point for the other eye is easily computed.

There is obviously a problem with hidden surfaces. It almost surely happens that there are surfaces which are visible in the right image which are not visible in the left. Since they are not present on the screen, shifting pixels around cannot produce them. Instead, gaps appear in the image wherever new surfaces become exposed. The extent to which this is a problem depends upon the image. The problem is similar to those described in the section on ray tracing stereo images.

The pixel shifting strategy is beneficial in applications where speed is critical. Interactive manipulations can have one of the stereo images computed and the others interpolated. Alternating which eye point sees the interpolated images helps prevent gaps from becoming a problem.

STEREO RAY TRACING

A variation of the method outlined here was first applied to speed up image generation for the frames of an animation sequence [Badt88]. Later it was adapted by Adelson and Hodges [Adel89, 92] for generating simultaneous stereoscopic left eye and right eye images. In this method, a technique called re-projection is used to infer the right eye view image from the ray-traced left eye image. The color of a pixel is determined using only the initial intersection ray and a shadow ray. The method does not allow for reflection and transparency rays [Deva91].

The algorithm proceeds from left to right across a scanline for the left eye view. A data structure is created for each pixel on the scanline for the right eye view. Each time an intersection occurs with an object and a ray cast from the left eye through a pixel, the lighting and texture mapping for that point is determined in the normal way. Then a re-projected ray is cast from the intersection point back to the right eye (see Figure 11). The pixel which intersects the re-projected ray is set to the color of the object determined from the left eye ray, with a correction for specular highlighting.

It is possible to have more than one point re-project to the same pixel in the right eye view. This can happen if there is an object which intersects the re-projection vector to the right eye, causing what Badt calls an overlapped pixel problem [Badt88]. The object with the closest intersection point takes precedence, and the color is determined in the usual way. The locations of the intersections with the pixel are rarely identical. There may be some way to use the multiple intersections to antialias. Adelson and Hodges choose the one closest to the center of the pixel and then antialias using nine rays per pixel [Adel92].

The re-projection of a right eye view pixel from the left eye view pixel is dependent on the z value of the image in the left eye pixel. Quite often the z values of two adjacent pixels in the left eye view are such that the second left eye pixel is re-projected more than one pixel away from the first. It can happen that sometime earlier or later in the scanline other pixels could have been or will be re-projected into this gap. The pixel becomes a 'bad' pixel; there may be a closer intersection point from the right eye which cannot be seen by the left eye, and hence the pixel may or may not have the correct information for the right eye image.

The data structure for the right eye would have an entry for every pixel in a scanline, each containing a Boolean flag which is set to true if there is re-projection to that pixel, and a field which holds the color value for the pixel. By processing the pixels from left to right and overwriting the scanline record every time a re-projection occurs, the correct object is always re-projected to the pixels in the right eye view. The bad pixel problem is solved by setting the flags of all the intervening pixels as false for the right eye view when a jump of more than one pixel occurs. Thus, all bad pixels are forced into becoming missed pixels; they are pixels corresponding to the right eye view which do not exist in the left eye view and must be ray traced for the right eye.

In [Adel92] the authors claimed an average speed-up of 80% over 30 scenes. Preliminary theoretical and experimental results suggest a speed-up of as much as 60% if transparency and reflections are included.

SCANLINE ALGORITHMS

A standard scanline polygon-fill algorithm makes use of an active edge list which is sorted and traversed by the y coordinate. Since the y coordinates of the polygons in the two separate eye views do not differ, only one active edge list

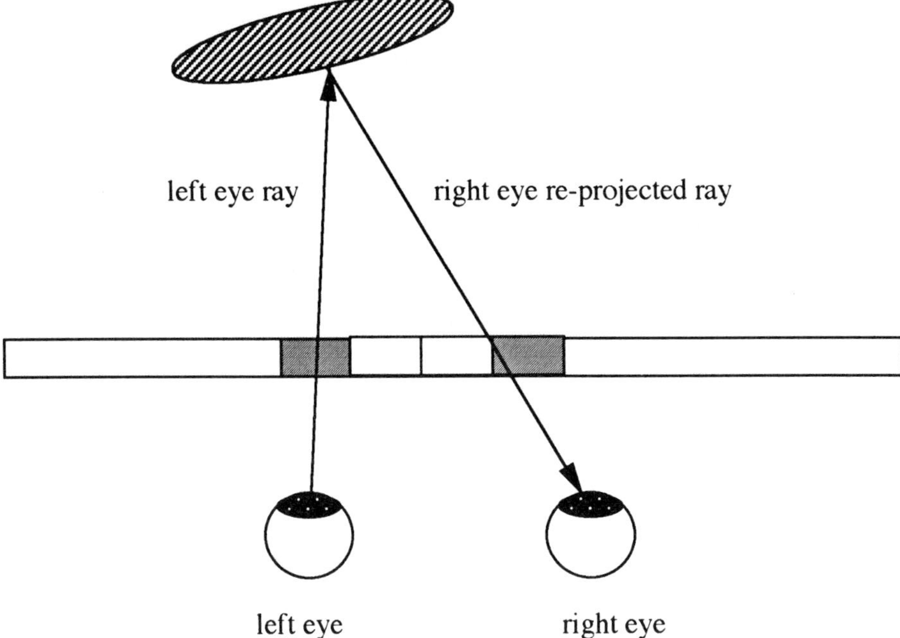

Figure 11. Re-projection.

need be kept for both eye views. This active edge list must keep separate data for the left eye x coordinates and the right eye x coordinates, and the polygon must be filled simultaneously in both eye views. All the work to update the active edge list can be shared, but the rest of the work must be done separately. For polygons with few sides this means that the improvement would be negligible, but for polygons with many sides significant work could be saved.

Either the scanline fill or the hidden surface modification can also include Gouraud shading by interpolating pixel colors along a given scanline. Since the normal vector to a polygon is independent of the observer, a vertex has the same color regardless of the viewer's position. Each vertex has the same color in both the left and right eye views, and since the height of the polygon does not change between eye views, the interpolation of color for the endpoints on a given scanline is shared between the two eye views. However, one eye view of the polygon can have more area than the other. Hence, the interpolation of color along the scanline must be done separately for each eye view.

Clipping Algorithms

The y coordinate of a line or polygon edge is the same in both eye views, so the y parametric equation for the line need only be calculated once. Thus, clipping the line against the top or bottom borders of the screen need only be done once for the pair. Unfortunately, clipping against the left and right sides must be done separately for each eye view. The stereo Liang-Barsky line clipping algorithm [Lian84] saves a considerable amount of work, since the top and bottom comparisons are a significant part of the calculations. The savings on the polygon clipping algorithm, however, are negligible, since the computation of intersection segments must be done separately for each eye view.

Backface Removal

Assume a normal to a polygon, $\vec{N} = [A, B, C]$, points away from the 'outward' face. A polygon is a backface relative to the eye point $\vec{L} = (X_v, Y_v, Z_v)$ if the outward face cannot be 'seen' from the eye point. Backfaces need not be rendered or passed to a hidden surface algorithm. The standard backface removal algorithm compares the normal $\vec{N}$ with a vector from the eye point $\vec{L} = (X_v, Y_v, Z_v)$ to a vertex P on the polygon. If $Q = \vec{N} \cdot (\overrightarrow{P - L}) < 0$, the polygon is a backface. If e is defined as the interocular distance, then the right eye coordinates are $R = (X_v + e, Y_v, Z_v)$ and $\vec{N} \cdot (\overrightarrow{P - R}) = \vec{N} \cdot \vec{P} - \vec{N} \cdot [\overrightarrow{L + e(1, 0, 0)}] = \vec{N} \cdot (\overrightarrow{P - L}) - Ae = Q - Ae$. We note that if the polygon is a backface for the left eye, then it is also a backface for the right eye. Similarly, if it is a front face for the right eye then it is a front face for the left eye (see Figure 12). Hence, since $e > 0$, if $Q < 0$ and $A > 0$ then the polygon is a backface for both eyes and can be removed or culled. If $Q > 0$ and $A < 0$, then the polygon is a front face for both eyes and must be retained. If neither is the case, then the signs of Q and $Q - Ae$ may be different and must be treated independently. The algorithm saves about 33% of the work of doing two separate backface removal operations.

Data Compression

The elimination of redundant image information is an important topic in communications and data storage requirements. Harrison and McAllister describe studies of both lossless and lossy compression of computer generated stereo pairs using the JPEG standard (see [Hari92]). The conclusion is that except in cases where there are only high frequency terms (such as a random dot stereogram) the JPEG standard appears to compress stereo pairs adequately without significant loss of depth even in the lossy case. There has been no investigation of the application of the new MPEG standard for the compression of stereo pairs. One would expect good results, since the left and right eye images are similar.

Color quantization is used to display images on graphics display devices when the frame buffer does not have a sufficient number of bit planes to represent all colors in the image, or it can be used to reduce or compress the amount of image data which must be transmitted over a network. A color quantization algorithm selects a set of colors based on those occurring in the original image and renders the image using these colors appropriately. This set must be such that it best represents the color information in the original image using some metric or measuring technique, i.e., the 'difference' between the original and the quantized

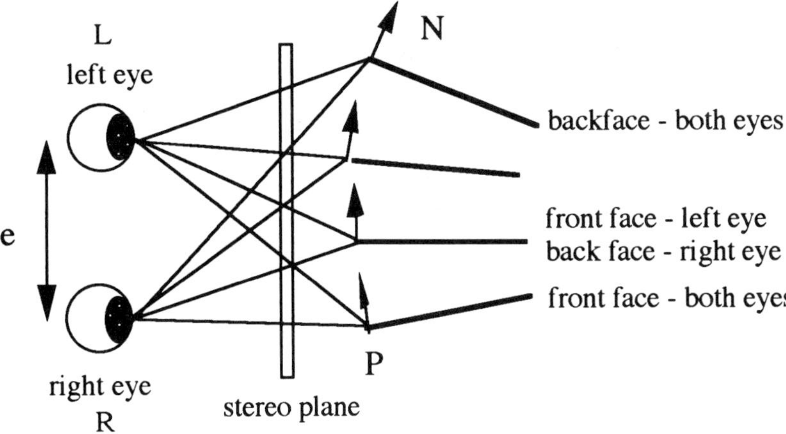

Figure 12. Backface removal.

image must be minimized according to some algorithm for measuring differences. This set is then loaded into the color lookup table (CLUT) for the frame buffer, and the index for the CLUT entry is then used instead of the actual 24-bit pixel value. Heckbert's paper [Heck82] is an excellent survey of several techniques.

Quantization can introduce extraneous contours in the image, since there may not be enough colors to produce 'smooth' shading. It can also introduce discontinuities and lack of definition in the image. Color quantization, when applied to stereo pairs, produces noise and loss of depth in certain cases [Hebb91]. Depending on the algorithm used, it can happen that the representative color subset *does not contain any of the original colors* if the image is coarsely quantized.

Color Quantization of Stereo Pairs

Using different CLUTs for each eye can produce corresponding features in the two views which are assigned different colors. This can lead to fatigue when viewing the stereo pair. Rather than combine the colors in an additive fashion, the eye perceives the colors shifting from the color in one view to the color in the other. This phenomenon, called binocular rivalry, is described in [Leve68].

If we use a single CLUT, a single set of representative colors obtained after processing both the views is used for rendering the quantized views. Here, the representative set is selected from a color histogram that has the color information of both the views. In general, stereo pairs do not differ widely in their color content. Thus, there are many colors common to both views. This means that each view gets more CLUT entries than is possible with the previous approach.

The smooth shading and specular highlights on three-dimensional objects in an image act as depth cues. Such an object is comprised of many colors. Quantization of these scenes leads to reduction in the colors present, and hence affects the depth cues in ways which depend on the particular algorithm. The quantization is manifested as bands or contours in the image. In extreme cases, the object loses most of its gradual shading and shows strongly demarcated regions. Such objects tend to flatten out and appear as two-dimensional objects in the 3D space seen by the viewer.

In certain situations, quantization leads to loss of boundary definition and introduction of discontinuities. Let A and B be two objects, where one partially obscures the other. Let their colors be C_A and C_B, respectively. If the distance between C_A and C_B is small, then both these colors can fall into the same quantization cell and hence get mapped to a single color. Thus, the boundary between the objects is lost. This can also happen when the image background color is close to the object color. In this case, parts of the object merge into the background. This can create nonsolid objects from solid ones.

Color Quantization of Animation

When quantization is applied to animation sequences, quantization of individual stereo pairs can cause a drift in the color of the objects. Sistare and Friedell [Sist89] used all the possible colors that can be generated in an animation sequence to build a static CLUT to be used for the entire animation sequence. However, this leads to increased quantization error in a single frame if methods similar to octree quantization are used, as each frame may not have all the colors that were used to build the CLUT. It may be possible to quantize over several frame sequences in parallel and then combine the resulting CLUTs. Methods are needed to allow weighting of specific frames to minimize differences between colors of frames at the boundaries of frame sequences, so that jump discontinuities in color do not occur.

MOTION BLUR IN STEREO ANIMATION

In computer animation we render a series of images, each representing a specific point in time. We discretize motion into single frames which can produce temporal aliasing; motion can appear to produce a strobing effect and be discontinuous. To reduce temporal aliasing, we simulate the image such as produced by a camera which records the motion during the opening of the shutter. We blur or smear the image in the direction of motion of the objects in the scene, the blurring being a function of the speed and direction of motion and frame time.

Motion blur is commonly achieved by one of three methods — stretching the object along the path of motion; stochastic sampling in the time domain; and supersampling over time. In the latter two cases ray tracing is used to render the blur. Patel and McAllister [Pate92] showed that traditional methods for creating motion blur can produce images with ambiguous depth when combined with stereo.

Monoscopic Motion Blur Techniques

In stochastic sampling each pixel is computed for a randomly determined point in time lying between two adjacent frame times. Aliasing is replaced by noise introduced to the correct average value. Note that we are effectively jittering the position of the object in space, and the average position is the average spatial position of the image over the frame time. Stochastic sampling has little extra cost but can produce grainy images; it places no limits on the path of motion — the path can be arbitrarily complex.

In supersampling several rays are passed through a given pixel, each for a different point in time. The resulting values are averaged to determine the pixel value. Nonadaptive supersampling reduces temporal aliasing, but there can always be objects moving faster than the time between each subframe. Adaptive supersampling continues subsampling until the change between rays is below a threshold. This can remove aliasing altogether but is computationally very costly. However, it avoids computing extra rays where they are not needed. Supersampling is very easy to implement. We simply render several subframes and then average the pixel values. This requires no modification to a generic raytracer.

Stretching uses a filter to scale the object in the direction of motion, i.e., we convert a time problem into a spatial one. Creating filters is feasible only for simple objects and simple paths. If the object representation overlaps from frame to frame, strobing is minimized or not noticeable. For rapidly moving objects, however, the resulting image can be very misleading, as the objects appear larger than they actually are. Implementation is also difficult. The path can not be arbitrarily complex, since the required filters are difficult to implement. Because of these problems, stochastic and/or supersampling is commonly used to produce motion blur in monoscopic computer animation.

Monoscopic Techniques for Stereo Motion Blur

If we apply the techniques described above in a straightforward way to render left and right eye views in a stereo pair, we find that the simulation of motion blur produces poor results when viewing single frames. When creating stereo images while using stochastic sampling, each eye sees different points on the object at a pixel location over time, creating discrepancies in the left and right views. Basically, the left eye sees a particular point on the object at a time t_1. The right eye may see that same point at a time t_2. If the object is moving we lose the correlation between the left and right views, as the position in space can change between t_1 and t_2. For moving objects, especially rapidly moving objects, there is no correlation between corresponding points in the two views, so the object appears flat along the view plane. It is similar to the situation in which each eye is presented with totally different images: no depth is perceived.

Supersampling produces images that are averages of several disparate images of the same object, making it difficult to fuse the views. Thus, the depth of the blur appears ambiguous. In supersampling, basically we average pixel values over a series of subframes. If the object is moving, the positions for the time frames we average are different for each view. However, there is some correspondence between the left and right views. Plate 22 is an example of supersampling applied for a stereo image. Note that the depth of the blur is ambiguous.

Simply scaling the object does not distort depth information. However, it looks unnatural and is misleading because it distorts object sizes. The stretched object method works well with stereo, because there is consistency in both views since it permits us to produce both eye views from a fixed point in time. Filters that blur along a continuous path of motion analytically are complicated and limited, and were not considered.

It is possible to improve supersampling by choosing a filter that emphasizes certain instances of the image, e.g., heavily weighting the filter toward the center position. If there are a small number of object positions, the visual system can usually fuse the image and see consistent depth. The resulting blur is not smooth, but the technique then requires no change to a raytracer.

A Proposed Solution

Patel and McAllister [Pate92] extended the object in the direction of motion, much like stretching. However, instead of actually scaling the object they superimposed a set of objects, each representing a spatial location for the original object at a particular time instant. A transparency is assigned to each instance of the object to achieve the desired motion blur. The object's size is not actually changed, but the superimposed object is effectively a stretched object.

Arbitrarily complex motion is possible. This appears to be equivalent to supersampling but is not. In supersampling the individual object instances are in different time frames. With complex motion, individual object instances all exist in the same time frame. To get a fading effect, transparency functions are used. Transparency is set for each 'subobject', and all are rendered. This method is computationally very expensive for three reasons — there are many more objects to render; each object is now transparent; and the maximum ray depth for the rendering must be increased. This has the advantage that no modification to the ray tracer need be made; the scene is simply modeled and rendered. This works well if only a few spatial locations are used, but depth can be ambiguous if too many subobjects with rapid motion are used. This is because the transparency also causes different depths to be averaged in at each pixel.

The technique of stretching has all of the advantages associated with distributed ray-tracing: shadows are motion blurred; the path of motion can be as complex as desired; and reflections, intersections, depth of field, etc., can be correctly rendered. However, the above algorithm does not produce a complete solution for rendering stereo motion blur.

Transparency creates other difficulties. We see through to the other side of the object. Using distributed ray tracing, the object is rendered accurately and then the results are averaged. With their method, parts of the objects that would be occluded may be visible. Similarly, objects behind the front object and moving at the same rate should be partially or wholly hidden. However, transparency allows us to see them.

Combining the monoscopic techniques with the re-projection technique described above may be possible. A satisfactory solution has not been proposed.

Conclusions

The improvement in technology and availability of stereo has galvanized research in stereo computer graphics. Areas such as stereo animation have motivated the development of stereo drawing devices, inspired research in data compression and algorithms for stereo motion blur, etc. Work on stereo interfaces is beginning to appear. The field of stereo computer graphics continues to be a rich area for researchers.

REFERENCES

[Adel91]
 Adelson, S.J., Bentley, J.B., Chong, I.S., Hodges, L.F., and Winograd, J., Simultaneous generation of stereoscopic views, *Comput. Graph. Forum*, No. 10, pp. 3–10, 1991.

[Adel92]
 Adelson, S.J., and Hodges, L.F., Visible surface ray-tracing of stereoscopic images, *Proc. 30th S.E. Regional ACM*, Raleigh, NC, pp. 148–156, April 1992.

[Ande90]
 Andersen, G.J., Focused attention in three-dimensional space, *Perception and Psychophysics*, Vol. 47, No. 2, pp. 112–120, February 1990.

[Badl86]
 Badler, N.I., Manoochehri, K.H., and Baraff, D., Multi-dimensional input techniques and articulated figure positioning by multiple constraints, *Proc. 1986 Workshop on Interactive 3D Graphics*, University of North Carolina, Chapel Hill, NC, October 23–24, 1986.

[Badt88]
 Badt, S., Jr., Two algorithms taking advantage of temporal coherence in ray tracing, *The Visual Computer*, Vol. 4, pp. 123–132, 1988.

[Barh91]
 Barham, P.T., and McAllister, D.F., A comparison of stereoscopic cursors for the interactive manipulation of B-splines, *SPIE Proc. Stereoscopic Displays and Applications II*, Vol. 1457, pp. 18–26, 1991.

[Beat87]
 Beaton, R.J., Dehoff, R.J., Weiman, N., and Hildebrandt, P.W., Evaluation of input devices for 3D computer display workstations, *SPIE Proc. True Three-Dimensional Imaging Techniques and Display Technologies*, Vol. 761, pp. 94–101, 1987.

[Beat88]
 Beaton, R.J., and Weiman, W., User evaluation of cursor-positioning devices for 3-D display workstations, *SPIE Proc. Three-Dimensional Imaging and Remote Sensing Imaging*, Vol. 902, pp. 53–58, 1988.

[Bier86]
 Bier, E.A., Skitters and jacks: Interactive 3D positioning tools, *Proc. 1986 Workshop on Interactive 3D Graphics*, University of North Carolina, Chapel Hill, NC, October 23–24, 1986.

[Brid87]
Bridges, A.L., and Reising, J.M., Three-dimensional stereographic pictorial visual interfaces and display systems in flight simulation, *SPIE Proc. True Three-Dimensional Imaging Techniques and Display Technologies*, Vol. 761, pp. 102–112, 1987.

[Burt88]
Burton, R.P., Becker, S.C., Broekhuijsen, B.J., Hale, B.J., and Richardson, A.E., Advanced concepts in device input for 3-D display, *SPIE Proc. Three-Dimensional Imaging and Remote Sensing Imaging*, Vol. 902, pp. 59–63, 1988.

[Butt88]
Butts, D.R.W., and McAllister, D.F., Implementation of true 3-D cursors in computer graphics, *SPIE Proc. Three-Dimensional Imaging and Remote Sensing Imaging*, Vol. 902, pp. 74–83, 1988.

[Carv91]
Carver, D.E., and McAllister, D.F., Human interface design for stereo CAD systems, *SPIE Proc. Stereoscopic Displays and Applications II*, Vol. 1457, pp. 54–65, 1991.

[Deho89]
DeHoff, R.J., and HildeBrandt, P.W. (for Tektronix, Inc.), Cursor for use in 3-D Imaging Systems, United States Patent Number 4,808,979, February 1989.

[Deva91]
Devarajan, R., and McAllister, D.F., Rendering of stereo images of implicit surfaces, *SPIE Proc. Stereoscopic Displays and Applications II*, Vol. 1457, pp. 37–53, 1991.

[Goge90]
Gogel, W.C., A theory of phenomenal geometry and its applications, *Perception and Psychophysics*, Vol. 48, No. 2, pp. 105–123, August 1990.

[Hari92]
Harrison, L., and McAllister, D.F., Problems with lossy compression of stereo pairs, *SPIE Proc. Stereoscopic Displays and Applications III*, SPIE/IS&T Electronic Imaging, Vol. 1669, pp. 39–50, 1992.

[Hebb91]
Hebbar, P.D., and McAllister, D.F., Color quantization aspects in stereopsis, *SPIE Proc. Stereoscopic Displays and Applications II*, Vol. 1457, pp. 233–241, 1991.

[Heck82]
Heckbert, P., Color image quantization for frame buffer display, *Comput. Graph.*, Vol. 16, pp. 297–307, 1982 (SIGGRAPH 82).

[Hodg87]
Hodges, L.F., and McAllister, D.F., True three-dimensional CRT-based displays, *Information Display*, Vol. 3, No. 5, pp. 18–22, 1987.

[Hodg90]
Hodges, L., and McAllister, D.F., Rotation algorithm artifacts in stereoscopic images, *Optical Engng.*, Vol. 29, No. 8, pp. 973–976, 1990.

[Hodg92]
Hodges, L., Tutorial: Time-multiplexed stereoscopic computer graphics, *IEEE Comput. Graph. and Appl.*, Vol. 12, No. 2, pp. 20–30, March 1992.

[Jule71]
Julesz, B., *Foundations of Cyclopean Perception*, Chicago: University of Chicago Press, pp. 10, 239–241, 1971.

[Kilp76]
Kilpatrick, P.J., "The use of a Kinesthetic Suppliment in an Interactive Graphics System," Ph.D. diss., University of North Carolina at Chapel Hill, 1976.

[Kim89]
Kim, W.S., Ellis, S.R., Tyler, M.E., Hannaford, B., and Stark, L.W., Quantitative evaluation of perspective and stereoscopic displays in three-axis manual tracking tasks, *IEEE Transactions of Systems, Man, and Cybernetics*, Vol. SMC-17, No. 1, pp. 61–72, January/February 1987.

[Leve68]
Levelt, W.J.M., *On Binocular Rivalry*, The Hague: Mouton, 1968.

[Levk84]
Levkowitz, H., Trivedi, S.S., and Udupa, J.K., Interactive manipulation of 3D data via a 2D display device, *SPIE Proc. Processing and Display of Three-Dimensional Data II*, Vol. 507, pp. 25–37, 1984.

[Lian84]
Liang, Y.D., and Barsky, B., A new concept and method for line clipping, *ACM TOG*, Vol. 3, pp. 1–22, 1984.

[Lips79]
Lipscomb, J., "Three-dimensional Cues for a Molecular Computer Graphics System," Ph.D. diss., Department of Computer Science, University of North Carolina, Chapel Hill, NC, 1979.

[Lips89]
Lipscomb, J.S., Experience with stereoscopic display devices and output algorithms, *SPIE Proc. Three-Dimensional Visualization and Display Technologies*, Vol. 1083, pp. 28–34, 1989.

[Lipt82]
Lipton, L., *Foundations of the Stereoscopic Cinema*, New York: Van Nostrand Reinhold, 1982.

[Love90]
Love, S., "Nonholographic, Autostereoscopic, Nonplanar Display of Computer Generated Images," Ph.D. diss., Department of Computer Science, North Carolina State University, Raleigh, NC, 1990.

[Mcal92a]
McAllister, David F., Minimizing absolute parallax in stereo graphics, *SPIE Proc. Stereoscopic Displays and Applications III*, SPIE/IS&T Electronic Imaging, Vol. 1669, pp. 20–30, 1992.

[Mcal92b]
McAllister, D.F., 3D displays, *Byte*, Vol. 17, pp. 183–188, May 1992.

[Mcal93]
McAllister, D.F., Ed., *3D Computer Graphics*, Princeton, NJ: Princeton University Press (in press).

[Mosh88]
Mosher, C.E., Jr., Sherouse, F.W., Chaney, E.L., and Rosenman, J.G., 3-D displays and user interface design for a radiation therapy treatment planning CAD tool, *SPIE Proc. Three-Dimensional Imaging and Remote Sensing Imaging*, Vol. 902, pp. 64–72, 1988.

[Naka89]
Nakayama, F., Shimojo, S., and Silverman, G.H., Stereoscopic depth: Its relation to image segmentation, grouping, and the recognition of occluded objects, *Perception*, Vol. 18, No. 1, pp. 55–68, 1989.

[Niel86]
Nielson, G.M., and Olsen, D.R., Jr., Direct manipulation techniques for 3D objects using 2D locator devices, *Proc. 1986 Workshop on Interactive 3D Graphics*, University of North Carolina, Chapel Hill, NC, October 23–24, 1986.

[Okos76]
Okoshi, T., *Three Dimensional Imaging Techniques*, New York: Academic Press, 1976.

[Pate92]
Patel, M., and McAllister, D.F., Combining motion blur and stereo, *SPIE Proc. Stereoscopic Displays and Applications III*, SPIE/IS&T Electronic Imaging, Vol. 1669, pp. 71–82, 1992.

[Rein90]
Reinhart, W.F., Beaton, R.J., and Snyder, H.L., Comparison of depth cues for relative depth judgements, *SPIE Proc. Stereoscopic Displays and Applications*, Vol. 1256, pp. 12–21, 1990.

[Robi91]
Robinett, W., and Rolland, J.P., A computational model for the stereoscopic optics of a head-mounted display, *SPIE Proc. Stereoscopic Displays and Applications II*, Vol. 1457, pp. 140–160, 1991.

[Roge80]
Rogers, D.F., and Satterfield, S.G., B-spline surfaces for ship hull design, *Comput. Graph.*, Vol. 14, pp. 211–217, 1980 (SIGGRAPH 80).

[Roge90]
Rogers, D.F., and Adams, J.A., *Mathematical Elements for Computer Graphics*, 2nd ed., New York: McGraw-Hill, 1990.

[Schm83]
Schmandt, C., Spatial input/display correspondence in a stereoscopic computer graphic work station, *Comput. Graph.*, Vol. 17, pp. 253–261, 1983 (SIGGRAPH 83).

[Sist89]
Sistare, S., and Friedell, M., A distributed system for near-real-time display of shaded three-dimensional graphics, *Proc. Graphics Interface '89*, pp. 283–290, 1989.

[Star91]
Starks, M., Stereoscopic video and the quest for virtual reality: An annotated bibliography of selected topics, *SPIE Proc. Stereoscopic Displays and Applications II*, Vol. 1457, pp. 327–342, 1991.

[Tilt87]
Tilton, H.B., *The 3-D Oscilloscope: A Practical Manual and Guide*, Englewood Cliffs, NJ: Prentice-Hall, 1987.

[Valy82]
Valyus, N.A., *Stereoscopy*, London: Focal Press, 1982.

[Wald86]
Waldern, J.D., Humrich, A., and Cochrane, L., Studying depth cues in a three-dimensional computer graphics workstation, *Int. Jour. Man-machine Studies*, Vol. 24, pp. 645–657, June 1986.

[Wick90]
Wickens, C.D., Kramer, A., Andersen, J., Glassner, A., and Sarno, K., Focused and divided attention in stereoscopic depth, *SPIE Proc. Stereoscopic Displays and Applications*, Vol. 1256, pp. 28–34, 1990.

[Wixs88]
Wixson, S.E., and Sloane, M.E., Managing windows as transparent pages in a stereoscopic display, *SPIE Proc. Three-Dimensional Imaging and Remote Sensing Imaging*, Vol. 902, pp. 113–116, 1988.

[Wixs90]
Wixson, S.E., Volume visualization on a stereoscopic display, *SPIE Proc. Stereoscopic Displays and Applications*, Vol. 1256, pp. 110–112, 1990.

[Wrig92]
Wright, J., and McAllister, D.F., Interactive design of rational Bézier tensor product surfaces in stereo, Technical Report, Department of Computer Science, North Carolina State University, Raleigh, NC 27695-8206, 1992.

[Yeh90]
Yeh, Y.Y., and Silverstein, L.D., Limits of fusion and depth judgement in stereoscopic color displays, *Human Factors*, Vol. 32, pp. 45–60, February 1990.

Synthetic Experience[†]

Warren Robinett

Warren Robinett

Abstract

A taxonomy is proposed to classify all varieties of technologically-mediated experience. This includes virtual reality and teleoperation, and also earlier devices such as the microscope and telephone. The model of mediated interaction assumes a sensor-display link from the world to the human, and an action-actuator link going back from the human to the world, with the mediating technology transforming the transmitted experience in some way. The taxonomy is used to classify a number of example systems.

Introduction

The Head-Mounted Display (HMD) has been used in two distinctly different kinds of applications — teleoperation, in which a human operator's senses are projected into a remote robot body; and virtual environments, in which the human can move through and interact with a three-dimensional computer generated virtual world. New uses for the HMD are currently being discovered, such as in-flight simulation, night vision goggles, microteleoperation, and augmented reality.

This paper proposes a taxonomy for classifying systems which incorporate a HMD. Systems are classified according to nine independent dimensions, each of which can take on a number of discrete values. The domain of this classification method is broad enough to also include technological precursors to the HMD, such as the telescope, microscope, television, and telephone.

This taxonomy attempts to impose some sense onto a very broad and very new area which is pregnant with unexplored possibilities. The method of extracting order from chaos is to cleave the set of possible systems into a small number of disjoint sets by imposing distinctions. Each of these distinctions corresponds to a dimension of the taxonomy. For example, the dimension called 'causality' distinguishes between teleoperation, in which the operator's actions affect the real

---

world, and virtual environments, in which the operator's actions affect only a simulated world. Other dimensions have to do with the sensory modalities used by the systems (vision, hearing, touch, and others), the nature of the representations (or models) of the environments surrounding the user, and displacements or scaling in time or space between the user's true position and the environment with which the user interacts.

The attempt to classify, or even talk about, devices which produce reproductions of sensory experience immediately introduces difficult issues in philosophy, psychology, and other fields. What is experience? What is reality? What is a representation of the world, or of an object? Is perfect reproduction of human sensory experience possible? Many more questions and issues of this sort could be listed here. Rather than be scared off by these difficult and complex issues, I have tried to mention the issues that I think are relevant to the discussion, and leave it to others to correct and clarify errors and omissions, if they desire. I hope this taxonomy can serve as a point of departure for us collectively to understand and develop Head-Mounted Displays into useful and widely-used tools.

The discussion in this paper is somewhat biased by my own experience in designing computer-simulated virtual worlds, and my lack of detailed knowledge of the work done over the last several decades in teleoperation, and perhaps other related fields. All of us in this diverse field have our specialties and our blind spots. My experience tells me that the distinctions that I put forward in this paper are important ones, and rather than waiting until I achieve broad knowledge of all the fields touching on virtual worlds, I put these ideas forward now to serve as a starting point for discussion.

The common theme of all these devices and systems is *technologically-mediated experience*. The older systems use optics or analog electronics to mediate and transform the user's experience, whereas the more recent systems rely heavily on computers and digital electronics. In both cases, the general model of technologically-mediated experience is the same (see Figure 1).

The new devices incorporating the HMD did not come out of nowhere, but are extensions and refinements of earlier devices and media. Media began to evolve thousands of years ago when prehistoric man created visual representations of the world, using paint. Painting was followed by the telescope, the microscope, photography, the phonograph, the telephone, film, television, and video games. Each of these devices derives its usefulness from being able to modify, record, or transmit some aspect of human sensory experience. For each of these devices, sensory experience is captured, processed, and then displayed to a human user.

The HMD is one step further along this evolutionary path. It improves on earlier visual media by being able to give the user a perception of a surrounding three-dimensional space, rather than just a look into a space from a fixed viewpoint. It is not simply a visual display technique, but rather a multisensory display technique (involving vision, the vestibular system, and the proprioceptive system) in which visuals depicting the surrounding 3D virtual world are generated so as to match the user's voluntary head movements.

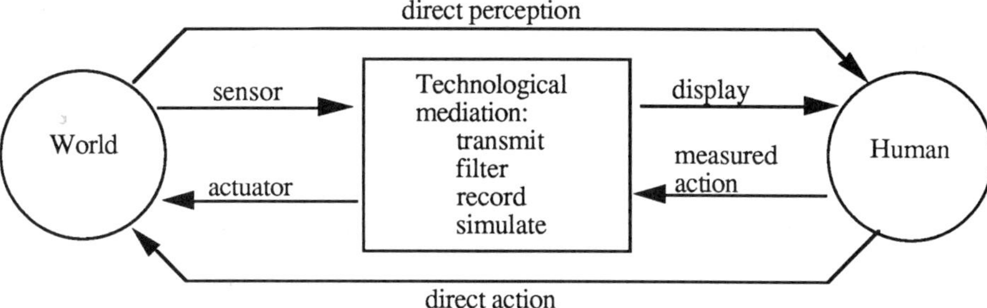

Figure 1. Technologically-mediated experience.

Two classes of experience are discussed, natural experience, i.e., directly perceiving the properties or behavior of something physically present in front of the perceiver; and synthetic experience, i.e., perceiving a representation or simulacrum of something physically real rather than the thing itself. Webster's Ninth New Collegiate Dictionary helps to clarify the term 'synthetic experience' by defining:

experience

> direct observation of or participation in events as a basis of knowledge;

> the conscious events that make up an individual's life;

> the act or process of directly perceiving events or reality;

synthetic

> devised, arranged, or fabricated for special situations to imitate or replace usual realities;

> something resulting from synthesis rather than occurring naturally;

synthesis

> the composition or combination of parts or elements so as to form a whole.

The term synthetic experience encompasses virtual environments, teleoperation, other uses of the HMD, film, the telephone, video games, and most earlier media. It is meant to be synonymous with the term technologically-mediated experience, used earlier. We limit the scope of synthetic experience to reproductions of sensory experience. We exclude verbal descriptions such as novels and oral storytelling.

We also exclude theater from this classification system, though there is clearly a common thread running from storytelling to theater to film. That theater is in one sense a natural experience of watching human actors, and at the same time a re-creation of a (hypothetical) earlier action, shows that it can be difficult to draw a distinct boundary between natural and synthetic experience. In the broadest sense, a student's mimicking of a tennis pro's serve is a reproduction of an earlier action, and role-playing in group therapy is a simulated experience.

However, we limit the scope of synthetic experience to technologically-mediated reproductions of sensory experience.

EXAMPLES OF SYNTHETIC EXPERIENCE

Some of the most important current applications of the HMD are landmarks that help to map out the scope of synthetic experience. These examples are meant to illustrate the breadth of synthetic experience and are not meant to be definitions.

Virtual reality uses a stereoscopic, wide-angle HMD to create the illusion of a three-dimensional surrounding fantasy world, a 3D video game that allows one or more players to get inside and interact with one another [Blan90];

Flight simulation also defines a simulated 3D world in which actions have effects, but in this case the simulation is intended to accurately model the behavior of a real aircraft so as to give the pilot experience in dangerous situations without mistakes being fatal;

Teleoperation uses devices such as, for example, an HMD and force-feedback handgrip that are electronically linked to a distant robot body with a robot arm and a pair of video cameras on the robot head. The robot head turns to mimic the operator's head motions, and the robot arm mimics hand motions, so that the operator's eyes and hands are effectively projected into the remote environment. The operator can look around and do things through the robot body. The remote environment may be a dangerous one, such as the bottom of the ocean, inside a nuclear power plant, or in space;

Microteleoperation replaces the human-scale anthropomorphic robot of ordinary teleoperation with a microscope and micromanipulator, so as to give the operator the sense of presence and the ability to act in the microscopic environment. The Scanning-Tunneling Microscope (STM) is well-suited to microteleoperation, since it uses a tiny probe scanned over the sample surface to capture a 3D image of the surface (at atomic resolution). The probe tip can also be used as a micromanipulator to interact with the sample material [Robi92];

Telecommunication is familiar to us through daily use of the telephone. Video teleconferencing extends this remote communication with other humans to include the sense of sight, and to allow communication among groups of people rather than just two at a time. The operator of a telecontrolled robot is able to speak and listen to another human in front of the robot;

Technological masquerade has been used to study intraspecies communication in animals by using recordings and sophisticated puppets to fool the animals into behaving as if they were interacting with another member of their species. This has been done extensively with recorded bird calls [Brig84], and also with a computer-controlled robot bee, which was able to direct real bees to specific locations far from the hive by moving in the patterned 'dance' that bees use to communicate and then dispensing a sweet liquid 'sample' of the (pretended) distant pollen [Weis89]. The connection with synthetic experience is that a human could potentially teleoperate a robot bee to attempt to communicate in real time with real bees;

Augmented reality uses a see-through HMD, in which half-silvered mirrors allow the user to see through directly to the real world, and at the same time spatially superimpose the virtual world on top of the real world. The superimposed virtual world may be labels or diagrams located at specific points in the real world [Caud92]. It can also be information derived from sensors, which is superimposed onto the user's direct view of the real world, for example helicopter pilots flying at night through canyons and using Forward-Looking Infrared (FLIR) sensors, who also have a direct view out into the darkness in case there is anything bright enough to see.

A *synthetic sense* is created when a sensor for a phenomenon that is imperceptible to human senses is linked to a display device. This gives the user the ability to perceive phenomena that are invisible, silent, and intangible without technological augmentation. Night vision goggles are an example. Another example, currently being prototyped, allows an obstetrician to use a see-through HMD to view data from a hand-held ultrasound scanner. The physician can see and touch the abdomen of a pregnant woman, and sees the data from the ultrasound scanner superimposed at the location from which it came, giving the perception of seeing into the living tissue [Robi91a].

A *sensory prosthesis* corrects, amplifies, or otherwise improves the fidelity of an ordinary 'built-in' human sense. Examples are corrective spectacles, sunglasses, and hearing aids. For people with defective or nonfunctional senses, *sensory substitution* can compensate for the disability. For example, the Opticon [Linv73] is an optical-to-tactile transducer array which allows blind people, after some training, to read from ordinary printed books by, in effect, running their finger over the printed text and feeling the black marks as raised bumps.

Dimensions of Synthetic Experience

The proposed taxonomy for classifying types of synthetic experience is shown in Table 1. The nine dimensions of the classification system are largely independent of one another. Thus, the space of all possible types of synthetic experience should be conceived as a matrix (with nine dimensions) rather than a hierarchy. The first five dimensions describe the basic nature of the technological mediation in a synthetic experience device, whereas the last four dimensions have to do with which sensory channels and motor channels are employed.

Causality

The first dimension of the classification system, causality, makes the most fundamental distinctions among the types of synthetic experience. The three possibilities are to transmit, record, or simulate experience. These categories correspond

Table 1. Classification system for types of synthetic experience.

Dimension	Possibilities	Examples
Causality	simulated recorded transmitted	flight simulator film teleoperation
Model source	scanned constructed computed edited	night vision goggles video game computational fluid dynamics film
Time	one-to-one accelerated (or retarded) frozen distorted	film time-lapse photography photograph edited video recording of event
Space	registered remote miniaturized (or enlarged) distorted	night vision goggles teleoperation microteleoperation (STM) STM with heights exaggerated
Superposition	merged isolated	augmented reality virtual reality
Display type	HMD screen speaker (many more – see Table 3)	virtual reality video game recorded music
Sensor type	photomultiplier STM ultrasound scanner (many more – see Table 4)	night vision goggles microteleoperation medical 'X-ray vision'
Action measurement type	tracker and glove joystick force-feedback arm (many more – see Table 5)	virtual reality video game teleoperation
Actuator type	robot arm STM tip aircraft flaps (etc.)	teleoperation microteleoperation remote piloted aircraft

to the way that we experience the world — not only do we experience the present, but we also remember the past and imagine the future. Replaying a recording has similarities with remembering: it is re-experiencing past events. Participating in an interactive simulation has similarities with imagining: it is trying out courses of action on an imaginary stage, perhaps to see what the consequences might be. Engaging in real-time transmitted experience through, for example, a teleoperator system, has similarities with normal active experience in the present: your actions affect the world [Robi91b].

The effect of voluntary actions is different in each of these cases. In a simulated virtual world (for example, in a flight simulator), actions have effects within that simulated world, but not in the real world. (There is no plane to crash; nobody dies.) In a virtual world which is a real-time reproduction of some part of the real world (for example, a pilot flying a remote-piloted aircraft), actions do affect the real world. (The plane can crash and burn.) In a recording of past events (for example, the 'black box' recording of what happened in an airliner crash), what happened was recorded, and actions by the user cannot change what happened. This dimension is called 'causality' because, for the three cases of simulated, transmitted and recorded experience, actions by the user cause effects in the simulated world, effects in the real world, or no effects at all.

This dimension might possibly be called 'time,' since recordings replay past events, transmitted experience takes place in real-time in the present, and simulations sometimes are used to predict future events. However, simulations are not necessarily of the future (for example, a simulation of continental drift), so it is best to name this dimension causality to capture the real differences between transmitted, recorded, and simulated experience.

Figure 2 shows diagrams of the primary data flow for transmitted, recorded, and simulated experience, with each shown as a special case of the diagram for technologically-mediated experience in Figure 1. In the case of transmitted experience, the diagram of Figure 1 is a good model for the data flow — the user observes the world through the sensor-display data path and performs actions that affect the world through the action-actuator data path. In the case of recorded experience, the sensor data is stored in some kind of memory device (such as magnetic tape), and at a later time this data is replayed through the display to the user. An actuator is not needed in this activity, and user actions are only needed to control the replay process itself. In the case of simulated experience, the primary data path is from the measured actions of the user, through the simulation, and back through the display to the user. Again, the actuator is not needed, and the sensor channel is needed only if the simulated virtual world is based at least partly on scanned-in data from the real world.

The fourth diagram shown in Figure 2 is a variety of transmitted experience, with a data path introduced to allow autonomous actions by a telerobot, under supervision of a human operator. An operator could alternate between passive real-time observation of the telerobot's actions, and taking direct control of the telerobot's actions as in normal transmitted experience.

In a system in which all of these data paths are present, all of these modes of operation are possible. In the UNC Nanomanipulator Project (see Robinett et al. [Robi92]), for example, in which a HMD and force-feedback arm control a Scanning Tunneling Microscope (STM), transmitted experience, recorded experience, simulated experience, and supervisory control are all possible. The user can directly control the STM tip through the force-feedback arm and modify the sample surface (transmitted experience). The user can record a snapshot or sequence of images of the surface and view them through the HMD at a later time (recorded experience). The user can manipulate simulated molecules through the force-feedback arm and HMD with no connection to the microscope (simulated experience). Future plans include allowing the user to initiate algorithmically-controlled modifications of the sample surface, with the possibility of intervening (transmitted experience with supervisory control).

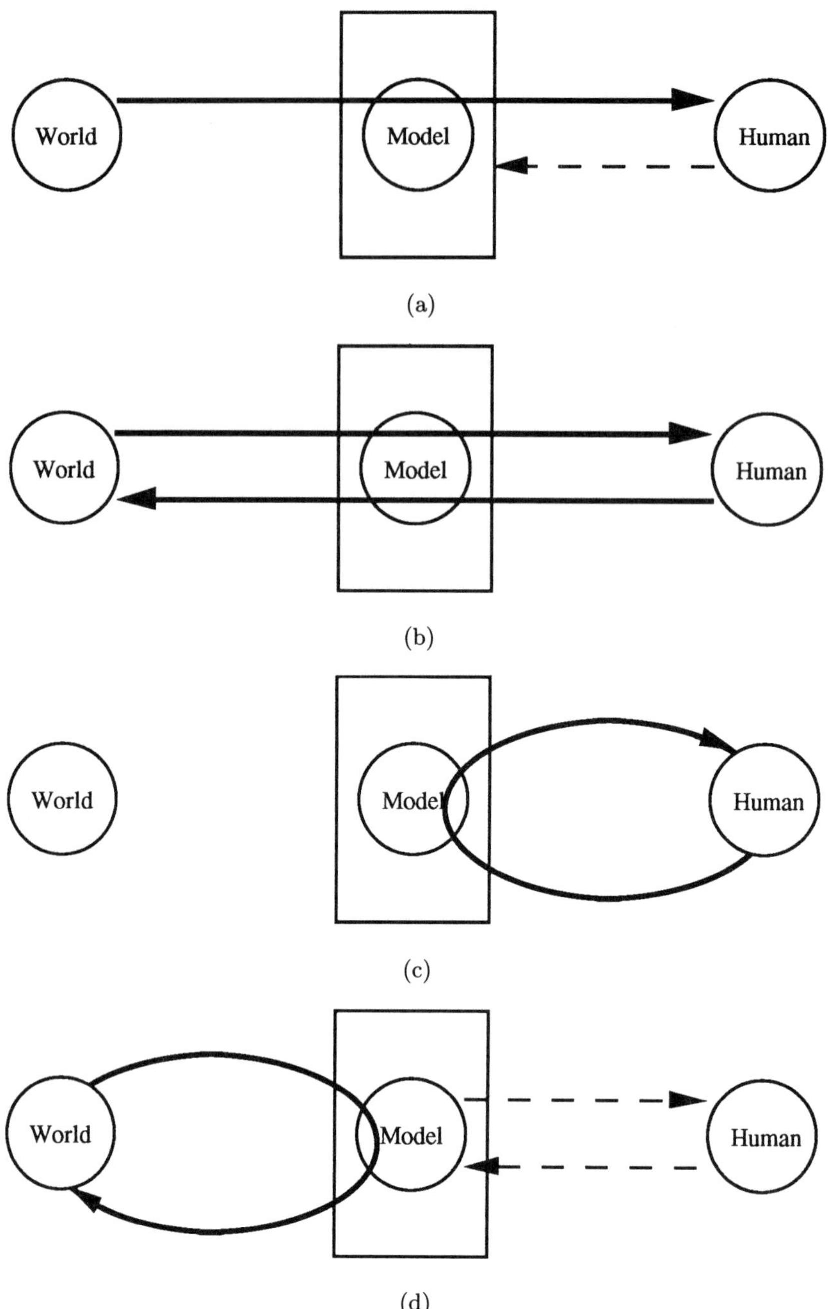

Figure 2. Data flow for types of mediated experience. (a) Recorded experience; (b) transmitted experience; (c) simulated experience; (d) robot (supervised by a human).

Model Source

In a synthetic experience, the human user perceives a virtual world which is defined by a (possibly changing) database called a model. This model is stored, at least transitorily, in some kind of memory device. The model defines what the virtual world looks like, sounds like, and feels like, according to which display devices are available.

There are three main sources for this model data. A sensor scans the real world to produce a model for later display to the user; a human artist or craftsman laboriously constructs a model, piece by piece; or a dynamic model is computed on the fly using a computational model. Examples of these three cases are live television, with the world scanned by the video camera; Disney-style animated cartoons, with each animation frame drawn by an artist; and computational fluid dynamics, where the simulation code generates new model data as needed. However, these cases are not exclusive, and a scanned-in model can be chopped up and edited to construct a model that is partly based on the real world, but is different. A good example of this is film, in which raw footage from the initial shooting is heavily edited, and some animated special effects are thrown in, to produce the final movie.

Time and Space

For data scanned in from the real world, in some cases (such as night vision goggles) the data is displayed in exactly the location from which it is derived, whereas in other cases (such as teleoperation) the scan space is displaced from the display space. The display space can also differ in scale from the scan space, as in microteleoperation. The mapping from scan space to display space may include a spatial deformation.

Furthermore, the scan and display can be aligned or displaced in time (transmitted experience versus recorded experience). Scan time and display time can also differ in time scale, as with time-lapse photography. Display time can be related to scan time by a nonlinear distortion mapping, for example, in the replay of an explosion where initial events occur more rapidly than later events. Distorted time modeling is used by researchers in telerobotics.

These possibilities are summed up by saying that, for both time and space, the scan and display are either aligned, displaced, differ in scale, or related by a distortion mapping, as shown in Table 2. The relationship of Table 2 to the overall taxonomy of Table 1 is that Table 2 emphasizes the similarity of the values which can be assigned to the two dimensions, 'time' and 'space', of the taxonomy.

Since this is a comparison of the time and space coordinates of the sensor and display, the comparison only makes sense when there is a sensor involved. A constructed model comes out of nothingness and therefore has no real world coordinates with which the display might align. Likewise, an edited model may have pieces that come from specific locations in the real world, but there is no way to match the whole of the model to the real world.

Table 2. Relative scale and displacement in time and space for sensor and display.

	Time	Space
Aligned	transmitted in real time one-to-one time scale live television	registered one-to-one scale night vision goggles
Displaced	recorded earlier one-to-one time scale TV rebroadcast of live event	remote one-to-one scale teleoperation
Scaled	recorded earlier accelerated (or retarded) time slow motion instant replay on TV	remote expanded (or miniaturized) microteleoperation
Distorted	recorded earlier distorted time TV event with dull parts edited out	remote distorted space microteleop, exaggerated Height

If we imagine two clocks displaying Greenwich Mean Time, one being scanned by the sensor and the other with the user beside the display, we can ask if the two clocks are displaying the same time and if they are running at the same rate. For transmitted experience, the two clocks must match from moment to moment, so a one-to-one time scale is required. In replaying a recording, the clocks can run at the same rate but display different times. However, as with a VCR, the recording might also be played back in slow motion, faster than normal, in reverse, or paused with the action frozen. All these varieties of time-progression are possible for any recording technique.

Since the distinction between transmitted and recorded experience is already covered by the causality dimension of the classification system, the time dimension of the classification system focuses on time scale, with the possibilities being one-to-one time scale, accelerated (or retarded) time, frozen time, and distorted time.

In the same way that we used two clocks to judge the time-offset and time scale differences between scan time and display time, we also use two spatial markers to judge the offset and scale difference between scan space and display space. For this we use a pair of three-dimensional coordinate axes, one scanned by the sensor and the other measuring the space the user occupies. For concreteness, let us imagine that the user wears a see-through HMD, which uses half-silvered mirrors to spatially superimpose the real and virtual worlds. In this case, the coordinate axes that are actually present in front of the user are seen by the user with an image of the scan-space coordinate axes optically superimposed. Both coordinate axes are ruled in centimeters. We now ask whether the two axes are aligned or displaced from one another, and whether they appear to be the same or different sizes.

The main possibilities are that relative to scan space, display space is registered, displaced, or expanded (or miniaturized). It is also possible to introduce various distortion mappings between scan space and display space. An example is microteleoperation using the STM, where we wish to exaggerate the height variations of the sample being scanned so as to make very slight height steps more obvious.

SUPERPOSITION

A virtual world can be merged, perhaps using half-silvered mirrors, with the surrounding real world. It may be convenient to combine the real and virtual worlds by using a video camera to capture an image of the real world and then performing a more sophisticated merge than is possible with optics. This example of using cameras to capture and merge the real world with a virtual one shows that the surrounding real world itself can be thought of as model, on an equal footing with the virtual world model, and the two models edited together if desired. A powerful technique is to spatially superimpose two models of the same region of space, creating a sort of three-dimensional Rosetta Stone through the spatial correspondence of pairs of matching points in the two models.

Data from multiple sensors can be fused into a single virtual world model. An example is a conference telephone call. This can be thought of as automatic real-time editing, in which the data from three or more sensors (microphones) is integrated and then displayed through the speaker in each user's handset. On the other hand, a display, particularly an HMD, can block out the real world and isolate the user within the virtual world.

SENSES AND SENSORS

Display type and sensor type are two of the dimensions of the classification system; a few examples are given in Table 1, where the classification system is defined. However, the complete range of displays can, in principle, cover every phenomenon that human sensory organs can detect. Likewise, the complete range of sensors encompasses all measurable or detectable phenomena. Table 3 lists human sensory channels and corresponding display devices, and Table 4 lists some sensors and the phenomena to which they are sensitive. Neither the list of display devices nor the list of sensors is exhaustive. Many of the sensors listed detect phenomena that are imperceptible to human senses. By linking such sensors to display devices, these imperceptible phenomena are rendered visible, audible, touchable, or otherwise perceptible to a human being. A sensor-display linkage of this sort creates a synthetic sense, an apparatus that extends human perception and awareness [Robi91a].

Using a HMD as a display device offers the possibility of mapping sensed phenomena to specific locations relative to the body of the user. This is what vision and hearing do, and for those sensors which are able to establish the location or direction of the phenomena they sense, this positional information can be interpreted through the visual (and auditory) channels of the HMD to depict the sensor data as emanating from specific locations in space.

Table 3. Human sensory channels and display devices.

Sensed phenomena	Sensory system	Display device
Visible light (400–700 nm)	vision	display screen (CRT, LCD, or other) head-mounted display (HMD) individual lights dials and gauges
Vibrations in the air (20 Hz–20 kHz)	hearing	speaker headphones headphones with spatialized sound
Force	'sense of touch'	force-feedback device
Vibration		buzzer
Surface texture		tactor array, air bladders
Temperature		heater, cooler, fan
Chemical composition of air	smell	Sensorama smell display
Chemical composition of food	taste	
Acceleration of body	vestibular system	motion platform
Limb and body position	proprioception	exoskeleton with forced movements
Internal state of body (hunger, thirst, fatigue, etc.)	interoceptors	intravenous medical device to monitor, control contents of bloodstream
Damage to body	pain	

There is a considerable number of imperceptible phenomena. Every one of them can be given a visible form, or sound, or tactile representation. Every detectable phenomenon can be given a perceptible representation, regardless of its remoteness in space, time, scale, or time scale, and regardless of what form of energy or matter is being detected. By linking sensors and displays to create synthetic senses, every phenomenon that exists can be rendered directly perceptible to the human senses.

What do these imperceptible things look like? Since they are imperceptible, a representation must be invented. Choices thus present themselves. In general, many different representations are possible for a given phenomenon, and different representations can be useful at different times. For example, a number of visual representations of molecules are used in different situations: touching sphere model, ball and stick model, solvent-accessible surface model, ribbon following the backbone of a protein. What these invisible things should look like is a graphic design problem that, in time, will be settled on the basis of informativeness, aesthetics, convention, and accidents of history.

Table 4. Sensors and what they sense.

Sensed phenomena	Sensor
Visible light	still camera
Visible light	video camera
Sound	microphone
Position of moving objects	radar
Distance to object	range-finder
Position and orientation of moving object	tracker (6 DOF)
Inside of human body	ultrasound scanner computer-aided tomography (CAT) scan nuclear magnetic resonance (NMR) imaging
Infrared light	night vision goggles
Ultraviolet light	UV detector
Xrays	fluoroscope
Magnetism	electronic compass
Radiation	Geiger counter
3D surface shape	3D laser scanner
3D topography of the earth	aerial photography and photogrammetry
3D surface of microscopic sample	scanning-tunneling microscope
Image of distant object	telescope
Chemical composition	gas chromatograph spectrograph
Movement and vibration	accelerometer gyroscope
Gravitation field variations	mass detector

ACTIONS AND ACTUATORS

In the same way that sensors and human senses are linked to cover all detectable phenomena, a linkage from manual and other input devices to actuators should be able to control any device or system designed to be controlled. This is a relatively unexplored area, with the main work so far done in teleoperation and remote piloted vehicles. Most other human tools, vehicles, environments, and instruments have their own idiosyncratic locally-operated control panels.

In a few years visual telepresence may be widely available, so that a person can move by virtual travel instantly to distant locations, just as is now possible with the telephone for hearing only. If, at that time, most controllable devices are linked to the communications network, then it will be possible for a person to project by virtual travel to a distant location and initiate actions there through actuators available at that site. For safety and security reasons, remote access will probably not be allowed for some types of devices, but for many devices it may make sense. Another issue is who has permission to control which devices. In spite of these probable limitations, we can still imagine a future world in which an enormous traffic of ghostly presences leap about the planet, manipulating distant parts of the world through briefly occupied robot bodies.

Table 5 lists human motor channels and some devices available to measure human actions. Some actuators that have so far been used in remote presence systems are a robot arm, the STM tip, and a remote piloted vehicle. Of course, there are many more devices and systems that could potentially be controlled over the communication network.

CLASSIFICATION OF SOME SPECIFIC SYSTEMS

Table 6 shows the synthetic experience types of a number of specific systems and devices. Comparing different lines in the table suggests variations and extensions for some of the systems. For example, a hybrid of film and virtual reality would give us 3D recording of earlier actions that the user could fly through and observe from any viewpoint. A hybrid of microteleoperation with the STM and the video cassette recorder would allow rapid events occurring at the microscopic scale to be rapidly scanned as they occur, and then later played back at a slower speed, pausing and backing up to observe interesting events.

The dimensions of the classification system are largely independent of one another, so it is possible to consider a given system and ask what kind of system results by changing it along one dimension. The main dependencies between the dimensions are that transmitted experience requires one-to-one time scale, recorded experience needs no actuator or action measurement (except to control the replay), and simulated experience needs no actuator. Also, the dimensions

Table 5. Human motor channels and measurement devices.

Motor channel	Behavior measurement device
hands	hand-tracker (6 DOF)
	hand-held pushbuttons
	instrumented glove
	keyboard
	mouse
	joystick
feet	foot-pedal
eyes (gaze-direction, blinking)	gaze-tracker
head position	head-tracker (6 DOF)
body posture	instrumented body-suit
voice	speech recognition
breath	breath controller
heartbeat	EKG machine

Table 6. Examples of how specific systems are classified.

	Causality	Model source	Time	Space	Super-position	Display	Sensor	Action measure	Actuator
Tele-operation	transmit	scan	one-to-one	remote	isolated	HMD, force feed-back arm	camera on robot head	force feed-back arm	robot arm
Microtele-operation	transmit	scan	one-to-one	expanded	isolated	HMD, force feed-back arm	STM	force feed-back arm	STM tip
Remote piloted aircraft	transmit	scan	one-to-one	remote	isolated	screen	video camera	joystick	flap actuators in aircraft
Flight simulation	simulate	computed	one-to-one	remote	isolated	HMD, motion base	satellite photo-graphy	cockpit controls	—
Virtual reality game	simulate	construct	—	—	isolated	HMD	—	tracker, glove	—
Video game	simulate	construct	—	—	isolated	screen, speaker	—	joystick	—
Augmented reality – helicopter	transmit	scan	one-to-one	registered	merge	HMD	FLIR	—	—
Night vision goggles	transmit	scan	one-to-one	registered	merge	HMD	photo-multiplier	—	—
Medical 'X-ray vision'	transmit	scan	one-to-one	registered	merge	HMD	ultrasound scanner	hand tracker	—
Telephone	transmit	scan	one-to-one	remote	merge	speaker	micro-phone	keypad	—

Table continued on following page

Table 6. (*Continued.*)

	Causality	Model source	Time	Space	Super-position	Display	Sensor	Action measure	Actuator
Live television	transmit	scan	one-to-one	remote	—	screen, speaker	camera, micro-phone	—	—
Film	record	edit	one-to-one	remote	—	screen, speaker	camera, micro-phone	—	—
Video cassette recorder	record	edit	one-to-one, fast, slow, frozen	remote	—	screen, speaker	camera, micro-phone	keypad	—
Time-lapse photo-graphy	record	scan	accelerated	remote	—	screen	camera	—	—
Photo-graphy	record	scan	frozen	remote	—	print	still camera	—	—
Painting	record	construct	frozen	—	—	canvas	—	—	—

of sensor-to-display relative time and space only apply to models scanned in by sensors from the real world.

Conclusions

The taxonomy presented in this paper, with its nine dimensions, offers a method for classifying devices that use technology to transmit, filter, record, or simulate experience. The taxonomy also helps to understand the relationships among existing synthetic experience devices, and to suggest as yet untried possibilities.

Acknowledgments. I thank my colleagues in the UNC Computer Science Department for their help and support, particularly the Head-Mounted Display team (Fred Brooks, Henry Fuchs, Gary Bishop, Rich Holloway, Jim Chung, Drew Davidson, Erik Erikson, Mark Mine, Jannick Rolland, and Doug Holmgren); the Nanomanipulator team (Stan Williams and Rick Snyder of UCLA, Bill Wright, Vern Chi, and Russ Taylor); and the Pixel-Planes team. Fred Brooks and Ivan Sutherland suggested modifications to earlier versions of the classification system presented in this paper. The anonymous reviewers also made many helpful suggestions and corrections. I also thank my friends and colleagues from the Banff Centre for the Arts, NASA Ames Research Center, The Learning Company, and Atari, where my ideas about computer-simulated worlds evolved. I thank Julius Smith, Scott Kim, Fred Lakin, Ken Harrenstien, and Ken Shoemake for many years of technical discussions, critiques, and support. This research was supported by the following grants: DARPA DAEA 18-90-C-0044, NSF Cooperative Agreement ASC-8920219, ONR N00014-86-K-0680, and NIH 5-R24-RR-02170.

REFERENCES

[Blan90]
Blanchard, C., Burgess, S., Harvill, Y., Lanier, J., Lasko, A., Oberman, M., and Teitel, M., Reality built for two: A virtual reality tool, *Proc. 1990 Workshop on Interactive 3D Graphics*, Snowbird, UT, pp. 35–36, 1990.

[Brig84]
Bright, M., *Animal Language*, pp. 55–108, London: British Broadcasting Corporation, 1984.

[Caud92]
Caudell, T.P., and Mizell, D.W., Augmented reality: An application of heads-up display technology to manual manufacturing processes, HICSS Conference, Honolulu, HI, January 1992.

[Linv73]
Linvill, J.G., Research and development of tactile facsimile reading aid for the blind (the Opticon), report to U.S. Dept. of Health, Education, and Welfare, Stanford Electronics Laboratory, Stanford University, Palo Alto, CA, 1973.

[Robi91a]
Robinett, W., Electronic expansion of human perception, *Whole Earth Rev.*, Vol. 72, pp. 16–21, 1991.

[Robi91b]
Robinett, W., Technological augmentation of memory, perception, and imagination, Virtual Seminar on the Bioapparatus, p. 17, The Banff Centre for the Arts, Banff, Alberta, Canada, December 1991.

[Robi92]
Robinett, W., Taylor, R., Chi, V., Wright. W. V., Brooks, F. P. Jr., Williams, R. S., and Snyder, E. J., The Nanomanipulator project: An atomic scale teleoperator, 1992 SIGGRAPH course notes for the course 'Implementation of Immersive Virtual Worlds', July 1992.

[Weis89]
Weiss, R., New dancer in the hive, *Science News*, Vol. 136, No. 18, pp. 282–283, 1989.

4 Hardware Architectures for Visualization

Architectures for 3D Graphics Display Hardware

Turner Whitted

Abstract

The interactivity required for effective visualization places high demands on graphics hardware. The traditional graphics pipeline has been stretched to extremes in order to meet this demand, but it is due for a restructuring. This overview examines the growing capability of graphics hardware, with special attention paid to rapid display of complex scenes, to addition of features that improve image quality, and to the flexibility needed to serve a wide range of graphics applications.

Introduction

Computer users have come to expect high levels of interactivity for all applications, but this is especially important for visualization purposes because interactivity increases the number of dimensions available in a presentation. A static plot can effectively depict no more than a scalar function of two variables. A dynamic display, on the other hand, permits effective presentation of scalar and vector functions in three dimensions, because the illusion of depth is enhanced by movement. Furthermore, the time axis provides an additional independent variable.

Currently, this 3D interactivity is gained through the use of high-performance display processors. While the evolution of these display processors has been driven by the increasing speed and diminishing costs of their components, their designs have become increasingly complex in response to the market for new features and because demand for performance is outstripping component speed. A narrow summary of progress in display processor architecture would emphasize the increasing speed of new designs. In a way that is appropriate, since most hardware designers are obsessed with speed. However, users need (and are finally getting) advanced features and flexibility as well as speed. While it is component speed that enables the inclusion of new features, architectural sophistication is the ingredient that makes them useful.

As a specific example, consider some of the factors that enhance the effectiveness of computer graphics in scientific applications. For software generated images, transparency has been a favorite feature for users trying to visualize complex physical phenomena, because it allows the viewer to see many interactions at once, even if they take place behind the nearest visible object. Figure 1 shows one frame from an animated sequence in which Cl_2 is broken down into monatomic form in its interaction with a monolayer of argon atoms. Without transparency the chlorine molecules would become invisible as they entered the argon layer. Transparency, however, is very difficult to implement in common display systems. Otherwise, this example places very few demands on the display system, since the amount of data being changed from frame to frame is small. In other cases features may be provided in the display system and still not help the application. For example, texture is a good method for encoding nongeometric results of physical simulations. High-end processors have begun to provide real-time texturing as a feature. An application in atmospheric modeling (see Figure 2) produces rectangular arrays of pollutant concentrations at three different altitudes. The concentration arrays make natural texture maps. The application database contains a grand total of only three polygons. However, each polygon is texture mapped, and each texture map changes at each frame. In this case the polygons-per-second rating is immaterial, but the texture mapping feature is of paramount importance. However, the limiting factor for this data set is not likely to be the display system, since the host computer must take on the task of reading a new set of texture maps for each frame. In this case, the performance and features of the display system have relativey little bearing on the workstation's ability to serve the application.

As we can see from these examples, useful performance in a 3D graphics display system cannot be narrowly defined. Adequate performance means adequate features as well. Since not all display processors incorporate advanced effects, it becomes important for users and designers alike to consider which characteristics of display systems enable these types of features and which ones preclude them. It is equally important to engage in at least a 'back of the envelope' level of analysis when matching display hardware to specific applications.

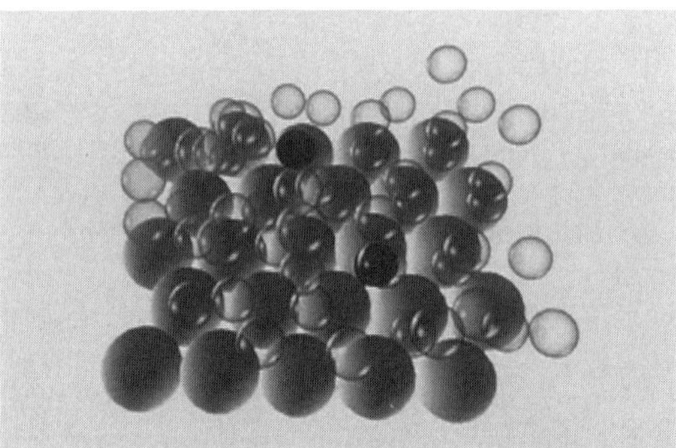

Figure 1. Simulation of photo-dissociation of chlorine molecules adsorbed on an argon substrate. Simulation and image by Professor Michael Prisant, Department of Chemistry, Duke University.

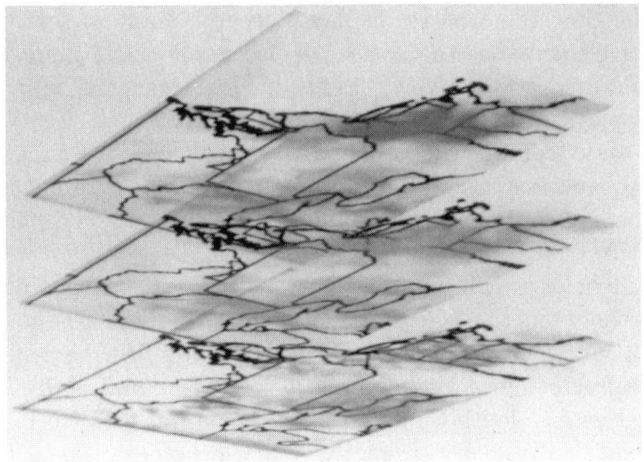

Figure 2. Ozone concentration in three different atmospheric layers. Simulation by Atmospheric Research and Exposure Laboratory, U.S. Environmental Protection Agency.

This paper is an overview of the state of the art of architecture and implementation of 3D graphics display systems. In this overview we will see that some limitations of graphics hardware are structural, i.e., they cannot be overcome without completely redesigning the hardware. In addition to structural issues, the overview covers some details of implementation, provides guides to analysis of performance, and includes descriptions of a few examples of the current generation of graphics hardware.

Basic 3D Engines

As with most new technology, 3D interactive displays first came in a variety of forms before converging to a standard configuration. The early standard contained circuitry for 3D transformations and projection connected to a second circuit for drawing straight lines on a CRT (Figure 3). In time these elements evolved from hybrids of analog and digital devices to entirely digital implementations as digital circuitry increased in speed and diminished in cost.

A major evolutionary step came with the replacement of calligraphic displays by raster scan displays. The utility of early vector-drawing displays was limited

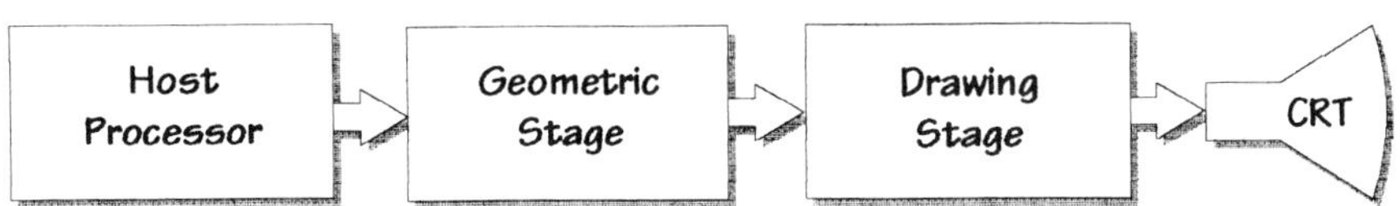

Figure 3. Basic display configuration.

by flicker. The time required to display a scene is more or less dependent on the number of elements in the scene. As scenes become more complex, the display time increases to the point that the image flickers too badly to be useful. Raster scan displays, on the other hand, contain a frame memory which decouples screen refresh time from drawing time. By drawing into one frame buffer while refreshing from another, i.e., double buffering, this decoupling is taken even farther, and display of dynamically changing data can be accomplished with few distracting artifacts.

A second benefit of drawing into a raster display is the option of filling in the pixels that lie between the edges. For drawings of surfaces, the filled display usually gives a better impression than a line drawing. As memory became less expensive, the frame buffer was extended from black and white to color, and was augmented with a depth buffer so that shaded images with hidden surfaces suppressed could be displayed interactively in a desktop workstation.

A steady series of incremental improvements have been applied to the basic 3D display system. In the interest of taking maximum advantage of parallel computing elements, the display hardware is typically stretched into a pipeline. The frame buffer is usually partitioned to reduce memory contention. The components in all cases are much faster, but design cleverness plays a major role as well [Moln90]. The advances of graphics algorithms have also crept into hardware. The number of advanced functions for shading, antialiasing, and conversion of higher-order surfaces to displayable primitives has been enhanced dramatically. Structurally, though, Figure 3 captures the essential elements of a real-time, 3D display system as well today as it did thirty years ago.

Thirty years of graphics hardware development has given us desktop and deskside workstations, with high resolution raster displays and a 3D graphics pipeline that evolved from line drawing systems. Not all graphics systems traveled along this path [Clar92]. In the days when generation of synthetic images for display on CRTs was a new idea, the raster scan pattern traced on the CRT was mimicked in the algorithms and image generation hardware. In fact, the distinction between algorithm and hardware was not evident. Watkins' classic scanline hidden surface algorithm [Watk70] was first presented as a simulation of hardware. Gouraud's smooth shading technique [Gour71] was presented as a modification to Watkins' hardware. Even Phong's dissertation [Phon73], in which he introduced a new and more realistic shading model, was accompanied by a preliminary design of hardware to implement the shader. In time, however, research and practice in realistic graphics moved almost completely into the domain of software-only implementations that did not run in anything close to real time. Gradually, however, many of the methods for realistic image synthesis have found their way into workstation display hardware.

A separate issue in the design of real-time display systems is the relationship between the graphics system and its host computer. Before the advent of workstations, graphics systems were implemented as terminals. Because of host-to-terminal bandwidth limitations, interactive performance demanded that the terminal maintain a local display list. With a display processor integrated into the workstation, the host can utilize an 'immediate mode' interface to the display pipeline and eliminate the terminal display list. There have been attempts by manufacturers, most notably Stellar and Ardent, to carry this integration to the point that simulation engines and visualization tools are housed in the same computer. Of course, in the most demanding scientific applications the entire workstation is generally used as a terminal attached to a larger host. In this case we are right back where we started, but with much higher performance [Myer68].

Algorithms and Structure

The 1974 survey by Sutherland, Sproull, and Schumacker [Suth74] described visible surface algorithms in terms of the sorting steps used to determine visibility. Not only did the paper point to (at that time) untried algorithms by identifying empty slots in its taxonomy, but it presented a more thorough analysis of performance than had previously existed.

Graphics architecture, both in theory and in the way it is implemented in either hardware or software, has grown in diversity and complexity to the point that a broader taxonomy and a different type of analysis is needed to understand the performance of the newer display systems. The purpose of this section is to map out a 'structural' taxonomy for graphics architectures. Like the paper by Sutherland et al. [Suth74], it is more a description of algorithms than of hardware and in fact may seem to blur the distinction between algorithms and architectures. We cannot escape the fact, though, that specific architectures are usually better suited to some classes of algorithm than to others. For example, the most popular hardware configuration is tightly tied to the z-buffer visibility algorithm. It makes a good starting point for a study of the relationship between algorithms, structure, and hardware.

THE EVER POPULAR PIPELINE

In Figure 4 the basic display system of the previous section is broken into its component parts. Most currently available incarnations of this pipeline function as a unidirectional, 'fire-and-forget' style of processor, in which geometric elements and display commands are funneled into the front end one at a time and thereafter shuttled through successive stages until an image takes form at the tail end without any further intervention by the earlier pipeline stages or the application program. This characteristic can yield extremely high performance, but at the same time is extremely restrictive.

As for the internal implementation, the geometric processing makes use of a few common arithmetic functions. The vertices of incoming polygons, each represented by a vector of four coordinate values, are transformed via matrix multiplication, composed of four inner product computations. Since the dynamic range of the incoming data is unrestricted, floating point representations are used. The most common cases of clipping, i.e., trivial reject and trivial accept, can be implemented with inner products, again using floating point arithmetic. Consider the clipping plane

$$Ax + By + Cz + D = 0$$

Substituting the point $< X, Y, Z, 1 >$ into the expression on the left hand side of the equation yields a zero only for points in the plane. Points on one side of the plane yield a positive number, and points on the opposite side yield a negative number. By orienting the plane so that positive values come from points inside the clipping volume and negative values from points outside, trivial acceptance and trivial rejection are rapidly computed using the same hardware that is used for coordinate transformation.

The lighting calculations use the Phong shading model

$$\text{intensity} = C_{\text{ambient}} + C_{\text{diffuse}}(\vec{N} \cdot \vec{L}) + C_{\text{specular}}(\vec{R} \cdot \vec{L})^n \tag{1}$$

or parts of it. The surface orientation vector, $\vec{N}$, is part of the vertex data for a polygon. The direction to the light source, $\vec{L}$, is part of the graphics state as are the various coefficients in the shading equation. The reflection vector, $\vec{R}$, can be computed on-the-fly. As in the case of other geometric operations, the common functions for shading are a pair of inner products. If the various coefficients are color vectors, then *intensity* is also a color vector.

Generally the surface orientation vector, $\vec{N}$, is replaced at this stage with the *intensity* vector. As Phong himself observed, the result obtained by interpolating the intensity term from the shading model is less satisfactory than interpolating the vectors used to produce the term and applying the shading function, once per pixel, at the end of the pipeline. Theoretically, there is no reason that the sampling rate of the shading function should be once per vertex or once per pixel. These design choices are simply a matter of convenience and serve to show that shading calculations are pretty much an afterthought in most systems, and that display system design is very much a matter of compromise.

The dynamic range of the geometric vertex components is still unrestricted after shading and requires floating point arithmetic. Finally, the perspective

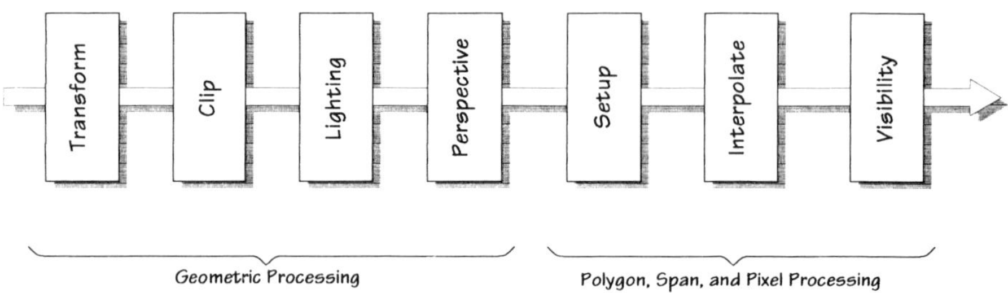

Figure 4. The classic pipeline.

divide maps all vertex values into a space that corresponds to display window boundaries plus a bounded Z range. From this stage to the end of the pipeline, the need for floating point arithmetic is eliminated.

The role of the drawing processor is to scan convert each polygon (often called 'tiling' or 'rasterizing') by interpolating depth and shading values across the interior of each polygon and to determine visibility on a per-pixel basis using a z-buffer. The drawing processor can maintain the maximum amount of precision in its setup and interpolation with fixed point arithmetic. The relative simplicity of fixed point arithmetic and the need for high data throughput generally leads designers to custom, fixed function hardware for tiling processors. The variety of tiler designs is astounding. One common characteristic of tiling hardware is the use of multiple processors, both to bring greater power to the problem and to provide parallel access to the frame buffer memory. A discussion of the other details of their implementation is deferred to a later section; for now we can treat them as black boxes.

Within the basic framework of the conventional pipeline there is enormous potential for extension and variation. For example, the floating point performance of some workstations is sufficient that the entire geometric section of the pipeline is relegated to the host [Apga88; Bord89]. This opens an option for more extensive user programming than a separate geometry processor would permit. Even with outboard geometry engines, extensions to the geometric processing include transformation of higher-order surfaces along with the operations to decompose them into polygons [Rock89]. Advanced shading features such as texture mapping can be included in the tiling function [Haeb90], [Lars90]. Two essential features, antialiasing and transparency, are seemingly incompatible with the pipeline architecture, but designers have managed to implement them anyway [Mamm89]. Of particular interest in scientific applications, data composed of volumetric samples instead of polyhedra can be displayed within the pipeline framework by replacing the tiling function by an operation called splatting [West89, 91], or even by adapting the tiler to emulate splatting [Laur91].

CHARACTERIZING DISPLAY SYSTEMS

Within the classic pipeline, one polygon at a time is present at each stage. At the end of the pipe all pixels within the bounds of a polygon are filled with a color value. At the opposite side of the architectural spectrum, ray tracing algorithms loop through one pixel at a time and query all potentially visible surface elements to determine which color should be loaded into the pixel. Ray tracing operations are almost entirely geometric, even though they need not do any coordinate transformation, do no clipping in the conventional sense, and, while they perform essentially the same function as a tiler, they share few common functions with conventional tilers.

Ray tracers are also very slow compared to almost any implementation of the classic pipeline. However, they are very simple, and they have the redeeming virtue that their visibility operators can be applied recursively. This enables the use of global illumination models that simulate specular reflection and transmission effects [Whit80]. Ray tracers have also been found useful in some visualization activities where volumes rather than surfaces are to be displayed [Levo90]. Global lighting effects require simultaneous access to all potentially visible surfaces surrounding a shaded point. Since the classic pipeline passes each surface element in isolation, global effects are precluded. This is one example of the relationship between structure and features.

That these two architectures are structural opposites is quite evident. The question at hand is how to characterize this 'oppositeness' in a useful fashion. Several proposals for classifying algorithms have been put forward, including the taxonomy based on sorting methods [Suth74]. More recent ones include those discussed in the following sections.

What we would like in a classification system is a set of independent axes which segregate architectures and shed some light on their performance. A taxonomy based merely on observed properties of systems usually yields dependencies, characteristics which appear to define properties of systems but which are, in fact, dependent on other factors. For example, what appear to be independent characteristics of hardware display systems, the order in which operations are performed, and the way memory is distributed in the system are actually tightly related. We could classify display systems based on either of the two, but including both does not tell us much. Here, briefly, are three proposals for classifying architectures, one based on distribution of interprocessor communications, one based on distribution of memory, and one based on order of loops.

Interprocessor Communication

Steve Molnar and his colleagues at the University of North Carolina propose a taxonomy based on the nature of interprocessor communications in multiprocessor systems [Moln91]. Given that multiple processors in both the geometric and drawing stages of Figure 3 are essential for high performance, Molnar suggests three reasonable configurations (given schematically in Figure 5):

Sort First

> In this case the drawing window is partitioned into equal-sized regions; one drawing processor is assigned to each region, and one geometric processor is paired with each drawing processor. Polygons are initially distributed to each geometry processor at random, but after transformation and bounds checking the polygon is transmitted to the processor pair which covers the region onto which the polygon projects. Then each pair of geometric and drawing processors displays all polygons which fall in their region. This is particularly effective for display of static scenes with a slowly moving viewpoint, since most polygons remain in the same partition from one frame to the next and interprocessor communications are small. Sort first suffers from load imbalance if polygons are concentrated in a few regions instead of evenly distributed over the display area.

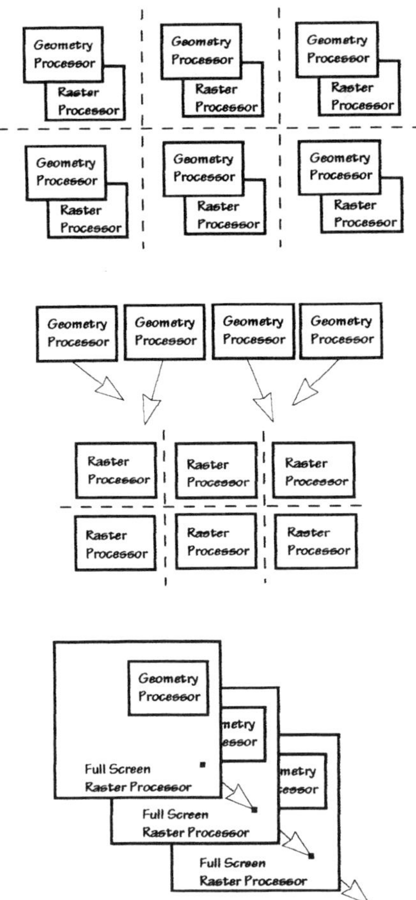

Figure 5. Display system configurations for sort first (top), sort middle (middle), and sort last (bottom).

Sort Middle

Here the display area is partitioned as before, with one drawing processor per region. However, the geometric processors are not paired with any drawing processor. Polygons are assigned to each geometric processor in round robin fashion. After all geometric processing, each polygon is transmitted to the drawing processor for the region into which the polygon falls.

Sort Last

For sort last configurations each drawing processor is paired with its own geometric processor, but every drawing processor now covers the entire display area. Polygons are assigned to geometric processors at random so the geometric load is evenly balanced. Since all drawing processors cover the entire image, there is no imbalance due to clustering. Although there is always the possibility of imbalance due to variation in polygon area, the random distribution of polygons tends to balance the distribution of polygon sizes. Note that the complete overlap of image areas requires a prodigious merge operation to generate a video stream.

As Molnar shows in his dissertation [Moln91] and in [Moln92], the performance of a sort last configuration scales linearly as processors are added. The key element of this architecture is not the rendering circuitry, but the compositing network for merging pixels. (Of course, connectivity is the distinguishing feature of any massively parallel architecture.) In order to keep shading costs constant, Molnar's proposed system defers shading until after compositing. This means that the geometric terms of Eq. (1) are passed through the network, sharply increasing the bandwidth needed in the compositing circuits over that which is needed if $< RGBAZ >$ is passed instead.

This classification scheme works well for arrays of processors tied together to implement the functions of the classic pipeline. It does a good job of differentiating designs that are likely candidates to produce extremely high polygon-per-second rates, but it is not sufficiently broad to include the range of alternatives that appear later in this discussion.

Memory Distribution

A gross characterization of display algorithms notes that either the display system must accumulate an entire image at the back end, as is the case with z-buffer algorithms, or must accumulate the entire object description of a scene at the front end, as is the case for ray tracing. Others, such as scanline algorithms, must accumulate pieces of the entire scene somewhere in the middle stages of processing. In Watkins' algorithm this accumulator is appropriately called the y-sort list, in which polygons are sorted according to vertical location in screen coordinates [Watk70]. We can label these various algorithms as front-end accumulators, back-end accumulators, or middle accumulators (Figure 6). The similarity between this and Molnar's classification is not entirely superficial, but classifying by memory distribution is intended not so much to predict rendering speed but to allow us to distinguish features supported by each class of architecture.

As noted before, back-end accumulators have memory cost determined only by image resolution and not by geometric complexity. Front-end accumulators can support global shading effects, since all surface elements are accessible at one time. List-priority algorithms, those which sort polygons to determine visibility prior to drawing, end up storing both the entire image and the entire geometric data base, seemingly the worst of both worlds. However, the fixed memory cost for a list priority algorithm is lower than that for a back-end accumulator like a z-buffer, so that list priority methods do make sense for applications that have small front-end memory costs. In many ways this classification by memory

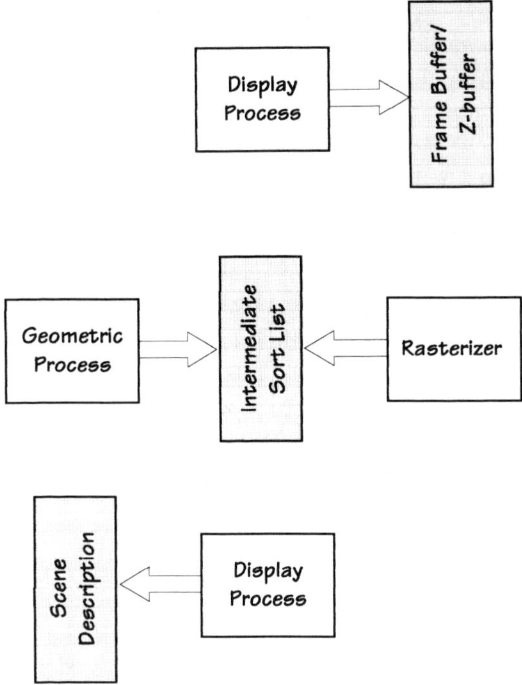

Figure 6. Back-end accumulators (top), middle accumulators (center), and front-end accumulators (bottom).

distribution seems like a sensible way to differentiate architectures. More importantly, because it keeps track of which intermediate results are collected at each processing step, it has the potential to predict which features will be supported by which architectures. However, it does not lead to any insight about contention and load balance in multiprocessor implementations.

Loop Order/Mapping Direction

The classic pipeline can be expressed as nested loops

$$\textbf{for } allpolygons$$
$$\textbf{for } allpixels$$
$$writepixels$$

while a ray tracer has the loop ordering reversed

$$\textbf{for } allpixels$$
$$\textbf{for } allsurfaces$$
$$writepixels$$

A more common label for these opposites is forward mapping and backward mapping, respectively. The usefulness of volume rendering algorithms has focused attention on mapping direction with some algorithms, e.g., splatting [West89], being of the forward mapping variety, and others, e.g., ray tracing, of the backward mapping variety. The terminology is processo-centric, in that forward refers to forward through the pipeline. If one considers the standard graphics viewing pyramid this terminology seems backward, since the forward mapping direction maps objects to images, and the backward mapping direction maps image samples to objects (Figure 7).

In practice, only a few rendering systems fall at the extremes of this classification. Ray tracing is almost purely a feed-backward technique, and splatting is almost purely feed forward. But the more common polygon-at-a-time z-buffer approach is generally implemented as a hybrid in which the transformation, shading, and tiler setup functions of the display pipeline operate in a feed-forward fashion and the tiler is internally a feed-backward mechanism.

Note that all forward mapping algorithms map to an accumulator. This means that a back-end accumulator must be forward mapping. In the case of the accumulate middle example, the algorithm is forward mapping into the y-sort list and backward mapping thereafter. This suggests that the mapping direction is actually a dependent axis and that the memory distribution classification might make a better taxonomy.

FEATURES AND STRUCTURE

The reason for being so picky about classification is that we wish to use it to distinguish characteristics that have a major effect on display system performance and features. For example, the polygon-at-a-time z-buffer algorithm accumulates the image at the tail end of the display pipeline. Since the size of the image accumulation buffer depends only on the display resolution, the z-buffer algorithm can display scenes of arbitrary complexity for a fixed memory cost. However, contention for the accumulation memory is the main performance bottleneck no matter how much parallelism is employed in the earlier stages of the display pipeline.

A ray tracing system, on the other hand, generates a single pixel at a time. It requires no accumulator at the pixel level. However, the algorithm cannot predict in advance which objects will be intersected by the ray tree associated with each pixel. This forces accumulation of the 3D scene at the front end, i.e., the geometric end of the display system. This requirement also leads to problems with ray-parallel, as opposed to object-parallel, accelerated ray-tracing architectures.

Scanline algorithms have a feed-forward front end in which geometric elements are accumulated in the y-sort list. The next step maps image scanlines backward into the y-sort list and creates yet another accumulator, the x-sort list, which is mapped to the image. This abrupt switching of mapping directions and the inclusion of at least two accumulators for intermediate results explains part of the difficulty of implementing scanline algorithms. However, it is the accumulation of intermediate results prior to the visibility and shading functions that allows scanline algorithms to incorporate transparency into the shading calculations.

A taxonomy based on mapping direction goes a long way toward focusing discussions of performance, memory costs, and complexity of common graphics display techniques. One might argue the taxonomy could be just as easily based

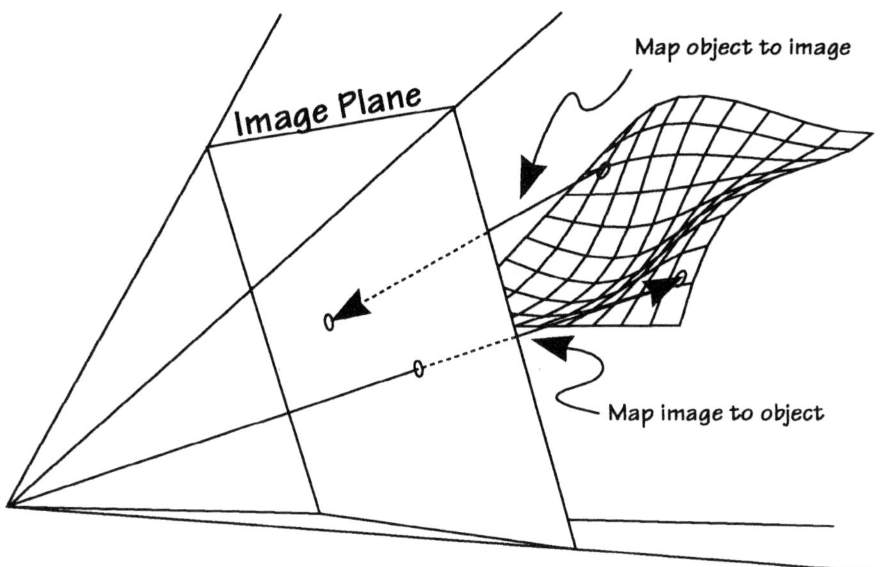

Figure 7. Opposites of mapping direction.

on the nature of the various accumulators used at the beginning, end, or middle
of the display process. Whether the classification is one of mapping direction or
of position of the accumulator is not nearly as important as the insight gained by
describing the processes in terms of their structure. It appears that a taxonomy
that can characterize both features and throughput, as well as the tradeoffs
between them, must account for interconnection between multiple processors as
well as the way that intermediate results are accumulated.

Nuts and Bolts: Components

Executives in the semiconductor industry like to remind the rest of us that
their products are becoming simultaneously faster, smaller, and less expensive.
Graphics hardware is the natural client for this trend, since graphics algorithms
are known to have an insatiable appetite for both memory and computing cycles.

At the component level, display hardware is no different than a general purpose
computer. It needs elements for computation, data transfer, and storage. It
does differ in the sense that unique classes of data storage can be identified and
optimized, e.g., a frame buffer, that particular data transfers take place regularly
and with a predetermined bandwidth, e.g., video refresh, and that certain fixed
calculations will be performed repetitively, e.g., matrix multiply. Interestingly,
these known specialized needs have given rise to specialized memory designs, but
have prompted little development of unique arithmetic elements.

This section discusses geometric processors, tiling processors, and memory organizations used in high-performance graphics systems.

High Speed Arithmetic

Since common practice is to implement geometric transformations as matrix multiplies, fast multiplier-accumulators are an obvious element of a high-performance graphics pipeline [Engl89]. In the interest of reducing cost, it would be handy to implement clipping and shading operations in the same elements [Clar82]. The common operation in these cases is a vector inner product. A coordinate transformation in homogeneous coordinates requires an inner product for each of the four terms in the result. The concatenation of two 4×4 matrices requires 16 inner products. Clipping requires at least one inner product per plane per vertex.

The ideal inner product engine is a multiplier/accumulator, an arithmetic element that computes an expression of the form

$$D = C + AB$$

An inner product of two four-element vectors requires four turns of the crank, with the C term acting as an accumulator. Since fast MAC chips are commodity items, building a geometry pipeline is conceptually as simple as adding control logic and a bit of memory.

High speed arithmetic elements with control logic and memory already included can substantially simplify the design of a geometric processor while reducing the overall system cost at the same time. DSP (digital signal processor) chips fit this niche reasonably well. Examples of DSPs include the AT&T DSP32 [AT&T88] and the Texas Instruments 320C30 [Texa90]. The distinction between a DSP and a general purpose RISC chip is subtle. Both are likely to have pipelined instruction units, both have streamlined instruction sets. Most RISC processors use the same external path for instructions and data, while a DSP is likely to adopt a Harvard architecture with separate instruction and data streams. DSPs may have 16- or 32-bit address spaces, instead of the 32- or 64-bit addresses of general purpose CPUs. DSPs usually support such features as bit-reversed addressing (useful for fast Fourier transforms) that would merely confuse the average programmer. What really distinguishs the two classes of CPU is the arithmetic unit and the number of internal buses that feed it. While a generic RISC CPU adds two integers together in a single clock period, or in some cases even multiplies two integers in a single cycle, DSPs simultaneously execute a single precision floating point multiply and a single precision floating point add in a single machine cycle. As Figure 8 illustrates, a typical DSP comes equipped with enough arithmetic elements and data paths to maintain a high processing rate.

The fragment of pseudocode below is a four-element inner product. The accumulate operations are delayed by one cycle, but the sequence can be dovetailed at the beginning and the end with another identical operation.

$$C_1 = A_1 B_1 \qquad \ldots$$
$$C_2 = A_2 B_2 \qquad S+ = C_1$$
$$C_3 = A_3 B_3 \qquad S+ = C_2$$
$$C_4 = A_4 B_4 \qquad S+ = C_3$$
$$\ldots \qquad S+ = C_4$$

Using the Texas Instruments TMS320C32 as an example, a 60-ns cycle time and 16 multiply/accumulate operations per vertex yields a theoretical peak rate of just over one million transformed homogeneous vertices per second.

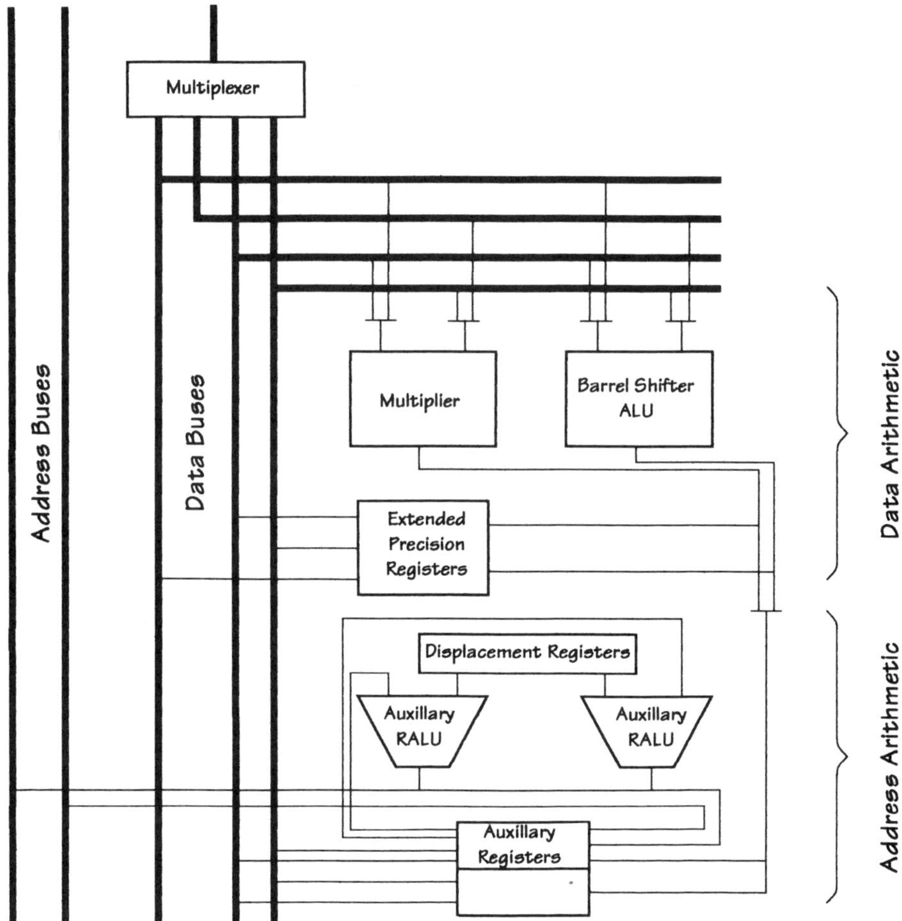

Figure 8. TI 320C30 DSP data paths.

While the inner product is the core element of transformation, clipping, and lighting, DSPs are general purpose devices that give a system designer the option to add features without altering the hardware in the front end of the display system. The idea of providing a programmable, integrated arithmetic engine is extended in the Intel i860 CPU. Internally the i860 is a 64-bit general purpose RISC CPU with a very powerful vector floating point unit attached (Figure 9). While DSPs are usually applied as geometric processors to be used in conjunction with other graphics processors, the i860 contains pixel processing hardware in addition to its pipelined floating point multiplier/accumulator. Some have promoted the i860 as a single chip graphics workstation [Grim89], but it has not caught on in this mode, at least partly because of anemic pixel processing and internal bus contention when programmers try to engage all elements of the chip simultaneously. Instead, the i860 is typically found in high-end display processors, as a programmable building block for the geometric stage of processing.

Assuming that the floating point operations can be vectorized, the i860 floating point unit will produce a single precision multiply/accumulate result every clock cycle [Marg90]. Using 40MHz parts, a four-element inner product takes only 100 ns. This yields more than twice the performance of the 320C30 for vertex transformation.

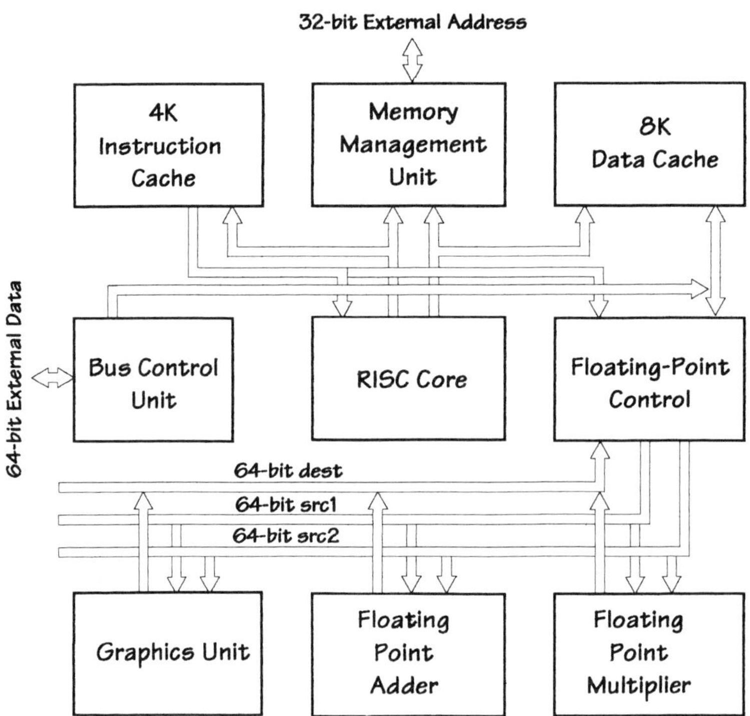

Figure 9. Major elements of Intel i860 CPU.

Among the overlooked features of any popular general purpose device are the programming tools available for them. C compilers are available for each of the chips mentioned in this section. While programming in a higher-level language is seldom efficient in cases where concurrency contributes to the performance of the chip, such tools can greatly reduce development time. In feature-laden advanced systems, higher-level languages are a programmer's only hope of maintaining order in the midst of overwhelming complexity. In spite of the potential open-endedness of display systems containing programmable elements, end users seldom have access to display processor code. Ironically, the heyday of user programmable systems was a time when difficult to program microcode engines were the dominant system elements [Levi84; Engl86]. Today, in an age of higher-level instruction sets and higher-level languages, manufacturers are apt to require that application programers remain a respectful distance from the hardware.

Memory

The first commercially available video frame buffer built from random access memory stored images at a resolution of $512 \times 512 \times 8$ bits. It cost $50,000. Today this system is a museum piece. Frame buffers with greater capacity cost a few hundred dollars and are common in personal computers.

The role of frame buffers has been augmented as their component prices have dropped. The original use of the frame buffer was to passively store images so that video circuitry could read it fast enough to refresh the CRT at standard video rates (i.e., 25 or 30 times each second). Even at low resolutions and low video rates, it was no small feat to maintain the needed refresh speeds. Here is a modest example in which the timing for refreshing a single scan line is taken from the NTSC video standard:

Memory access time:	100 nsec
Memory resolution:	$640 \times 480 \times 8$
Video frame rate:	30 Hz, interlaced
Active time for a scanline:	63 usec

Simple arithmetic shows that reading 640 8-bit pixels along a scanline requires a memory access time of less than 95 nsec. Allowing for register setup margins and other delays, the only way to maintain this rate is to access two pixels simultaneously. One could argue that a better solution is to use faster memory, but the best available speed for high density dynamic RAM is only about twice as fast as the time in the example. Of more interest to most of us is an example tied to workstation display rates:

Memory access time:	60 nsec
Memory resolution:	$1280 \times 1024 \times 24$
Video frame rate:	72 Hz, noninterlaced
Active time for a scanline:	12 usec

In the second case the video clock rate is over 100 MHz, and the frame buffer must deliver a new 3-byte pixel to the video stream every 9.5 nsec. This example hints at the basic dilemma of frame buffer design: storing lots of bits is not the issue; accessing lots of bits in parallel is required [Whit84]. However, the advance in RAM technology is toward more densely packed memory at constant speed. Neither of these examples mentions the problem of getting images into the frame buffer. In the case of interactive systems, the front end of the frame buffer is being bombarded with accesses as the display process attempts to update or replace the stored image several times each second. Access to the frame buffer is a major bottleneck for display systems, and advances in standard memory technology do not address the problem.

To eliminate the contention caused by video readout, semiconductor manufacturers introduced a form of dynamic memory chip specifically for frame buffer applications. Bits in a dynamic RAM chip are stored as a rectangular array laid out in rows and columns. Internally, to read a single bit a single row from all columns is read simultaneously, and the result from a single column is selected from this operation. VRAMs, also called Video RAMs, take advantage of this characteristic by providing a second access port, in which the result of the simultaneous all-column read is latched into a shift register and then clocked out of the chip at video rates without otherwise affecting the operation of the chip. This means that video refresh is not the memory access bottleneck that it would be in frame buffers constructed from conventional DRAM. It does not relieve the contention from the display processor end of the frame buffer.

Front end contention can only be reduced by partitioning the frame buffer and giving each partition an independent data path. The most obvious partition is to split the image into contiguous regions and to treat each region as an independent frame buffer. Unfortunately, the pattern of access to frame buffer locations is usually very coherent, i.e., if any given pixel is addressed, the most likely next address will be one of its neighbors. This pattern holds for both image writing and video refresh. Consequently, the most successful organization for parallel access frame buffers is an interleaved arrangement, in which each partition holds every Mth column of every Nth row of the image. This partition, first proposed by Fuchs [Fuch77], has been extended by others [Clar80] and is widely used in commercial display systems.

Other specialty chips do not have quite the impact on architecture as VRAM, but they do combine enough common functions to lower the cost of display systems. For example, video controllers and RAMDACs (chips which combine the function of video lookup tables with digital-to-analog converters) reduce the amount of 'glue' logic needed to complete a frame buffer. While these chips mostly benefit the low end of display systems, they are nevertheless indicative of how higher levels of integration change the physical aspects of graphics systems.

TILERS

Scan converting, that is tiling, a polygon is a fairly simple function. Polygon edges are sorted from top to bottom, edges are tracked from pixel row to pixel row by forward differencing, and the span between edges is interpolated, again by forward differencing (Figure 10). Hopefully the cost of setup for forward differencing can be amortized across enough pixels that it does not become the bottleneck.

There are a lot of ways to build a flawed tiler. One of the most common is to confuse 'fixed point' with 'integer'. Tilers can use fixed point arithmetic, but sloppy implementations that snap vertices to pixel centers produce irritating artifacts, especially in a changing scene. As Figure 10 illustrates, the very first increment along each edge must bring the edge interpolants into alignment with the first scanline crossed by the edge. Similarly, the first increment along each span must bring the span interpolants up to the exact value for the first pixel encountered by the span. Since cumulative round-off error in forward differencing is slope dependent, the increment values as well as interpolant accumulators must have sufficient precision to handle the worst case. This type of exacting interpolation costs bits and cycles but is essential for a properly working tiler.

A look at numbers shows why the speed of tiling is a major concern for graphics hardware designers. Consider a single triangle covering 50 pixels when projected. The display system must contend with three vertices, three edges, an average of 10 spans, and 50 pixels. Even for such a small triangle, the potential bottlenecks are in the tiler.

It is no surprise, then, that parallelism is essential for a high-performance drawing engine. For triangles, setup for both edges and spans can be done once per polygon, allowing setup to be shared by several interpolators. Since

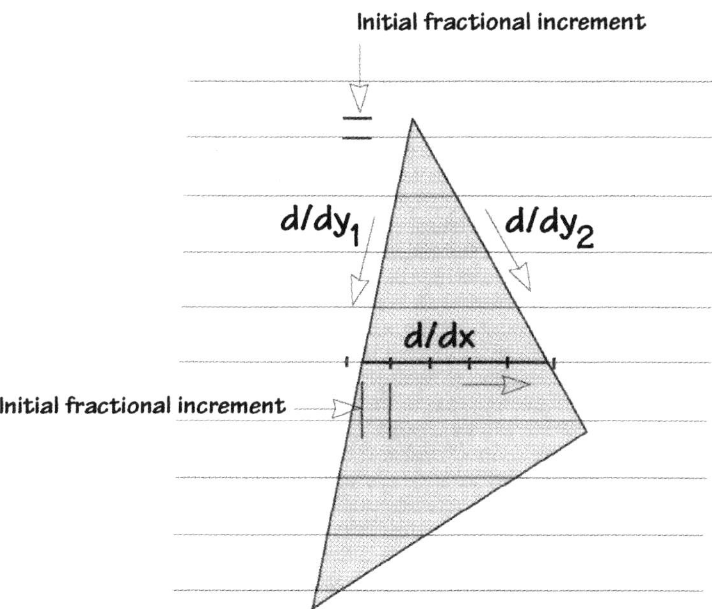

Figure 10. Triangle scan conversion by forward differencing.

partitioned frame buffer memory is needed to reduce contention, it is common to partition the tiler so that each memory partition has its own interpolator. Some variation of this approach is used in most commercial display systems [Akel88; Potm89; Kirk90].

An extreme in parallelism is to put tiling logic at each pixel. In the Pixel Planes systems [Fuch85] the tiler is literally inside of custom, logic-enhanced frame memory chips. Instead of forward differencing, the tiler contains a distributed linear expression evaluator, with logic at each pixel to compute a unique value as a function of the pixel coordinates. The sequence in Figure 11 shows how a linear expression for a half-plane formed by extending each edge is evaluated for each edge in turn. An ordering convention is chosen so that the half-plane for which the linear expression is less than zero is defined to be on the 'inside' of the edge. The intersection of these inside half-spaces is the interior of the triangle. A flag for each pixel is ANDed with the sign of the linear expression to compute the intersection. After setting the flags for the interior of the polygon, a separate linear expression for depth is evaluated for all pixels, and for those where the flag bit is '1' the depth is compared with the previous depth value and conditionally written. Several systems (see [Apga88; Fuch89]) use this technique or variations.

Analysis

On the surface, performance analysis for display systems is simple. To predict the time required to create an image, break the display process into primitive operations, multiply the number of times each primitive operation is executed by the time for each operation, and sum the products [Park80]. Total times are reduced by executing the primitive operations concurrently, i.e., through the use of parallel hardware.

A popular form of concurrent execution is functional parallelism. Here, each type of primitive operation is implemented in a separate processor. Not only does this yield concurrent execution, but it permits each processor to be optimized for a particular task, further reducing execution time. In practice, the optimization permitted by functional parallelism is only moderately exploited. This is partly because the similarities of many graphics operations permit a single type of device (e.g., a multiplier/accumulator) to efficiently perform a variety of operations.

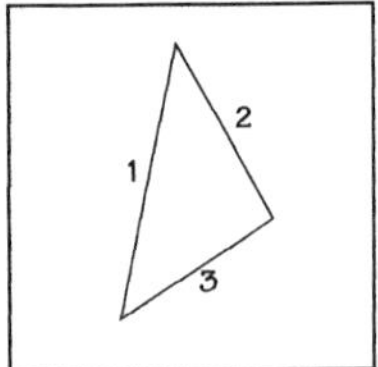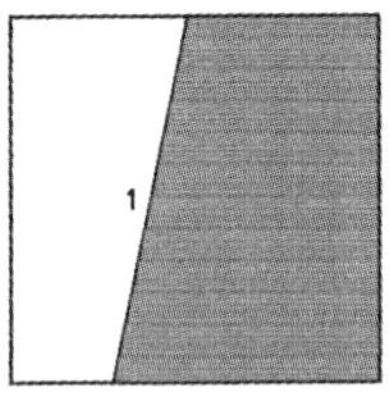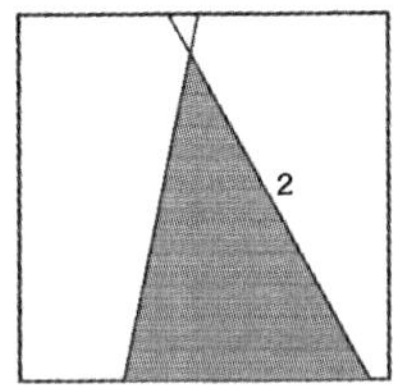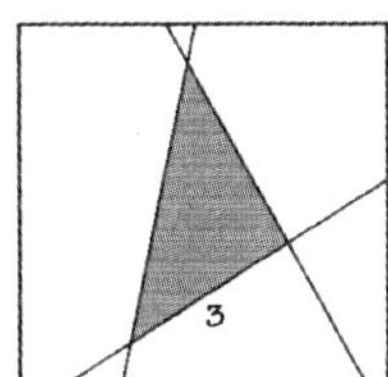

Figure 11. Triangle scan conversion by linear expressions.

While concurrent execution in parallel hardware gives faster execution, contention interrupts the flow of processing and slows it down. In display systems we see contention for processors, contention for data paths, and contention for memory. Since the most popular form of display processor is image based and uses a large image memory, it is natural that the most serious bottleneck in these systems is contention for image memory.

One of the first published analyses devoted specifically to the performance of shaded display systems is [Park80]. Parke's analysis starts with a simple model for the tiling process using single processor display systems

$$T_t = P_n P_t + S_n S_t + E_n E_t + G_n G_t \tag{2}$$

where
T_t is the total time to complete an image
P_n is the number of pixels
P_t is the time per pixel
S_n is the number of spans
S_t is the time per span
E_n is the number of edges
E_t is the time per edge
G_n is the number of polygons
G_t is the time per polygons

Parke uses this as a starting point to model the expected performance of different parallel architectures. Here we follow his analysis for a particular architecture, in which multiple tiling processors are associated with individual partitions of an interleaved frame buffer memory. For this example, the association is fixed and one-to-one. To begin with, $P_n = k_d(res_x)(res_y)$, where the vertical and horizontal resolution of the display window is fixed and k_d, the average depth complexity, is a function of the scene data base and viewing parameters. Assuming the data base is composed of quadrilateral polygons, then $E_n = 4G_n$. The number of spans is $S_n = k_g G_n \sqrt{P_n/G_n}$, where k_g is a geometric constant that Parke estimates to be about 1.2. Now, for a nearly square array of tiling processors with M rows and N columns, P_n for each processor is divided by MN, since interleaving in a square pattern tends to balance the workload for any distribution of the scene data over the display window. Similarly, the number of spans per processor is divided by M, the number of rows. Ultimately, the object of the exercise is to plug in the P_t, S_t, E_t, and G_t terms based on a count of operations needed for each element, and determine values of M and N for a given performance goal. One problem revealed by this analysis is a bias toward making M larger than N to take advantage of greater parallelism for span interpolation. Succumbing to this bias, however, introduces an orientation dependency in the interleaved frame memory that will upset the load balance between pixel processors for small polygons.

Of course, the preceding analysis considers only scan conversion costs and ignores the geometric processing. However, transformation, clipping, lighting, and perspective costs are incurred on a per vertex basis. We can add a vertex term to Eq. (2) of the form $V_n V_t$. For parallel geometric processing elements, the vertex time can simply be divided by the number of processors if the vertices are evenly distributed among the processors. However, if functional parallelism is employed in the geometric pipeline then the operations must be grouped so that each processor handles approximately the same number of operations for each vertex [Akel88].

Before proceeding to analysis of more complex systems, let us plug in some reasonable numbers to the simple expression to derive an important structural characteristic of common display systems. In a uniprocessor system the costs for each operation are weighted by the cost of each operation and summed to produce the total cost. In parallel implementations the operations are executed concurrently, and processor balance is an issue. If operations were assigned randomly to identical CPUs, then communications overhead might become the overwhelming consideration. However, the functional specialization with current display processors somewhat warps our analysis.

As we have seen, the dominant operations at each stage of the geometric pipeline are so similar that no specialization is warranted. The tiling engine, however, is a very specialized beast and is generally constructed from specialized pieces. For the sake of analysis, assume that the geometry pipeline is implemented from one or more general purpose floating point CPUs. Further assume that a single type of custom processor handles both edge and span setup and interpolation. Finally, assume that a fairly simple processor is intimately tied to the frame buffer memory to implement the conditional read-modify-write operation needed for visibility. (These are not really assumptions, they are merely a reflection of current technology.) In this case the question is how much computational power and data path bandwidth is required in each of the processing stages.

Now add to these assumptions some actual component speeds and characteristics of typical scene data bases. Assume a database of 1,000 quadrilaterals, a frame update rate of 10 per second, a geometry engine that can do a multiply/accumulate in 100 nsec. For the drawing engine, ignore setup costs for now, but assume that the interpolators can do an integer add in 50 nsec, and that frame buffer access time is 100 nsec. Next assume that the object is scaled so that it fills 60% of a 1K×1K window with an average depth complexity of 2. This works out to an average polygon area of 1,200 pixels and about 35 spans of 35 pixels each per polygon. Then the numbers of elements flowing through the display system for each frame are

$$G_n = 1,000$$
$$V_n = 4,000$$
$$E_n = 4,000$$
$$S_n = 35,000$$
$$P_n = 1,200,000$$

Akeley and Jermoluk [Akel88] estimate the numbers of floating point operations required to move a vertex through the pipe to be a little over 100. To be really conservative, assume that adds and multiplies cannot be overlapped. Then our geometry engine can crank out 100,000 transformed, lighted, and clipped vertices per second, about twice the needed throughput. There is no need for parallelism in the geometry stage. Go now to the very back of the pipeline, where the tiler must do z-buffer type read-modify-write operations at the rate of 12,000,000 pixels per second. Again being conservative, we expect each memory chip and any arithmetic unit associated with it to do this operation in about 500 nsec. To meet this rate, we use a 2×3 interleaved memory. A single span interpolator can feed this array with 10M pixels per second, a rate that falls about 20% short of the needed performance. We have to include two span interpolators, and for convenience we assign each one to a row of the 2×3 array. The edge interpolation rate is two per span, or about 700,000 integer adds per second, small enough that it could be folded back into some other arithmetic unit [Whit81]. Note that the degree of parallelism grows as data progresses through the pipeline. This inverted funnel shape is common in raster display systems.

What we have just done is use analysis to design a display system. Presumably the size and number of polygons was derived directly from a target application. However, the behavior of an application cannot be described so tersely.

Carlbom's dissertation [Carl82] is all encompassing, based on an abstract model of interactive graphics applications. In it she makes the important observation that performance is heavily dependent on the application itself. Perhaps because it is difficult, more complete analysis seems not to have captured the interest of graphics hardware developers. While manufacturers seem to prefer benchmarks, they are not generally considered to be successful. Since any display system is a compromise anyway, more detailed analysis may not be worthwhile.

Case Studies

Designing any complex computing system is a balancing act. Rarely does an elegant concept translate to a clean, fast, and flexible implementation. This is partly because of the sheer complexity of computing systems, and partly because of the difficulty of optimizing any design for a wide range of operating conditions. It is true for display systems in spite of their supposed 'special purpose' status. The best way to expose the tradeoffs of display system design and to discover what works well and what does not is to review machines that have already been built.

This section is a review of several different display hardware implementations, all but two of them commercial products. In some cases, examining successive generations of the same line of product is more useful than reviewing one or the other in isolation. The list includes the Silicon Graphics GTX and VGX processors, the AT&T Pixel Machine, the Hewlett-Packard TVRX display processor, and Pixel-Planes 4 and 5. For the two Silicon Graphics systems, the difference between the two generations of design are particularly interesting, since it demonstrates how restructuring can eliminate a bottleneck. The Pixel Machine design contains both extreme strengths and weaknesses. The two Pixel Planes designs are noncommercial research machines built at the University of North Carolina at Chapel Hill. Pixel Planes 4 was the first full implementation of the innovative processor-in-memory concept that has come to be associated with the Pixel Planes algorithm. Pixel Planes 5, misnamed and only loosely related to the earlier series of machines, is an exercise in providing flexible connectivity within a display processor. Finally, the Hewlett-Packard display system, while structurally similar to others that conform to the traditional pipeline, has unique implementation details that shed some light on how its designers chose to solve performance problems.

SUN MICROSYSTEMS GS

While Sun Microsystems is not well known for its 3D products, it has for a number of years offered a variety of graphics acceleration options. The GS accelerator has a modest price and modest performance. It is included here as an extremely straightforward low-end system [Sun90].

Functionally, the GS implements the classic pipeline with a single TI 320C30 as the geometry stage (Figure 12). The drawing engine utilizes a single fixed point ASIC for pixel address generation and three identical drawing/tiling ASICs. The frame buffer memory is 8-way interleaved spatially for parallel access. Each pixel is 48 bits deep and can be organized in a variety of ways by enabling different video lookup tables in the RAMDACs.

For the purposes of this discussion, the important characteristic of the GS is its internal structure. A single geometric processor fans out to three parallel tiling chips, which further expand to an eight-way parallel frame buffer access path. This is precisely the 'inverted funnel' structure discussed in the analysis section. This arrangement is found in more complex systems as well.

One noteworthy aspect of the GS design is its small physical size. The GS occupies two 5×9 inch circuit boards sandwiched together. When plugged into a standard SPARCstation 'pizza box', the board set occupies all three available SBus slots. Putting real-time 3D capability in a generic desktop unit rather than an expensive deskside workstation represents a step toward universal inclusion of 3D features.

SILICON GRAPHICS GTX

When introduced in 1989, the IRIS 4D/GTX from Silicon Graphics [Akel89] provided the highest throughput available. The performance goal for the system was set for 100,000 shaded, four-sided, 10 pixel by 10 pixel polygons per second. Table 1, taken from [Akel88], reflects the designer's own analysis of the performance needs in the geometric stage of the pipeline. The analysis in [Akel88] is not as detailed as it could be. For example, multiply/accumulate functions are overlapped in most hardware but are counted separately. The useful number for analyzing a system like this is the time taken for each function, not the amount of floating point arithmetic performed for each function.

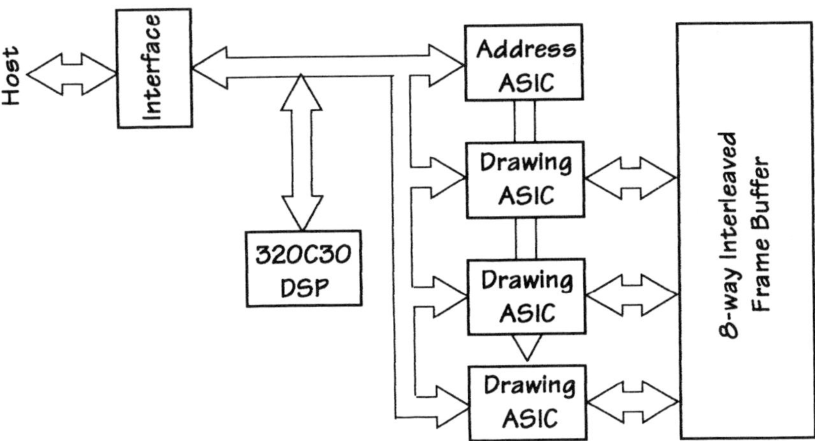

Figure 12. Sun Microsystems GS.

Structurally, the GTX is no different than earlier offerings from SGI, but the use of faster components yields more than double the performance. Rather than dedicating a pipeline stage to each of the functions in the table, the geometric section is a serial array of 5, 20 Mflop microcoded floating point units, as illustrated in Figure 13. Display primitives are fed into the front end of the array from the host processor through a format conversion and interface module. A FIFO is included in each of the pipeline stages to buffer fluctuations in the flow of data.

The drawing engine for the GTX is a more elaborate version of the inverted funnel described previously. At the narrow end a single polygon processor sorts vertices, decomposes arbitrary polygons into axis aligned trapezoids, and computes slope values for each edge. The edge processor uses seven interpolators, one for each of x, y, z, *red*, *green*, *blue*, and *alpha*, to walk along each edge producing span endpoints and slopes. Note that in the SGI system y is a dependent

Table 1. Performance requirements for the Silicon Graphics IRIS 4D/GTX.

Function	Number of operands	Number of operations	Rate (Mflops)
Vertex transformation	400,000	16 mult., 12 add	11.0
Normal transformation	400,000	9 mult., 6 add	6.0
Normal normalization	400,000	3 mult., 2 add, 1/sqrt(), 3 mult.	9.5
Lighting	400,000	12 mult., 10 add, 5 compare, 1 table lookup	11.0
Clipping	400,000	6 compares	2.5
Perspective divide	400,000	8 operation recip., 3 mult.	4.5
Viewport	400,000	3 mult., 3 add, 3 float to int conv.	3.5

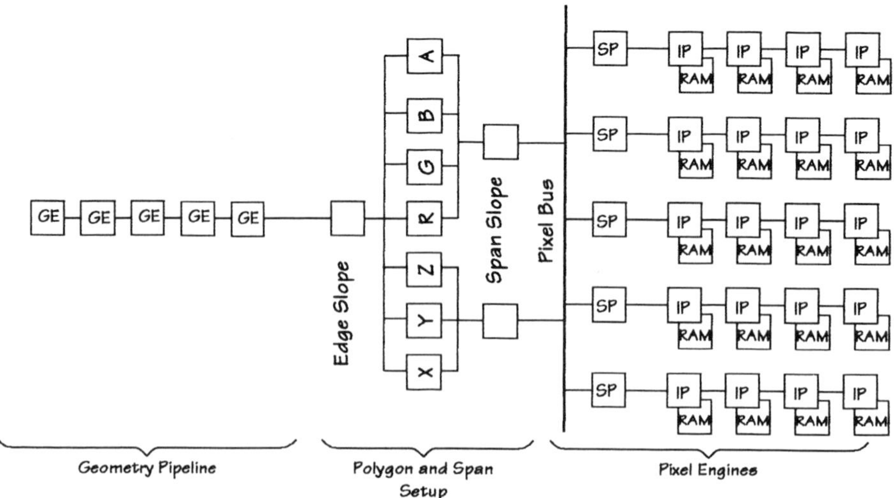

Figure 13. Silicon Graphics GTX display pipeline.

edge variable rather than x, because the edges are scanned horizontally to create vertical spans. Span processors are interleaved horizontally, each one handling every fifth column of the image array. Each span processor is connected to four image engines, which are interleaved vertically so that each one addresses every fourth pixel of every fifth column. As spans are interpolated, each pixel is written to one of the four image engines, which performs pixel level z-buffer or compositing operations. The stated goal of 100,000 100-pixel polygons per second imposes a need to write 10 Mpixels per second. At its peak rate, the GTX produces one span every 500 nanoseconds and generates 40 Mpixels per second. This 1-5-20 fanout progression has the flavor of a data 'impedance matching' network, which matches the high arithmetic speed of the pipeline with the relatively long (in the range of 100 nanoseconds) image memory access time.

PIXEL-PLANES 4

The pixel planes algorithm tiles polygons by evaluating a sequence of linear expressions that define the polygon's edges and the plane equations for polygon depth [Fuch82]. Similar expressions define interpolated color across the polygon face. The first three generations of machines based on this algorithm were laboratory breadboards for proof of concept. Pixel-Planes 4, completed in 1986, was a full scale implementation.

The logical layout of the system (Figure 14) is simple, with only three major elements: a geometry processor and linear expression generator; a massively parallel linear expression evaluator and its associated drawing controller; and a controller for assembling pixels into a video stream. The geometry processor and linear expression generator is an off-the-shelf array processor. As primitives are passed to the drawing engine, linear expressions are generated instead of slopes for each interpolant. The processor-in-memory array can then evaluate the expression at all pixels simultaneously. The task of the drawing controller is to arrange a sequence of these simple operations so that they implement complex rasterizing functions.

Pixel-Planes 4 is able to maintain a display rate of 40,000 shaded polygons per second at 512×512 resolution, modest performance by current standards. What is remarkable about the system, however, is the range of functions that can be cast as a sequence of linear expression evaluations. Users have been able to incorporate shadow casting, direct rendering of spheres, texture mapping, and CSG operations within the Pixel-Planes framework [Fuch85].

One can argue that the massive parallelism is not particularly cost effective for scenes composed of large numbers of small polygons. Using the standard 10 pixel by 10 pixel polygon as a test case, the 262,144 Pixel-Planes 4 processors achieve only .04% utilization. While this argument is oversimplified, it has prompted other designers to build versions in which a scaled-down rectangular array stamps out a footprint of pixels better matched to average polygon size [Apga88].

SILICON GRAPHICS VGX

The most significant difference between the GTX and its successor, the VGX model (see Figure 15), is in the arrangement of the geometry section. Rather

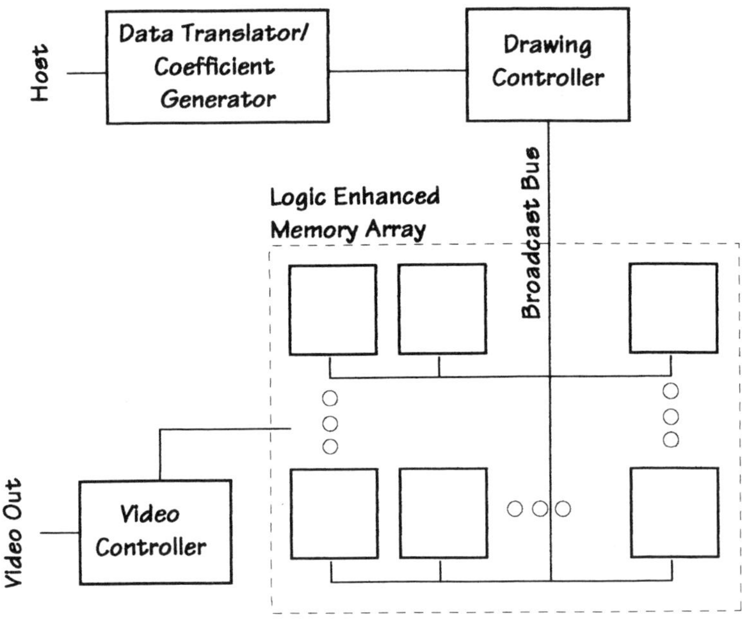

Figure 14. Pixel Planes 4.

than a single data path through the processor, four parallel data paths through a SIMD processor make the transformation pipeline wide and shallow rather than narrow and deep.

The VGX transformation unit is optimized for triangle or quadrilateral strips. This is a reasonable design decision, given the frequency of occurrence of this data type. Subdivided parametric surfaces, swept surfaces, surfaces of revolution, and surfaces reconstructed from contour data are all represented efficiently by polygon strips.

Once the first two vertices of the first triangle are passed from the host to the transformation unit, each succeeding vertex completes a new triangle composed of itself and the two preceding vertices. In the VGX, each new vertex is parcelled out to a different processor in round robin fashion. Because the geometry engine is a SIMD processor, each vertex is handled identically. This necessitates a vertex sequencer at the output of the transformation unit to reassemble the vertices into triangles for the tiling stages.

Now compare the speed of the VGX geometric stage to that of the GTX. The five geometric processors of the GTX have a total peak computational capacity of 100 Mflops. The VGX geometry hardware uses four Texas Instruments 74ACT8867, a part whose peak rate is 32 Mflops, for a total peak rate of 128 Mflops. The real performance gain of the VGX comes from transforming shared vertices in triangular or quadrilateral strips about half as often as does the GTX.

The same hardware used for the geometry stage is repeated (with different microcode) in the polygon and edge processors of the VGX. Adding texture map

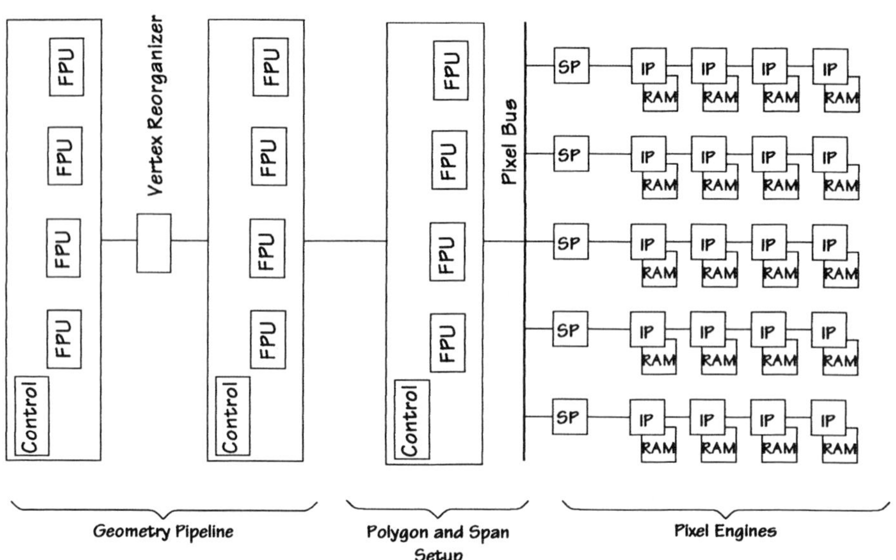

Figure 15. Silicon Graphics VGX.

indices as interpolants permits texture mapping. Since the texture lookup is done in the interleaved pixel processors, 20 copies of each texture must reside in the frame buffer. That the addition of texture mapping imposes an extra computational load on the pixel processors is obvious. However, since the entire rasterizer is designed for linear interpolation in screen space, distortion in texture patterns appears if large polygons are texture mapped. Consequently, an additional burden is placed on the geometry engine, since it must dice large texture mapped polygons into smaller ones on which the distortions are less noticeable.

An interesting innovation, optional in the VGX, is the accumulation buffer, which enables a variety of effects by storing intermediate results of multiple passes through the pipeline [Haeb90]. It is instructive to compare this feature to the capabilities of the Stellar GS-1000, which gained essentially the same capabilities by including the frame buffer memory in the address space of the host computer [Mamm89]. The beauty of the accumulation buffer is that it is fitted into what is logically an 'outboard' display processor, i.e., one which is tied to its host only at the front end. As an example of its usefulness, consider that realistic shading effects are generally expressed as sums of expressions like those in Eq. (1) [Cook84]. The application programmer cannot get at the internals of the VGX to program such loops in the shading code, but with the accumulation buffer the shading loops can be brought outside the rendering operation and programmed from the host end. Programmers are just now learning how to use this type of feature.

Hewlett-Packard TVRX

With the TVRX display processor, Hewlett-Packard takes a different approach to high-performance graphics. At the component level it combines a variety of off-the-shelf components, in addition to custom VLSI. Both the geometric and tiling stages are modular. From one to four geometric processor modules can be installed. The configuration shown in Figure 16 with four modules bears some resemblance to the wide input path of the SGI VGX, but in order for the system to be modular each module must be independent. Consequently the TVRX must be conscious of boundaries between polygons so that vertices of one polygon do not get distributed to two different modules. Each geometry module contains an Intel i860, a TI 320C30, and local memory. In normal operation, the i860 is responsible for transformation, clipping, lighting, and subdividing higher-order surfaces into polygons. The 320C30 is mainly used for conversion of floating point coordinates to fixed point. Depending on the mix of operations, however, the TVRX may reassign a particular operation from one processor to the other, 'shifting gears' to balance the load.

The TVRX tiling engine is unique and has enough innovative features to merit a chapter of its own. Unlike tilers, which set up a forward difference increment for each interpolant, the TVRX's interpolators compute normalized distance along an edge or a span. Then each interpolated component is evaluated using an expression of the form

$$X_i = X_1 + d_i(X_2 - X_1)$$

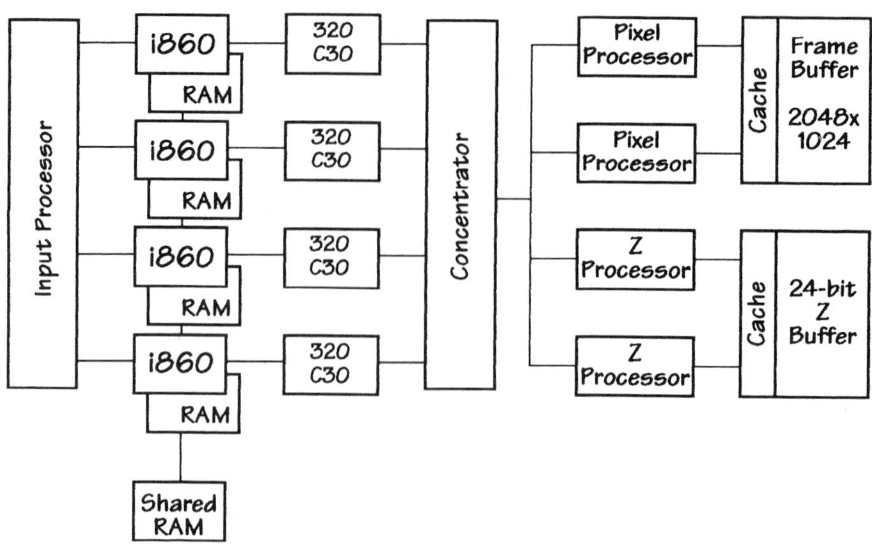

Figure 16. Hewlett-Packard TVRX display processor.

Conventional interpolation costs one add per sample per component. In the TVRX the cost is a multiply and an add per sample per component, but the result is very accurate and does not require a lot of precision in each interpolated component. While the expression above is for linear interpolation, the TVRX handles perspective interpolation with some additional per sample overhead, including a divide. Note, however, that the per component overhead is the same for perspective as it is for linear interpolation. Moreover, texture mapping imposes no extra burden on the geometry stages, since arbitrarily large polygons can be texture mapped without distortion.

The TVRX also stores gamma corrected colors in the frame buffer rather than using the video lookup tables for gamma correction during video scanout. Normally this would cause a problem, since the gamma corrected values must be read, modified, and rewritten in any compositing operation. To overcome this, circuitry is included to undo the gamma correction whenever a pixel is read.

The TVRX is not as finely tuned for raw polygon throughput as the Silicon Graphics VGX, but it is feature-rich, and robust in the sense that it maintains high performance for a range of data and operation mixes. Furthermore, throughput of the geometric stage can be scaled, up to a limit imposed by contention at the concentrator, by adding independent processors.

AT&T Pixel Machine

The Pixel Machine capitalizes on the low cost of AT&T's fast DSP32 signal processing chip. The DSP32 is similar in character to the TI 320 series DSPs [AT&T88]. The basic idea of the Pixel Machine is to harness large numbers of these processors to dramatically speed up a variety of graphics and imaging operations [Potm89]. As illustrated in Figure 17, the gross structure of the Pixel Machine is deceptively similar to the Silicon Graphics GTX. However, since each node is a user programmable, general purpose floating point CPU, the range of operations to which the system can be applied is unlimited.

The Pixel Machine is the only display system described in this survey that carries floating point computing to the pixel nodes. Consequently, it is most often thought of as a ray-tracing machine. In fact, the standard definition of a ray-tracing engine is an array of floating point processors [Gaud88; Nish83; Ulln83].

What is interesting and unique about the Pixel Machine, in addition to the raw floating point performance (820 Mflops fully configured), is the way its designers manage memory. The 16-bit address space of the DSP32 requires that archaic techniques be dusted off and put back to use. Program overlays, paged data, and the use of the workstation host as a virtual memory server are among the techniques used.

PIXEL PLANES 5

Although it makes use of the pixel planes algorithm in enhanced memory chips for tiling, Pixel Planes is primarily a collection of general purpose CPUs, in this case the Intel i860. What sets this most recent incarnation of Pixel Planes apart are the gross structural differences between it and its predecessors. Since the backbone of the system is a high speed ring network that gives every processor access to every other one, it is not possible to characterize the structure in a conventional sense. Since the system was intended as a testbed for evaluating different architectures, this is no surprise.

Pixel-Planes 5 (see Figure 18) contains an array of general purpose nodes which are suitable for geometric transformation, shading, or even ray tracing if

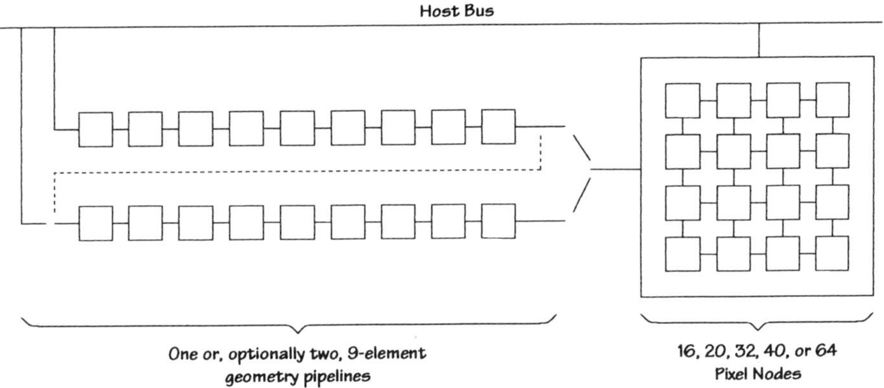

Figure 17. AT&T Pixel Machine.

that is desired. A second element type contains 128×128 fragments of a frame buffer, with the associated linear and quadratic expression evaluator as part of the frame buffer's enhanced memory chip. As commonly used, a portion of the GPs (which might mean geometry processor or general purpose, depending on who one asks) are devoted to transforming polygons, which are then transmitted to the appropriate frame buffer section for tiling.

While it is impossible to describe the normal operation of Pixel-Planes 5, there are some nifty functions that have been programmed into it. In particular, programmers have adopted a 'shade last' methodology. In the case where lighting calculations are performed at each vertex, the cost of shading is proportional to the number of vertices, vertices are shaded even if they later are hidden, and the result just does not look very good unless polygons are very small. Furthermore, shading at vertices and texture mapping at the pixel level does not work very well unless highlight terms are kept separate and added to pixel color only after texture mapping. In response to all of this, Pixel-Planes 5 programmers compute lighting terms for each pixel after all visibility is resolved. While this insures a fixed shading cost, the per pixel overhead is high. In Pixel Planes, however, the per pixel parallelism is also high, and shading in the 128×128 SIMD pixel processor is very fast.

There are some potential bottlenecks in the system. First, since the image plane is tiled by noninterleaved, 128×128 partitions, even though rendering processors are dynamically allocated there is a prospect of load imbalance if the scene is concentrated into a number of regions that is smaller than the number of renderers in the system. The possibility of contention among GPs as

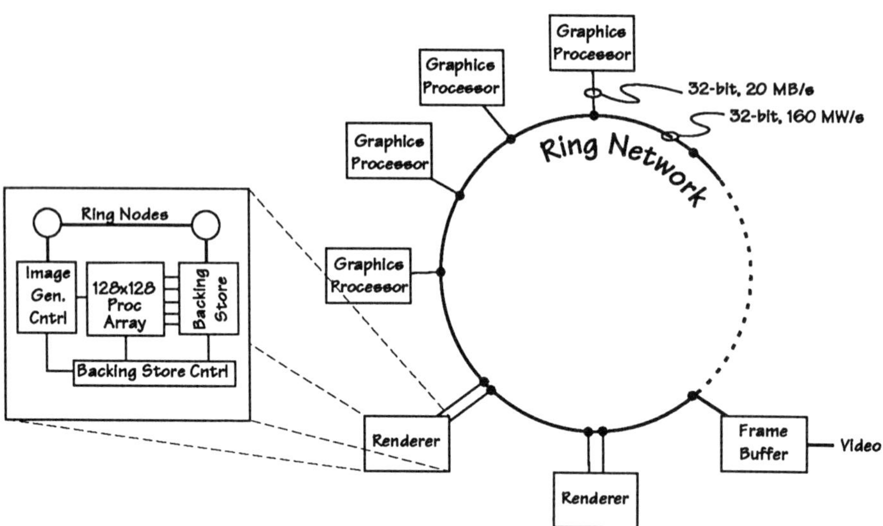

Figure 18. Pixel-Planes 5 physical layout.

they attempt to send transformed geometry to the same renderer is alleviated by buffering all intermediate data in the GP and waiting for a message from a master GP to send specific results to a renderer rasterizing a specific image region. This is a conscious trade of increased latency for decreased contention.

Speculation

In several places this paper has strongly hinted that perhaps the classic pipeline has been stretched to the breaking point, and that designers ought to be searching for a more flexible replacement. On this point there is general agreement, even from those who owe much to the pipeline [Clar92]. Indeed, there are numerous proposals for retiring the pipeline. Some of them address physical limitations to performance. Others reflect the fact that adding new rendering features within a conventional framework is getting to be like the tail wagging the dog.

A good bit of current R&D effort is still directed toward increased polygon display rates. These efforts will definitely succeed.

A major challenge is to fold global illumination into the real-time hardware feature set. This effort might succeed as well, but not within the current feed-forward framework [Abra88]. For one thing, the popular algorithms for global illumination, ray tracing, and radiosity are iterative in nature. Designers of real-time display systems hate that kind of nondeterminism.

On the one hand, we can speculate that the next generation of graphics hardware will be difficult to design. On the brighter side, this is the first time in 30 years that graphics architects have had the opportunity to start from scratch.

Acknowledgments. Participants in the special topics course on Graphics Architecture at the University of North Carolina at Chapel Hill instigated the preparation of these notes. Additional material was provided by Nick England and Leonard McMillan of Sun Microsystems and Andy Goris of Hewlett-Packard. Professor Steve Molnar of the University of North Carolina at Chapel Hill reviewed the draft and suggested numerous improvements.

REFERENCES

[Abra88]
Abram, G.D., Westover, L., and Whitted, T., Accelerated rendering, *Proc. Ausgraph '88*, pp. 93–98, 1988.

[Akel88]
Akeley, K., and Jermoluk, T., High-performance polygon rendering, *Comput. Graph.*, Vol. 22, pp. 239–246, 1988 (SIGGRAPH 88).

[Akel89]
Akeley, K., The Silicon Graphics 4D/240GTX superworkstation, *IEEE Comput. Graph. and Appl.*, Vol. 9, No. 4, pp. 71–83, July 1989.

[Apga88]
Apgar, B., Bersack, B., and Mammen, A., A display system for the Stellar Graphics supercomputer model GS1000, *Comput. Graph.*, Vol. 22, pp. 255–262, 1988 (SIGGRAPH 88).

[AT&T88]
AT&T, *WE DSP32C Digital Signal Processor Information Manual*, 1988.

[Bord89]
Borden, B.S., Graphics processing on a graphics supercomputer, *IEEE Comput. Graph. and Appl.*, Vol. 9, No. 4, pp. 56–62, July 1989.

[Carl80]
Carlbom, I.B., System Architecture for High-Performance Vector Graphics, Ph.D. diss., Department of Computer Science, Brown University, 1980.

[Clar80]
Clark, J.H., and Hannah, M., Distributed processing in a high-performance smart image memory, *VLSI Design*, Vol. 1, No. 3, pp. 40–45, 4th Quarter 1980.

[Clar82]
Clark, J.H., The geometry engine: A VLSI geometry system for graphics, *Comput. Graph.*, Vol. 16, pp. 349–355, 1982 (SIGGRAPH 82).

[Clar92]
Clark, J.H., Roots and branches of 3-D, *BYTE*, Vol. 17, No. 5, pp. 153–164, 1992.

[Cook84]
Cook, R.L., Shade trees, *Comput. Graph.*, Vol. 18, pp. 223–231, 1984 (SIGGRAPH 84).

[Engl86]
England, N., A graphics system architecture for interactive application-specific display functions, *IEEE Comput. Graph. and Appl.*, Vol. 6, No. 1, pp. 60–70, January 1986.

[Engl89]
England, N., Evolution of high performance graphics systems, *Proc. Graphics Interface '89*, Canadian Information Processing Society (Morgan Kaufman in US), June 1989.

[Fuch77]
Fuchs, H., Distributing a visible surface algorithm over multiple processors, *Proc. ACM Annual Conf.*, Seattle, WA, pp. 449–451, October 1977.

[Fuch85]
Fuchs, H., et al., Fast spheres, shadows, textures, transparencies, and image enhancements in Pixel-Planes, *Comput. Graph.*, Vol. 19, pp. 111–120, 1985 (SIGGRAPH 85).

[Fuch89]
Fuchs, H., et al., Pixel-Planes 5: A heterogeneous multiprocessor graphics system using processor-enhanced memories, *Comput. Graph.*, Vol. 23, pp. 79–88, 1989 (SIGGRAPH 89).

[Gaud88]
Gaudet, S., Hobson, R., Chilka, P., and Calvert, T., Multiprocessor experiments for high-speed ray tracing, *ACM TOG*, Vol. 7, pp. 151–179, 1988.

[Grim89]
Grimes, J., Kohn, L., and Bharadhwaj, R., The Intel i860 64-bit processor: A general-purpose CPU with 3D graphics capabilities, *IEEE Comput. Graph. and Appl.*, Vol. 9, No. 4, pp. 85–94, July 1989.

[Haeb90]
Haeberli, P., and Akeley, K., The accumulation buffer: Hardware support for high-quality rendering, *Comput. Graph.*, Vol. 24, pp. 309–318, 1990 (SIGGRAPH 90).

[Kirk90]
Kirk, D., and Voorhies, D., The rendering architecture of the DN10000VS, *Comput. Graph.*, Vol. 24, pp. 299–307, 1990 (SIGGRAPH 90).

[Lars90]
Larson, R., Morrison, B., and Goris, A., *Hardware Texture Mapping*, Graphics Technology Division, Ft. Collins, CO: Hewlett-Packard Co., 1990.

[Laur91]
Laur, D., and Hanrahan, P., Hierarchical splatting: A progressive refinement algorithm for volume rendering, *Comput. Graph.*, Vol. 25, pp. 285–288, 1991 (SIGGRAPH 91).

[Levi84]
Levinthal, A., and Porter, T., Chap — a SIMD graphics processor, *Comput. Graph.*, Vol. 18, pp. 77–82, 1984 (SIGGRAPH 84).

[Levo90]
Levoy, M., Efficient ray tracing of volume data, *ACM TOG*, Vol. 9, pp. 245–261, 1990.

[Mamm89]
Mammen, A., Transparency and antialiasing algorithms implemented with the virtual pixel maps technique, *IEEE Comput. Graph. and Appl.*, Vol. 9, pp. 43–55, July 1989.

[Marg90]
Margulis, N., *i860 Microprocessor Architecture*, Berkeley: Osborbe/McGraw-Hill, 1990.

[Moln90]
Molnar, S., and Fuchs, H., Advanced Raster Graphics Architecture, Chap. 18, pp. 855-922, in Foley, J., van Dam, A., Feiner, S., and Hughes, J., *Computer Graphics: Principles and Practice*, Reading, MA: Addison-Wesley, 1990.

[Moln91]
Molnar, S., Image Composition Architectures for Real-Time Graphics, Ph.D. diss., Dept. of Computer Science, The University of North Carolina at Chapel Hill, August 1991.

[Moln92]
Molnar, S., Eyles, J., and Poulton, J., PixelFlow: high-speed rendering using image composition, *Comput. Graph.*, Vol. 26, pp. 231–240, 1992 (SIGGRAPH 92).

[Myer68]
Myer, T.H., and Sutherland, I.E., On the design of display processors, *CACM*, Vol. 11, No. 6, pp. 410–414, June 1968.

[Nish83]
Nishimura, H., Ohno, H., Kawata, T., Shirakawa, I., and Omura, K., LINKS-1:

A Parallel Pipelined Multimicrocomputer System for Image Creation, *Proc. 10th Symposium on Computer Architecture* (Stockholm), pp. 387–394, New York: ACM, 1983.

[Park80]
Parke, F.I., Simulation and expected performance analysis of multiple processor z-buffer systems, *Comput. Graph.*, Vol. 14, pp. 48–56, 1980 (SIGGRAPH 80).

[Phon73]
Phong, B.T., Illumination for Computer Generated Pictures, Ph.D. diss., Computer Science Dept., University of Utah, July 1973. Condensed version in *CACM*, Vol. 18, No. 6, pp. 311–317, 1975.

[Potm89]
Potmesil, M., and Hoffert, E., The pixel machine: A parallel image computer, *Comput. Graph.*, Vol. 23, pp. 69–78, 1989 (SIGGRAPH 89).

[Rock89]
Rockwood, A., Heaton, K., and Davis, T., Real-time rendering of trimmed surfaces, *Comput. Graph.*, Vol. 23, pp. 107–116, 1989 (SIGGRAPH 89).

[Sun90]
Sun Microsystems, SPARCstation 2GS/SPARCstation 2GT Technical White Paper, November 1990.

[Suth74]
Sutherland, I.E., Sproull, R.F., and Schumacker, R.A., A characterization of ten hidden-surface algorithms, *ACM Computing Surveys*, Vol. 6, pp. 1–55, March 1974.

[Texa90]
Texas Instruments, *TMS320C3x User's Guide*, 1990.

[Ulln83]
Ullner, M.K., Parallel Machines for Computer Graphics, Ph.D. diss., California Institute of Technology, Pasadena, 1983.

[Watk70]
Watkins, G., A Real Time Hidden Surface Algorithm, Ph.D. diss., Computer Science Dept., University of Utah, 1970.

[West89]
Westover, L., Interactive Volume Rendering, *Proc. Chapel Hill Workshop on Volume Visualization*, May 1989.

[West91]
Westover, L.A., "Splatting: A Parallel, Feed-Forward Volume Rendering Algorithm", Ph.D. diss., Dept. of Computer Science, University of North Carolina at Chapel Hill, Chapel Hill, NC, 1991.

[Whit80]
Whitted, T., An improved illumination model for shaded display, *CACM*, Vol. 23, pp. 343–349, June 1980.

[Whit81]
Whitted, T., Hardware enhanced 3-D raster display systems, *Proc. 7th Canadian Man-Computer Communications Conference*, Waterloo, Ont, pp. 349–356, June 1981.

[Whit84]
Whitton, M.C., Memory design for raster graphics displays, *IEEE Comput. Graph. and Appl.*, Vol. 4, No. 3, pp. 48–65, March 1984.

Biographies

Biographies

State of the Art in Computer Graphics –
Aspects of Visualization

David F. Rogers

David F. Rogers is Professor of Aerospace Engineering at the United States
Naval Academy. In 1959, he earned a Bachelor of Aeronautical Engineering
degree from Rensselaer Polytechnic Institute and subsequently was awarded the
M.S.AE and Ph.D. degrees from the same Institute.

Dr. Rogers is the author of three textbooks on computer graphics, includ-
ing *Mathematical Elements for Computer Graphics* and *Procedural Elements for
Computer Graphics*. He is a member of SIGGRAPH, ACM, the Society of Naval
Architects and Marine Engineers, and an Associate Fellow of the American Insti-
tute of Aeronautics and Astronautics. Dr. Rogers is the founder and former Di-
rector of the Computer Aided Design/Interactive Graphics Group at the United
States Naval Academy. He is editor for the Springer-Verlag Series *Monographs in
Visual Communication* and is a founding editor of *Computers & Education*. He
also is a member of the editorial boards of *The Visual Computer* and *Computer
Aided Design Journal*.

Professor Rogers was co-chair of the BCS/ACM International Summer Institutes on State of the Art in Computer Graphics held in Stirling, Scotland in
1986; Exeter, England in 1988; and Edinburgh, Scotland in 1990. He was also
cochairman of ICCAS '82, The International Conference on Computer Applications in the Automation of Shipyard Operation and Ship Design. He is a member
of the International Program Committee for ICCAS. He was also cochairman of
the International Program Committee for Computer Graphics Tokyo '85. He is

a member of the AIAA Technical Committee on Interactive Graphics and habitually serves on the organizing committees or technical program committees of computer graphics conferences worldwide.

Professor Rogers was Fujitsu Research Fellow at the Royal Melbourne Institute of Technology in Melbourne, Australia in 1987 and a Visiting Professor at the University of New South Wales, Sydney, Australia in 1982. He was an Honorary Research Fellow at University College London in England during 1977–78, where he studied Naval Architecture.

Professor Rogers was one of the original faculty who established the Aerospace Engineering Department at the United States Naval Academy in 1964. He has both an experimental and a theoretical research background. He has research interests in the areas of highly interactive graphics, computer aided design and manufacturing, numerical control, computer aided education, hypersonic viscous flow, boundary layer theory, and computational fluid mechanics.

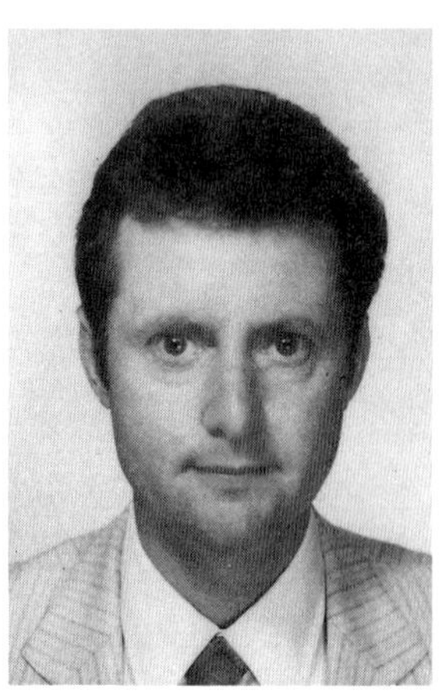

Rae A. Earnshaw

Rae Earnshaw is Head of Computer Graphics at the University of Leeds, with interests in graphics algorithms, human–computer interface issues, scientific visualization, graphics standards, fifth-generation graphics software, workstations and display technology, mathematics of computer graphics, CAD/CAM, graphics system building, and education issues. He has been a visiting professor at Illinois Institute of Technology, Chicago, USA; Northwestern Polytechnical University, China; and George Washington University, Washington DC, USA.

Dr. Earnshaw was a director of the NATO Advanced Study Institute on 'Fundamental Algorithms for Computer Graphics' held in Ilkley, England, in 1985, and a co-chair of the BCS/ACM International Summer Institutes on State of the Art in Computer Graphics held in Stirling, Scotland in 1986; Exeter, England in 1988; and Edinburgh, Scotland in 1990. He was a director of the NATO

Advanced Study Institute on Theoretical Foundations of Computer Graphics and CAD held in Italy in 1987. He is a member of ACM, IEEE, CGS, EG, and a Fellow of the British Computer Society.

Dr. Earnshaw has authored and edited 15 books on graphics algorithms, computer graphics, and associated topics, and published a number of papers in these areas. He chairs the Scientific Visualization Group at the University of Leeds, is a member of the editorial board of *The Visual Computer*, vice-president of the Computer Graphics Society, and chair of the British Computer Society Computer Graphics and Displays Group.

Ingrid Carlbom

Ingrid Carlbom is Manager of Visualization Research at Digital Equipment Corporation's Cambridge Research Lab. She is currently collaborating with a neuroscientist at Children's Hospital in Boston, MA, building a system for modeling neuronal dendrites from transmission electron microscopy. From 1980 to 1986 she was a member of professional staff at Schlumberger-Doll Research, Ridgefield, CT, where from 1981–1983 she was Program Leader managing research in graphics and geometric modeling. While at Schlumberger, her research concerned geometric modeling techniques for subsurface formations. Her current research interests include scientific visualization, geometric modeling, medical and biological imaging, and computer graphics system architecture. Dr. Carlbom received a Ph.D. in Computer Science from Brown University, a M.S. in Computer Science from Cornell University, and a Fil. Kand. from the University of Stockholm, Sweden. She is a member of ACM, SIGGRAPH, and IEEE.

Roy Hall

Roy Hall is an Assistant Professor of Computer Graphics at Cornell University in Ithaca, NY. Professor Hall joined Cornell's Program of Computer Graphics in 1988. He has a background in architecture and structural engineering from Rensselaer Polytechnic Institute, and in computer graphics from Cornell University. His current research concentrates on the relationship between designer and computer in industrial and architectural design applications. He has extensive experience in image synthesis algorithms and color reproduction. In addition to research at the Program of Computer Graphics, he teaches courses in both the design and technologies sequences in the Department of Architecture. Formerly Director of Software Development for Wavefront Technologies, Professor Hall has written several commercial image generation systems, and is the author of *Illumination and Color in Computer Generated Imagery*.

Tosiyasu L. Kunii

Tosiyasu L. Kunii is currently Professor of Information and Computer Science at the University of Tokyo. He started work in raster computer graphics in 1968, which led to the Tokyo Raster Technology Project. His research interests include computer graphics, database systems, and software engineering. He has authored and edited over 30 computer science books and published over 120 refereed academic/technical papers in computer science and applications areas. He received the B.S., M.S., and D.S. degrees from the University of Tokyo.

David F. McAllister

David F. McAllister is Professor of Computer Science at North Carolina State University in Raleigh, NC. He received his B.S. in Mathematics from UNC at Chapel Hill in 1963, his M.S. in Mathematics from Purdue University in 1967, and his Ph.D. in Computer Science from UNC at Chapel Hill in 1972. His areas of interest include stereo computer graphics, numerical analysis, performance evaluation, and fault-tolerant software systems. He is a member of ACM, IEEE, Eurographics, SID, and SPIE.

Gregory M. Nielson

Gregory M. Nielson is a Professor of Computer Science and Adjunct Professor of Mathematics at Arizona State University, where he teaches and does research in the areas of computer graphics, computer aided geometric design, and scientific visualization. He has lectured and published widely on the topics of curve and surface representation and design; interactive computer graphics; scattered data interpolation; and the analysis and visualization of multivariate data. He has collaborated with several institutions, including NASA, Xerox, and General Motors, and he is a participatory guest scientist at Lawrence Livermore National Laboratory. Professor Nielson is on the editorial board of several journals, and he currently chairs the IEEE Computer Society Technical Committee on Computer Graphics.

Warren Robinett

Warren Robinett is a designer of interactive computer graphics software and hardware. In 1978, he designed the Atari video game "Adventure", the first graphical adventure game. In 1980, he was co-founder and chief software engineer at The Learning Company, a publisher of educational software. While there he designed "Rocky's Boots", a computer game which teaches digital logic design to 11-year-old children. "Rocky's Boots" won Software of the Year awards from three magazines in 1983. In 1986, Robinett worked as a research scientist at NASA Ames Research Center, where he designed the software for the Virtual Environment Workstation, NASA's pioneering virtual reality project. In 1989 he moved to the University of North Carolina as manager of the Head-Mounted Display Project, continuing to work in virtual reality.

Dietmar Saupe

Dietmar Saupe gained his Dr. rer. nat. in Mathematics in 1982 at the University of Bremen. He was Visiting Assistant Professor of Mathematics at the University of California, Santa Cruz, 1985–87, and since 1987 has been Assistant Professor of Mathematics at the University of Bremen. There he is a researcher at the Dynamical Systems Graphics Laboratory, with main interests in mathematical computer graphics, visualization, and experimental mathematics. He has been involved as speaker and course organizer in five past SIGGRAPH courses on fractals and is coauthor/coeditor of *The Science of Fractal Images*, 1988, and *Fractals for the Classroom*, 1991, both from Springer-Verlag. He is one of the contributors to the exhibit "Frontiers of Chaos", which is being shown worldwide under the auspices of the Goethe-Institute. Dr. Saupe is a member of the DMV, ACM, and SIGGRAPH.

Val Watson

Val Watson is Chief of the Workstation Applications Office in the Fluid Dynamics Division of the NASA Ames Research Center. He is responsible for the application of high performance graphics workstations in support of fluid dynamics research. His current emphasis is on the development of visual analysis tools to aid in understanding the computer simulations of complex three-dimensional flow fields. Several computer programs developed at Ames for flow visualization are being widely used by the aerospace industry.

Val is currently chairman of the Interactive Computer Graphics Technical Committee for the American Institute of Aeronautics and Astronautics and a member of the Board of Directors of NCGA. He received a B.S. in Mechanical Engineering and M.S. in Aeronautics from UC Berkeley, and a Ph.D. in Aeronautics and Astronautics from Stanford University.

Turner Whitted

Turner Whitted is co-founder and technical director of Numerical Design Limited, a company that produces image synthesis software. He is also Research Professor of Computer Science at the University of North Carolina at Chapel

Hill, where he directs student research on geometric modeling and volumetric rendering. From 1978 to 1983 Dr. Whitted was a member of the Computer Systems Research Laboratory at Bell Labs, where he developed rendering systems and algorithms, including the widely-used technique of recursive ray tracing. For several years he has served as a member of the SIGGRAPH conference technical program committee. From 1981 until 1987 he was an associate editor of *ACM TOG*. He received B.S.E. and M.S. degrees from Duke University and a Ph.D. in Electrical Engineering from North Carolina State University.

Index

INDEX